THE RISE OF A★M★E★R★I★C★A

Fighting the Next American Revolution and the Constitutional Crisis

By John D. Diamond

Authors & Artists Publishers of New York, Inc
3 Kimberly Drive, Suite B
Dryden, New York 13053 USA
www.AuhtorsandArtistsPublishersofNewYork.com
www.AAPNY.com

Copyright © 2006 John D. Diamond
Al rights reserved, including the right of reproduction in whole or in part, without the written permission of the publisher. Requests for such permission should be addressed to Authors & Artists Publishers of New York Inc., 3 Kimberly Drive, Suite B, Dryden, New York 13053 USA

Cover Design Gary Hoffman
Book Design Gary Hoffman

Manufactured in the United States of America

Library of Congress Cataloging-in-Publication Data
Diamond/ John D
American History, Constitutional History, American Politics, Christianity

Every effort has been made to identify copyright holders and give the appropriate information about material included in this book. In the event of an oversight please notify the publisher and corrections will be made in the next edition. The beliefs stated in this book are those of the author and do not necessarily represent those of the publisher.

9 8 7 6 5 4 3

ISBN 978-0-9724922-8-7

www.TheRiseofAmerica.com
www.JohnDDiamond.com

To my son Shawn,
that I might leave you
a better America.

THE RISE OF A★M★E★R★I★C★A
Fighting the Next American Revolution and the Constitutional Crisis

Historical Cycle of the World's Great Civilizations
Preface
Foreword
Introduction
1. Stolen History
2. What Do Americans Believe?

America's Rise
3. The First American Revolution
4. The U.S. Constitution
5. The Second American Revolution
6. The American Civil War
7. The Third American Revolution

America's Fall
8. The Fourth American Revolution
9. The Fifth American Revolution
10. The Battle Behind the Battle
11. America's Enemies
12. The Warren Court

America's Future
13. The Next American Revolution
14. Restoring Our Constitution
15. Conclusion

The Historical Cycle of the World's Great Civilizations

1. Bondage (Physical, Spiritual or Both)

2. Spiritual Faith

3. Great Courage

4. Liberty

5. Abundance

6. Complacency

7. Apathy

8. Dependence on Government

9. Bondage (Physical, Spiritual or Both)

Where Does America Fit into this Cycle?

Preface

When I first began work on *The Rise of America* series, I sought to examine and prove three historical truths:

1. That America was founded as a Judeo-Christian nation whose government and laws were to be guided and directed by Judeo-Christian principles.

2. How the Supreme Court has illegally and unconstitutionally ripped power from the hands of a predominantly Judeo-Christian people and has essentially outlawed the system of government that our founding fathers had created.

3. How the outlawing of Judeo-Christian principles by the Supreme Court has resulted in the debasing of our culture and society, and there is the danger of turning God himself against America.

It is the author's contention that America is presently experiencing both a constitutional crisis and a moral crisis, and that the former has created the latter. Furthermore, this constitutional crisis and moral crisis are endangering America's future.

My first editor stated that while she understood what I was attempting to do with the book and how the issues were related, she suggested that I focus on each of the following three themes separately.

In the books of the series, the topics will be discussed as follows: In the first book, *The Rise of America: Fighting the Next American Revolution*, I was able to focus upon the Constitutional Crisis. The second book, *The Rise of America: Fighting the Next American Civil War*, could focus on America's moral crisis. In the third book, *The Rise of America: My God, My God, why have You forsaken Us?*, I could focus upon America's present spiritual crisis.

In this series I hope to prove two immutable truths. That history always repeats itself and that mankind oftentimes fails to learn from the mistakes of the past. It is my hope that by reading these books in order, the reader will be better able to not only examine each of these subjects independently, but also able to see the progression and recognize the domino effect that has taken place in America over the last sixty years.

Foreword

[1] *"Fear can hold you prisoner, hope can set you free... Hope is a good thing, maybe the best of things, and no good thing ever dies. I will be hoping that this letter finds you, and finds you well."*

Andy Dufresne (Tim Robbins),
The Shawshank Redemption

Soon after the attacks on America on September 11th, there began in the media a debate concerning the role of God and religion in American society. Since I was already working on my Master's degree in Education, and since the study of American history has always fascinated me, I began a research project that ultimately resulted in the writing of this book.

While studying the vast resources needed to complete *The Rise of America*, I found myself experiencing a number of different emotions—sadness, frustration, hopelessness, helplessness and fear. But the emotion that I felt most was indignation. Indignation is defined as **a righteous anger that is a reaction to injustice.** I felt:

- Anger when I compared what this great nation once was with what it is now.

- Anger at the people and institutions that have caused it to become the way it is presently.

- Anger at the previous generation of Americans who stood by and did nothing while our Constitution was being destroyed.

- And most of all, anger at myself for not being a good citizen by knowing and defending our Constitution.

If while reading this book you find yourself experiencing any or all of these emotions, I apologize in advance. Use these emotions as encouragement to play a more active role in the affairs of your society and government.

Once the research was complete and I began to contemplate the possibilities, I experienced yet one more emotion: Hope!

When I finished most of my research and looked back at all the different emotions I had experienced, I had to make a decision. Which of these emotions would I use as the motivation for writing this book?

Since sadness, frustration, hopelessness, helplessness and fear are all negative emotions, which often do more to paralyze and discourage than motivate, and since indignation itself is still a somewhat negative emotion, hope would be the emotion that motivated me most.

Hope is often the light at the end of the tunnel. It combines both desire and expectation. Therefore, hope is a positive. Once indignation had served its purpose, all that was left was hope:

- **Hope** that this book will reach and touch those it should.

- **Hope** that those it does reach will be motivated enough to act on their convictions.

[2] *"Hope that is seen is not hope; for why does one still hope for what he sees? But if we hope for what we do not see, we eagerly wait for it with perseverance . . . Therefore, since we have such hope, we use great boldness of speech . . . and we desire that each one of you show the same diligence to the full assurance of hope until the end, that you do not become sluggish, but imitate those who through faith and patience inherit the promises."*

The Apostle Paul

Introduction

In this book, we are going to take a long, hard look at both the rise and fall of the American system of government. We will seek to understand the type of government that our founding fathers established, and we will see how the constitutional Republic that they created has all but been destroyed, and how we are no longer a government "of the people and by the people." Rather, we are a government "of the court and by the court."

We will examine our founding fathers' understanding of these questions and their perception of the relationship that should exist between morality, religion and government in America.

Revolution

You may be wondering why the subtitle of this book is *Fighting the Next American Revolution*. I will explain this in detail as the book progresses. For now, though, it is important to know and understand what the term "revolution" means. Webster's New World dictionary defines Revolution as:

> [1] "Overthrow of a government, form of government, or social system by those governed... with another government or system taking its place."

Often when we think about a "revolution," we think of bringing a change to a government through forceful or violent means. While often this is the case, as with the American Revolution and the conflict with the British, or the Russian Revolution of 1917, a country can at times experience a "revolution" so gradually that the people did not even realize a revolution ever took place.

James Madison warned us that throughout history, when many countries have been taken over by tyrants, it wasn't always the result of bloody and violent uprisings, but more commonly through silent and gradual tactics that took away one freedom at a time.

> [2] "Since the general civilization of mankind, I believe there are more instances of the abridgement of the freedom of the people by gradual and silent encroachments of those in power, than by violent and sudden usurpations."

As we begin to examine America from before its inception to the present, I believe the evidence will prove that America has experienced a "gradual and silent" *coup d'état*. It is the author's contention that during our relatively brief history, America has experienced no less than five major revolutions, by which our government and our society have been radically altered. Three of these "revolutions" were actually *coup d'états* that took place at the hands of the Supreme Court, without the consent of the American people and contrary to the type of government that our founding fathers created. History and historians remember these times as turbulent, but historians have rarely identified these periods as revolutions.

However, those of us who live in the beginning of the twenty-first century have the privilege of hindsight. They say that hindsight is 20\20. As twenty-first century Americans, we are now able to look back through history at these times and events and examine the effect they have had on the shaping of modern American government and society.

For now we simply must understand that the word "revolution" simply means: "A change in the form of government, or social system... with another government or system taking its place." We will build upon this idea as the book progresses.

As the definition tells us, in order for a revolution to occur, it is not necessary that the government be replaced by another government, but simply that the "form of government" or "social system" be replaced by a different form of government or social system than the one originally established.

America has only experienced one "revolution" in which the government itself was violently overthrown and replaced, that being the American Revolution of 1775–1783. However, we as a nation have experienced several smaller and less notable revolutions, in which the direction of our nation has been radically altered without the consent of the people and contrary to the principles established in the Constitution. The effects of these revolutions continue to negatively affect our society to this very day.

If we are going to restore America to its former glory, we are going to have to try to get away from the political and ideological name-calling. This does nothing more than divide us, even on issues where we see eye to eye. This may be hard to accomplish since many Americans are firmly entrenched in their political and ideological positions; however, we have to understand that the future of America and the future of our children is at stake. We must therefore find some common ground. This issue is far too important for partisan politics.

I do not believe that the blame for the degeneration of American society can be placed *solely* on the shoulders of Republicans or Democrats. Nor do I believe that we can attribute this crisis exclusively to the actions of liberals or conservatives.

The degeneration of American government and society, and the crisis that we are presently facing, is primarily the result of socialism and secularism. This sentiment is presently being expressed by Protestants, Catholics and Orthodox Jews alike.

Former Alabama Attorney General, and now federal judge, Bill Pryor has identified the crisis for us.

> [3] "This crisis has two faces. First is the increasing secularization of our country, and second is the erosion of self-government. The primary catalyst for both trends is, in my judgment, the *Supreme Court of the United States...* Our challenge...in this next millennium will be to... restore the American experiment as understood by George Washington, James Madison, and Abraham Lincoln."

The Rabbi Daniel Lapin, founder of the Pacific Jewish Center, an Orthodox synagogue in Venice, California, said the following:

> "The reality today is that while we still have a choice, the choice is between a benign America based upon Judeo-Christian principles and on the other side is a very aggressive, sinister and power hungry secular fundamentalism that wishes to inject its tentacles into every single aspect of American life."

As we will examine in this book, socialism and secularism are two political ideologies from which our founding fathers and the American people tried very hard to protect America. This was their motive behind drafting and ratifying the 1st and 10th Amendments to the Constitution. Our founding fathers understood that socialism and secularism are two political ideologies that always lead nations into tyranny, oppression and ultimately destruction.

We will examine how America has evolved from a government that derived its power from the consent of the people, to a people who now derive their power and their civil rights from the consent of the federal government.

America at War!

As a military veteran, I took an oath to: "Support and defend the Constitution of the United States against all enemies, foreign *and domestic*... So help me, God." But this begs the question: Who are these enemies of the Constitution? Are there foreign enemies who would destroy our Constitution? Does Al-Qaeda have the power to seize our civil and constitutional rights? No. Our overseas enemies cannot take our freedoms and civil liberties away from us. Only America's "domestic" enemies could pull off such a feat. So many times we focus only on America's foreign enemies, while forgetting that America also has "domestic" enemies.

Most of America's past leaders have understood that America was far too powerful ever to be destroyed by our foreign enemies. If we ever lost our freedoms, it would be because we brought it upon ourselves. Listen carefully to the words of Abraham Lincoln:

> [4] "America will never be destroyed from the outside. If we falter and lose our freedoms, it will be because we destroyed ourselves... Shall we expect some

transatlantic military giant, to step over the ocean, and crush us at a blow? Never!—All the armies of Europe, Asia and Africa combined, with all the treasure of the earth in their military chest; with a Bonaparte for a commander, could not by force, take a drink from the Ohio, or make a track on the Blue Ridge, in a trial of a Thousand years. At what point, then, is the approach of danger to be expected? I answer, if it ever reach us, it *must spring up amongst us*. It cannot come from abroad. If destruction be our lot, we must ourselves be its author and finisher. As a nation of freemen, we must live through all time, or die by suicide."

We must understand that America is at war! However, this war is not being fought on some foreign soil, with tanks and planes. It is being fought here at home. It is being fought in our courts, it is being fought in our schools and it is being fought in our churches. I am not referring to a war against terror, but a war for the very soul of America. It is a war of ideology and it is a war for the political, spiritual and moral direction of this nation.

For over 80 years there has been a silent war raging in America, between those who believe in the type of America that our founding fathers created and those whose single goal is to destroy it. And the battleground for this war is our society, our schools, our churches and our government.

As we progress throughout this book, we will see how the "American form of government" and the "social system" that our founding fathers created has been gradually overthrown and ultimately destroyed, and how another form of government has evolved and replaced it, especially with regard to our civil and state rights.

During the debate over the Ten Commandments monument in Alabama, Greta Van Susteren was asked by Bill

O'Reilly, host of *The O'Reilly Factor,* whether or not she believes the monument should stay or go. She replied, "I don't have a dog in this fight," indicating that it does not matter to her one way or the other. You may feel the same way when it comes to this specific issue. However, if you are an American citizen, you do have a dog in this fight, whether you realize it or not.

Religious freedom is but one of the civil rights that our founding fathers sought to ensure and protect by drafting the Bill of Rights. The other freedoms include things such as the freedom of speech, freedom of the press, rights of assembly and petition, the right to bear arms, protection to own private property and the right to a fair trial, among others. You may not consider yourself a staunch supporter of religious freedom, but I am sure that there are some civil rights that you do not want the federal government to infringe upon. Therefore, every American who loves the freedoms and liberties that our founding fathers fought and died for does have a dog in this fight!

If the federal government is willing to attack our religious freedoms and those who believe in the same Judeo-Christian principles as our founding fathers, which makes up one of the largest, if not the largest, groups in America (around 90%, by most polls), do you truly think that one of the civil rights such as the right to own property, as guaranteed in the 5th Amendment, is not next? Think again!

On Thursday, June 23, 2005, in the case of *Kelo vs. City of New London* the Supreme Court ruled that the government can now legally seize peoples' homes and businesses for private economic development without the consent of the home or business owner.

You read that right—*the government can take your private property*! That is what five unelected Justices of the U.S.

Supreme Court ruled when they rewrote the Constitution and took away our private property rights. Justice Sandra Day O'Connor got it exactly right when she wrote the following in her dissenting opinion:

> "Any property may now be taken for the benefit of another private party, but the fallout from this decision will not be random. The beneficiaries are likely to be those citizens with disproportionate influence and power in the political process, including large corporations and development firms. As for the victims, the government now has license to transfer property from those with fewer resources to those with more."

Who do you think is going to suffer from this ruling? The rich? Somehow I do not see them going into Beverly Hills and bulldozing down some movie star's house to put up a shopping mall. It will be you and I and all other Americans with limited resources to fight these large corporations and development firms in court. Where are all the Labor Unions with their political muscle now? Will they stand true to their principles and defend the common man against the large corporations, which will undoubtedly dump on the "little guy"? It is time some of our union dues are put to good use to take back our government.

Do you still think your freedom and liberties are not at risk? Are you still naive enough to believe that the U.S. Government operates with the consent of the American people? No freedom is more fundamental in America than the freedom to own property. In polls released just after this ruling, 91% of Americans disagree with the Supreme Court's ruling that allows large corporations and development firms to confiscate our private property for their own private and personal use.

Protecting private property rights was a central reason our founding fathers declared independence in 1776. *World Book* Encyclopedia has this to say about the meaning of the 5th Amendment to the Constitution:

> [5] "The amendment also forbids the government to take a person's property for public use without fair payment. The government's right to take property for public use is called *eminent domain.* Governments use it to acquire land for highways, schools, and other public facilities."

It has been a long-established precedent that the government may buy private property to acquire land for highways, schools, and other public facilities. The American people have long understood and accepted this, because highways and schools benefit the general public.

Now, 214 years after the Constitution was established, the Supreme Court has decided that your property may be taken by anyone with more money than you, in order to build a casino or a shopping mall. *Eminent domain* used to mean that the government could take your property for public use; now it can take your property and give it to anyone who simply wants to make money off your land, thus destroying the 5th Amendment. Similarly, the Supreme Court has also destroyed the 1st and 10th Amendments to the Constitution.

The American people must realize that most of our elected representatives are so engulfed in partisan politics that they are unwilling or unable to take *our* government back from the Supreme Court.

The politicians in Washington have known about these unconstitutional seizures of power for over 60 years. But instead of defending the American people against these abuses of power, they sit on the fence, afraid to take a stand for anything that may cost them votes in the next election. Meanwhile, the American people suffer from their inaction and lack of courage. Calling on the Supreme Court to give our rights back is like appealing to a thief to bring back your property. Our founding fathers realized that you can only appeal to tyrants for so long before you are forced to take matters into your own hands.

The Declaration of Independence says, "Governments are instituted among Men, *deriving their just powers from the consent of the governed.*" Our founding fathers believed that government has to receive consent from the governed. If we do not wake up soon and realize that the U.S. government has not received any consent from the American people to burn the American flag, take the word "under God" out of the Pledge of Allegiance or illegally confiscate our property, you can pretty much kiss the America that our founding fathers created goodbye.

In Nazi Germany, the people stood around while Hitler exterminated millions of Jews. Why did they not say or do anything? *Because they did not have a dog in this fight.* After all, their government was not actively persecuting them and, as a result of not standing up for what was right, their country was destroyed.

Martin Niemller (1892–1984), German Protestant pastor and theologian, had this to say on behalf of the German churches:

> [6] "When Hitler attacked the Jews... I was not a Jew, therefore, I was not concerned. And when Hitler attacked the Catholics, I was not a Catholic, and therefore, I was not concerned. And when Hitler attacked the unions and the industrialists, I was not

a member of the unions and I was not concerned. Then, Hitler attacked me and the Protestant church—and there was nobody left to be concerned."

Mankind has historically shown that we are self-centered. If there is an injustice taking place that does not directly affect us or those we care about, we will often not allow ourselves to be too concerned with it.

However, those who seek to oppress those around us will eventually begin to oppress us, given the chance. We must not allow this to happen any longer. Here we must be reminded of the following quote from Winston Churchill:

> [7] "Study history, study history. In history lies all the secrets of statecraft. While each day brings new adventures and new mistakes, if we do not learn from our mistakes, then we are doomed to repeat them. It often seems to me that our leaders do not learn from their mistakes or the mistakes of their predecessors."

After understanding these truths, it is my hope and prayers that others in their chosen career fields (teachers, police, politicians, judges, lawyers, sports figures, reporters, and religious leaders) will be bold and courageous enough to stand up for the truth and no longer sit on the sidelines, complaining about everything going or around us. As American citizens, we have the constitutional power to fix the problems we are experiencing—but the time is growing short.

We may feel, and rightly so, that we ourselves are not part of the problem, but the question is, are we going to be part of the solution? British statesman Edmund Burke (1729–1797) once said, "All that is necessary for evil to triumph is that good men do nothing..." If the America that we know and love is going to survive, the good can no longer sit idle. It is time to take control! It is time to let our collective voices be heard!

It is time to fight the next American Revolution.

Chapter 1

Stolen History

> [1] *"A nation which does not remember what it was yesterday, does not know what it is today, nor what it is trying to do. We are trying to do a futile thing if we do not know where we came from or what we have been about."*
>
> **President Woodrow Wilson**

When I initiated research on this subject, I began by reading about the history of America and its founding fathers—much of which can be found in the library of Congress. I wanted to understand why the early settlers and colonists came to America and attempt to determine the type of government and society they intended to establish.

When I looked at the condition of America for the first 150 years after this nation was founded, and compared it to present-day America, I find it hard to believe that we are living in the same nation, which is supposed to be governed by the same Constitution.

If America as a nation has experienced such a major ideological, political, social, spiritual and constitutional transformation over the last 150 years, how then did these changes take place throughout history? Who changed it? Who authorized it?

The only way I could accurately answer this question was to study American history, not from the perspective of comparing one point in time to another, but to slowly examine the transformation of our nation from point to point along the historical timeline. This is the only way to see the degree of change that has occurred, but it is also the only way to accurately determine when and how the transformation took place and who was responsible.

I am, admittedly, a history buff. I love watching any kind of movie, TV show or documentary having to do with history. At times I will be watching a program dealing with, for example, the 1942 bombing raids over Germany. During the show they will often interview a pilot who took part in the raids.

Since these raids occurred over sixty years ago, the pilot will now be an 84-year-old man. The program shows this man standing next to his plane at the age of 22, while interviewing him at age 84.

It sometimes fascinates me to see how this man looked back then, compared to now. Sometimes the change is so dramatic that it is hard to tell that you are looking at the same person. I began to wonder how in the world this man's appearance had transformed so significantly from 1942 to today. While the two photos reveal the degree of change, it leaves important unanswered questions. How did this transformation take place? At what rate? How did it happen, and when?

If, in the 1942 picture, we see a perfectly healthy young

man with a full head of black hair, and in the present-day picture we see that he is now bald except for a patch of gray hair and that he is now missing a left arm and has a large scar on his forehead, we are left with many questions unanswered.

How old was he when he started losing his hair? When did it start turning gray? How did he lose his arm and get the scar on his head? If we only look at the before and after pictures, these questions remain unanswered. We are aware of the amount of change that has taken place, but are unable to pinpoint when the changes occurred.

Therefore, the best way to determine how his appearance has changed throughout time would be to examine successive pictures of the man every year between the ages of 22 and 84.

If, in the photo at age 23, we see the scar and his arm missing, we may surmise that he was injured in the war. If the injuries are not seen until year 54, we may rule out a war injury and consider a possibility more like an automobile accident. If we see the scar at age 45 but the arm is not missing until age 78, we know that the two injuries are unrelated.

While these "snapshots" themselves cannot answer all the questions, they are helpful in determining when the injuries took place, and give us a much better starting point, should we choose to investigate further.

I have found this same technique helpful in evaluating the transformation that has taken place in America, especially with regard to American ideology, our spiritual condition and our constitutional rights. The fact is, these three are more closely linked than they may appear.

If we only look at America shortly after it was founded and compare it to modern day America, important questions remain unanswered. How did this ideological transformation take place? At what rate? When? Who was responsible?

Who authorized it?

To discern in the most accurate way how much America has changed since inception with regard to our civil rights, we must start by examining the type of nation that was originally created and then periodically research American history. Through observing these "snapshots" of American history, we will be better prepared to understand not only how much America has changed with regard to civil rights, but we will also see how, when and who was responsible for the changes.

To understand where America is going, it is critical to know where we have been. It is almost impossible to see how far we have fallen unless we establish some point of reference. President Woodrow Wilson once said:

> [2] "A nation which does not remember what it was yesterday, does not know what it is today, nor what it is trying to do. We are trying to do a futile thing if we do not know where we came from or what we have been about."

Looking Back

I have learned, over many years of study, that people tend to base much of their beliefs upon what someone else has told them. This is true in society, and it is also true theologically. Rarely does anyone actually take the time anymore to research a given topic for themselves. That is the problem with living in a society where so much of our time is monopolized with the non-essentials. We usually find a book or a commentary from someone whom we perceive to be an expert in a given field to see what *they* have to say about the issue, then we simply accept it as fact. After all, this is much faster and easier than actually researching the subject for ourselves.

We sit under the guidance and direction of teachers, professors, politicians, ministers and priests and take for granted that they know what they are talking about and that what they are saying is true. But do we truly know these people? How can we know if these people have some prejudice or other ulterior motive for what they are saying (or *not* saying)? What if they have a hidden agenda? Could they themselves have been deceived? The only way to know for sure is to independently research the topic for ourselves.

This same approach is paramount if we desire to know and understand what actually transpired in America's past; specifically, the events involved in the founding of this great nation and the relationship that our founding fathers thought should exist the states and the federal government, and between a nation and its God.

What we learn is that since the late 50s or early 60s, secularists in the field of education have dominated positions of authority in most educational institutions and have systematically removed America's Judeo-Christian heritage from most public school American history textbooks.

As Tim Lahaye, author of the *Left Behind* series, writes in his book, *Faith of our founding fathers*:

> [3] "A U.S. federal judge was fascinated by the testimony of the expert witness on the stand as he described the distortion of history in the state-approved textbooks. The judge had always been led to believe that students and their parents could trust their schoolbooks. Consequently, it was difficult for him to believe that the religious history of America had been systematically stolen from our nation's

texts. Dr. Paul C. Vitz, New York University psychology professor, had just finished a research project for the U.S. department of education on 60 of the most popular textbooks and our public schools. It is estimated that 87% of the nation's elementary school children use the books."

As Dr. Vitz tells us in his book, *Censorship: Evidence of Bias in our Children's Textbooks*, [4] "The most striking thing about these texts," states Dr. Vitz in Judge Brevard Hand's court in Mobile, Alabama, "is the total absence of the Christian religion in them. He goes on to point out that other beliefs are mentioned—the Jewish, Amish, Mormon, and Catholic faiths—but little or no mention is made of the Evangelical Protestants who founded this nation."

This tactic is known as "exclusion" and secularists use it not only in our educational institutions, but also in the media, the courts, and in the church.

After Professor Vitz finished his research, he reported his findings about this secular bias in our public school textbooks to the U.S. Department of Education:

> [5] "Secular bias is primarily accomplished by *exclusion*, by leaving out the opposing position. Such a bias is much harder to observe than a positive vilification or direct criticism, but it is the essence of censorship. It is effective not only because it is hard to observe—it isn't there—and therefore hard to counteract, but also because it makes only the... secular position familiar and plausible."

Restoring History

History books are unique from other textbooks because

history, for the most part, does not need to be re-written, especially by those individuals 200–400 years removed from the actual events. It is always better to let the actual participants of the era tell us what they have to say, as opposed to some secular educator 200–400 years in the future, interpreting and rewriting what our founding fathers "really meant." As if they have some special understanding and insight about the founding of America that the founders themselves did not.

Ideally, one would simply need to add more pages to the history textbook as events unfold. For example, a history textbook from the 1930s would simply need additional pages added as World War II unfolded. This process could be continued up to the present day.

However, for the sake of brevity, we must minimize the amount of material placed in the American history textbooks, lest the students be overwhelmed by the volume of information. One history textbook I bought, which was written in 1928, stated:

> [6] "The early chapters of the book have been shortened to make room for fuller treatment of the industrial revolution and recent history."

Imagine how much history has had to be removed to make room for new, more current information. Herein, then, lies the problem. It's up to *the individuals who edit the books* to determine what history stays and what history is left out: what *they* feel is and was relevant to the founding of the nation.

Since many of those in charge of editing American history textbooks do not see the relevance or the correlation between America's Judeo-Christian past and how it affected the founding of the nation, America's true heritage and its impact on its formation was one of the first things to be removed. We are left with a generation of Americans who have no idea what our country's true past looked like. As a result, many of the people I have talked to have little, if any, understanding of the influence that religion had upon the founding of this country and the establishment of its form of government. Gary Palmer, President of the Alabama Policy Institute tells us:

> [7] "It has been the consistent practice of the totalitarians, the atheists, and the materialists to concentrate on undermining, ridiculing, or eliminating the basic truths of religion. They know that once these go, all the derivative truths and practices that depend on these primary principles become virtually meaningless."

I began my research by searching for the oldest public school history textbooks that I could find. I went to public libraries, to dusty old bookstores; I even bought about twenty old history textbooks from EBay. These textbooks ranged in publication date from 1866–1928. Of course, I wanted to see what the history textbooks before World War II had to say about the faith and purpose of those who formed this country, since shortly after World War II, the campaign to officially kick God out of American schools, government and the public square began. What truly amazed me was that I even found several "secular" public school history textbooks, which have nothing to do with religion, that have shed considerable light on our nation's past.

When one reads what was written in American history textbooks more than one hundred years ago about America's forefathers and the founding of this great nation, and compare it to what is written today about these same events, one cannot help but see that there has been a biased attempt to remove our Judeo-Christian heritage from the minds and hearts of the people of this nation. What Professor Vitz reported to the U.S. Department of Education about the systematic removal of our Judeo-Christian heritage was absolutely true.

As I have already stated, it is always better to let the actual participants of a given period tell us what they have to say, rather than listen to someone else's interpretation rewritten to suit their purposes. For that reason, I will let the Americans of the past tell us in their own words how America once looked.

This forces me to quote many books, but in this way, at least readers may independently research and validate these claims for themselves. My intent here is to show exactly what our school children were being taught 100–150 years ago, as opposed to what they are being taught today.

Christianity was so pervasive in the American culture of those days that the astute French observer Alexis de Tocqueville—the first to explore the relationship between religion and American democracy—reporting on his travels to America in the 1830s, provided a widely quoted analysis:

> [8] "Upon my arrival in the United States, the religious aspect of the country was the first thing that struck my attention; and the longer I stayed there the more I did perceive the great political consequences resulting from this state of things, to which I was unaccustomed. In France, I had almost always seen the spirit of religion and the spirit of freedom pursuing courses diametrically opposed to each other; but in America I found that they're intimately united, and that they reigned in common over the same country.

Religion in America takes no direct part in the government of society, but nevertheless it must be regarded as the foremost of the political institutions of that country; for if it does not impart a taste for freedom, it facilitates the use of free institutions. Indeed, it is in the end the same point of view that the inhabitants of the United States themselves look upon religious belief. I do not know whether all the Americans have a sincere faith in their religion, for who can search the human heart? But I am certain that they hold it to be indispensable to the maintenance of Republican institutions. This opinion is not particular to a class of citizen or to a party, but it belongs to the whole nation, into every rank of society."

Alexis de Tocqueville realized what the American people of the day already knew —that the principles of the Bible upon which this country was founded form the foundation of American society and freedom.

It is interesting to note that Alexis de Tocqueville says "This opinion is not particular to a class of citizen *or to a party*, but it belongs to the whole nation, into every rank of society." He states that every political party and every class of people held to these convictions.

Recently I saw a T-shirt showing a picture of some of our founding fathers; it read: *The Original Right-Wing Extremists*. The leftist media today refer to those who hold to the traditional American values of our founding fathers as the "far right" or as "Extremists."

The secularists in the schools, courts, media and the pulpits have moved America as a whole so far to the ideological left that what was considered mainstream at the time America was founded, and as recently as fifty years ago, is now considered "far right" and "ultra-conservative" by many in the press today.

Therefore, before we go any further, let us examine where the American people find themselves ideologically.

Chapter 2

What Do Americans Believe?

> [1] *"God cannot sustain this free and blessed the country which we love and pray for unless the church will take right ground. Politics are a part of a religion... Christians must do their duty to the country as a part of their duty to God... He will bless or curse this nation according to the course they take."*
>
> **Charles G. Finney**

Do the majority of Americans believe in God and want His blessing upon this nation, or is this just the opinion of a small group of people? If you listen to those in the secular media, religion plays a small and insignificant part in the lives of most Americans. The success of Mel Gibson's movie The Passion of the Christ should be enough to prove otherwise.

To properly understand where most Americans stand on the issues of God, faith and religion, let us look at a Gallup poll. The following is taken from *First Things, the Journal of Religion and Public Life*. You must ask yourself if you find yourself in the majority or the minority in this poll.

> [2] "In 1988, the highly respected Gallup Organization reported that nine Americans in ten said they never doubted the existence of God, eight in ten said they believed they will be called before God on Judgment Day to answer for their sins, eight in ten believed that God still works miracles, and seven in ten believed in life after death. Moreover, 90 percent prayed, 88 percent believed that God loved them, 78 percent said they had given 'a lot' or 'a fair amount' of thought to their relationship with God during the past two years, and 86 percent said they wanted religious training for their children.
>
> Natural law? Seventy-nine percent believed that 'there are clear guidelines about what's good and evil that applies to everyone regardless of the situation.' Traditional moral standards? Gallup found 36 percent were conservative on the subject, 52 percent moderate, and only 11 percent liberal.
>
> Almost half of all Protestants described themselves as born-again Christians. How can that much faith exist in a secular society?
>
> If 84 percent of its people believe that Jesus Christ was what He said He was, doesn't that by definition qualify the United States as a Christian country? A mere 8 percent of Americans were without a religious preference, and even they, in the words of

Gallup, "express a surprising degree of interest in religion and religious belief." (That figure was reconfirmed in a 1994 Gallup poll.)

Gallup polls taken in 1991 showed a modest rise in religiousness in America over the previous three years. Christians were 82 percent of the adult population. (This figure held steady three years later, with 58 percent of the population being Protestant and 25 percent being Catholic.) About seven out of ten adults reported membership in a church or synagogue (a level reached in the 1970s that remained the same in 1994). Eighty-six percent of teens said they believed that Jesus Christ is God or the Son of God, and 73 percent considered regular church attendance an important aspect of American citizenship. Fifty-nine percent of interviewees said they agreed completely that a personal faith in Jesus Christ was the *only* assurance of eternal life, and another 17 percent agreed 'somewhat.' Eighty-one percent believed the Bible to be the literal (32 percent) or inspired (49 percent) word of God.

The Catholic sociologist Andrew Greeley, after announcing similar data in 1993 from an international study, declared, 'In some countries, most notably Ireland and the United States, religious devotion may be higher than it has ever been in human history.' In the first place, the polling data declare emphatically and unanimously that the United States continues to be a Christian nation—at least of a sort. The level of faith in the Christian gospel expressed by Americans is, indeed, in Gallup's words, 'simply amazing.' Gallup concluded that 'the degree of religious orthodoxy found among Americans is simply amazing... Such a nation cannot by any stretch of the imagination be described as secular in its core beliefs.' And yet Billy Graham could declare that America was no longer a Christian or Protestant nation. It is, he said, 'a secular country in which thousands of Christians live and have substantial influence.'

Is modern America secular or Christian? We seem to be the most religious nation in the advanced industrialized West, but at the same time appear to be blatantly, even aggressively, secular. Scholars, clergy, judges, journalists, and others have pondered the paradox for years."

These polls surprised me, because I have believed that our nation has become more and more secular over the last 40 years. I began to wonder how I had the impression that America was a mostly secular country when the people who make up America say they still hold to traditional Judeo-Christian beliefs and values.

Who Is Responsible?

In this book it was my original intention to speak more on America as a whole rather than focus upon individuals or groups. However, since a nation is made up of individuals and groups of individuals, the line often gets blurred, especially when certain groups and organizations have made it their life's work to destroy the U.S. Constitution.

My prime motivating reasons for writing this book are two-fold. First, to show how the American system of government that our founding fathers guaranteed us in the Constitution has been destroyed by a civilian army whose allegiance and loyalty was to a hostile foreign power.

Second, to prove how these people have turned America as a nation away from God, and as a result, are in grave danger of turning God against America. The truly sad thing is that this is not the fault of the people of America; it is the government (and particularly the Supreme Court) that must shoulder the blame.

America can be seen as a ship traveling in a certain direction. It is either getting closer to God, or farther from Him. At times throughout American history, certain individuals and groups have been able to turn this nation as a whole away from God without the consent of the American people.

For 50 years or more, socialist and secularists in the press, media, church and the educational systems have done everything they can to rewrite history and totally ignore America's true historical past, and as a result, we have forgotten what type of nation we once were. The Courts have basically rewritten our Constitution in order to reflect a more socialist and secular worldview, and many in the pulpit are preaching a message that is far from "Christian."

It should not be hard to believe that such a small number of people would be able to alter the course of an entire nation. Even scripture shows that something small has the ability to change the course or direction of something much larger.

> [3] "We put bits in horses' mouths that they may obey us, and we turn their whole body. Look also at ships; although they are so large and are driven by fierce winds, they are turned by a small rudder wherever the pilot desires."

As we see, it is not hard to turn an object that is large, like a horse and a ship, using something that is very small. The same is true with our government and the American

Republic, created by our founding fathers. Once you know where the controls are, a small group of people can alter the course and direction of an entire nation.

Before we go any further, I would like to clarify one point in order to alleviate any confusion. I have said that there are those in America who have sought to turn America away from God, yet in the Gallup polls we see that at least 90% of Americans believe in God and that the majority hold to at least some type of religious faith. Therefore, before proceeding we must make a distinction between "America" and "American(s);" between "America" as a government institution and "American(s)" as a people.

Think of America as a ship. A ship is neutral; that is, it does not care in which direction it is traveling. The decision with regard to direction is up to the people on board.

Let us say that 99 out of 100 people aboard the ship want it to head north. However, if there is one person on this ship who does not want the ship to travel in this direction, all he has to do is find the rudder controls and take them over, thus giving him control of the entire ship. He then has the power to turn the entire ship around so that it is now sailing in the wrong direction, contrary to the will of the rest of the people.

When a person takes over the controls of a ship and turns it away from its predetermined destination, it is said the ship has been hijacked, which means [4] "to seize control forcibly… in order to go to a nonscheduled destination."

The people on the ship may realize that the ship has been turned from its original course and is now heading south, which is opposite to the direction that they wanted to go. Those who want to go north may turn toward the north in an attempt to show which direction they desire to go, but the ship is, in fact, sailing farther and farther to the south despite the fact the 99% of those on board are opposed to going in this direction.

The only recourse the people have is either to abandon ship or find out who hijacked the ship's rudder and wrest control of the ship away from him, returning the ship to its original course.

The same can be said about America. Our country is neutral; that is, the land in which we live does not care in which political, social or spiritual direction it is traveling. Our founding fathers intended to leave the decision with regard to America's direction up to the people who live in this country.

The America that we live in today is traveling in a direction that is 180 degrees different to the political, social and spiritual direction it was when our founding fathers created it. Our country is not even the same as it was as much as 80 years ago.

To briefly prove this point, let us look at the debate over Creation v. Evolution in American public schools.

Since long before the founding of the American government, every public school in America had taught the biblical account of creation to explain the origin of man and the origin of the universe. With the publication of Darwin's *Origin of Species*, in 1855, states all across America began passing laws that made the teaching of evolution illegal. In the state of Tennessee, this was known as the "Butler Law."

In 1925, a science teacher named John T. Scopes was convicted of teaching evolution to his students. This became known as the "Scopes Monkey Trial." It took the jury just nine minutes of deliberation to find him guilty, and he was fined $100.

As history proves, in 1925, the teaching of creation was common practice and the teaching of evolution was illegal in many states. Eighty years later, we find the exact opposite to be true. Today, evolution is taught in every public school in the nation and the teaching of the biblical account of creation to explain the origin of man and the origin of the universe is illegal.

Now, if this reversal of policy had been the result of the American people's decision, the change would be acceptable, but the American people have not even been consulted—the change has been forced upon us by a Supreme Court that has ignored 225 years of historical and judicial precedent in order to socially engineer American society and culture.

The reversal of everything our founding fathers stood for politically, socially and culturally began in earnest in the year 1925, when America was invaded and infiltrated by a civilian army whose allegiance and loyalty were elsewhere. Their goal—destroy the Constitutional Republic that our founding fathers created, and replace it with a socialist/totalitarian state to be ruled by a handful of judges. Therefore, if we are to defeat this enemy, we must understand how it operates.

As we have seen through the illustration of a ship, a relatively small number of people may control something very large with access to the rudder. The tactic that the socialists and totalitarians would use would be two-fold.

First, increase the amount of power given to the Supreme Court by the founding fathers and the Constitution, and install the Court as the "rudder" for American society. Second, take political and ideological control of the Court, therefore steering America in any direction that they desire.

Once they had taken control of the federal courts, they could then challenge any law that the American people had enacted, thereby thwarting the will of the people and setting themselves up as the supreme rulers of the American people.

An ongoing conspiracy has existed to overthrow the Constitutional Republic that our founding fathers created. A communist front organization called the American Civil Liberties Union (ACLU) is but one of the organizations that has led the way in our country's overthrow. Therefore, it is important to understand who they are and the tactics they have successfully used since 1925.

The ACLU is a socialist/communist front organization that for nearly a century has been on a mission to alter the American government from a Constitutional Republic into a socialist state, in which everything is controlled by the government. The ACLU's founder, Roger Baldwin, makes no apologies for his position:

> [5] "We are for *Socialism*, disarmament, and ultimately for abolishing the state itself... We seek the social ownership of property, the abolition of the propertied class [private ownership of property], and the *sole control* of those who produce wealth. *Communism* is the goal... I don't regret being part of the communist tactic. I knew what I was doing. *I was not an innocent liberal.* I wanted what the communists wanted and I traveled the United Front road to get it."

Contrary to what they would have us believe, the ACLU does not simply come to the defense of people who have had their civil liberties violated. Its primary strategy is to get someone to violate any opposed law enacted by the American people through the proper democratic process, so that the law may be challenged in court. The sole motivation behind this tactic is not to get the offending party acquitted, but to get the Supreme Court to rule the law enacted by the American people as "unconstitutional."

Understanding Their Tactics

As we saw earlier, in 1925, a science teacher named John T. Scopes was convicted of teaching evolution to his students. However, this was not simply a case of a science teacher violating the anti-evolution laws and getting caught; it was a staged event from the very beginning, the sole purpose of which was to challenge the people's constitutional right to enact laws banning the teaching of evolution. The following is taken from the University of Missouri-Kansas City School of Law:

> [6] "The Scopes Trial had its origins in a *conspiracy* at Fred Robinson's drugstore in Dayton. George Rappalyea, a 31-year-old transplanted New Yorker and local coal company manager, arrived at the drugstore with a copy of a paper containing an American Civil Liberties Union (ACLU) announcement that it was willing to offer its services to anyone challenging the new Tennessee anti-evolution statute.
>
> The conspirators summoned John Scopes, a twenty-four-year old general science teacher and part-time football coach, to the drugstore. As Scopes later described the meeting, Rappalyea said, 'John, we've been arguing and I said nobody could teach biology without teaching evolution.' Scopes agreed. 'That's right,' he said, pulling a copy of Hunter's *Civic Biology*—the state-approved textbook—from one of the shelves of the drugstore (the store also sold school textbooks). 'You've been teaching them this book?' Rappalyea asked. Scopes replied that while filling in for the regular biology teacher during an illness, he had assigned readings on evolution from the book

for review purposes. 'Then you've been violating the law,' Rappalyea concluded. 'Would you be willing to stand for a test case?' he asked. Scopes agreed. He later explained his decision, 'the best time to scotch the snake is when it starts to wiggle.' Herbert and Sue Hicks, two local attorneys and friends of Scopes, agreed to prosecute.

On the first business day of trial, the defense moved to quash the indictment on both state and federal constitutional grounds. This move was at the heart of the defense strategy. The defense's goal was not to win acquittal for John Scopes, but rather to obtain a declaration by a higher court—preferably the U.S. Supreme Court—that laws forbidding the teaching of evolution were unconstitutional. (That goal, however, would not be realized for another 43 years, in the case of *Epperson vs. Arkansas*)."

The ACLU was not trying to get Mr. Scopes acquitted; it wanted the laws forbidding the teaching of evolution to be ruled unconstitutional. Since the Supreme Court did not yet have the legal or the constitutional authority to stick its nose in states' business, it would be another 43 years before the ACLU would get the ruling it desired. This strategy has been employed over and over by the ACLU and other socialist groups in order to override the American people's right to govern their respective societies. They intentionally and deliberately stage a crime scene to get someone arrested, so that the law enacted by the American people may be challenged in court. This tactic is still being employed to this day.

In 1982, Michael Hardwick was placed under arrest for sodomy when police found him having oral sex with another man. However, when the district attorney decided not to prosecute, Mr. Hardwick sued the attorney general of Georgia, stating that he wanted to be prosecuted for his activities. Why would an individual insist on being prosecuted? It was clear that the same tactic was being used as in the Scopes case. Mr. Hardwick was not trying to get acquitted; he simply wanted Georgia's sodomy laws to be ruled unconstitutional by the federal courts.

Following decisions by the lower federal courts, the case ultimately reached the Supreme Court, which ruled in the 1986 case *Bowers vs. Hardwick* that the Constitution *does not* confer a fundamental right upon homosexuals to engage in sodomy. But those opposed to laws enacted by the American people continue to stage such cases until they can get a majority of judges to overturn 225 years of historical and judicial precedent. It would take only 17 years for their tactic to work.

On September 17, 1998, police found two men having anal sex in an apartment in the suburbs of Houston. However, this was not a case in which law enforcement was searching bedrooms, looking for people committing sodomy. This was a staged crime scene from the very beginning, the purpose of which was to rule sodomy as a constitutional right.

Harris County sheriff's department had received a report that there was a man going crazy with a gun in John Lawrence's apartment. When the police arrived, since they had probable cause to believe that a crime was being committed, they entered Mr. Lawrence's "unlocked" apartment and found the two men having sex.

When it was learned that there had never been a man with a gun, the neighbor, Roger Nance, admitted that he had lied and served 15 days in jail after pleading no contest to charges of filing a false police report. This case would make it to the Supreme Court five years later.

In the case of *Lawrence vs. Texas*, the Supreme Court

found somewhere in the Constitution that our founding fathers intended to include sodomy as a constitutionally protected civil right. I refer to this particular case not to argue for or against state sodomy laws, but to illustrate how the Supreme Court over the last 60 years has continually and consistently ignored 225 years of historical and judicial precedent in order to reach a predetermined decision in its social engineering of American society and culture.

During the American Revolution, a man named Lieutenant Enslin was tried for attempting to commit sodomy with another soldier, named John Monhort. He was found guilty and sentenced to be dismissed from the military with "public disgrace." George Washington, who would soon be the President of the Constitutional Convention, himself approved of the sentence with "abhorrence and detestation."

During the time of the Constitution's ratification by the original thirteen states, sodomy was illegal in all of the states. In 1961, all 50 states had outlawed sodomy. Therefore, for the Supreme Court to now attempt to say that sodomy is a civil right that the framers of the Constitution sought to protect is ridiculous. As the Supreme Court Justices had said in their 1986 Bowers v. Hardwick decision:

> "Against this background, to claim that a right to engage in such conduct is 'deeply rooted in this Nation's history and tradition' or 'implicit in the concept of ordered liberty' is, at best facetious."

This was clearly a case in which the Supreme Court wanted to rewrite both history and the Constitution. For the last 60 years, the Supreme Court has been on a mission to destroy the Constitution and the traditional Judeo-Christian values that our founding fathers held so dear.

The majority of Americans believe in traditional American values. They believe in the Constitutional right of self-government. Polls show that the majority of Americans believe in the same system of government that our founding fathers stood for.

However, socialists and secularists in all segments of society have been on a campaign to remove God from America's past, while at the same time continuing to try to keep Him out of every aspect of present-day American life. This includes, but is not limited to, the banning of school Christmas plays, the singing of Christmas carols, the removal of nativity scenes and crosses from places where they have stood for decades and, in some cases, centuries.

Do you find yourself offended by T-shirts and bumper stickers that say GOD BLESS AMERICA, or are you more likely to display them? Do you want God to bless America? Do you agree with the total secularization of America?

The individuals who are presently warring against traditional American values are clearly in the minority. Unfortunately, the 90% of us who do believe in the traditional Judeo-Christian principles on which this country was founded have practically laid down and allowed a small minority to dictate public policy.

The reason the minority has been able to dictate policy to the majority is actually quite sad, and I find myself as much to blame as the next person. The less than 10% of those who want God removed from society and government are far more zealous about their cause than the remaining 90% that are in their support of our Judeo-Christian heritage.

For the last 40 years, whenever our Judeo-Christian values, traditions and symbols have been systematically removed from all facets of American life, it is this minority that has made the most noise. When politicians and judges sit in their offices and hear from the small percentage of those opposed to God and 2 or 3% of the 90% who support Him, who do you think their votes and court rulings are going to favor?

If the American people truly want God to bless America and want to enjoy the freedoms and civil rights guaranteed in the Constitution, then we are each going to have to play a more active role in the affairs of our government.

Two hundred years ago, Edmund Burke said, "All that is necessary for evil to triumph is that good men do nothing..." And for the last 40 years, that is exactly what has happened.

In the early 1800s, America experienced a religious revival known as the "Second Great Awakening." One of the key figures was lawyer-turned-evangelist, Charles G. Finney.

Mr. Finney clearly states for us what the role of those who believe in God should be with regard to our government.

> [7] "God cannot sustain this free and blessed country which we love and pray for unless the church will take right ground. Politics are a part of a religion... Christians must do their duty to the country as a part of their duty to God... He will bless or curse this nation according to the course they take."

We must turn this country around. However, in order to accomplish this, we must understand who has hijacked our Constitution and seized control of our country in order to return America to its original political, social and spiritual direction.

As we will consider in depth in the following chapters, America was a nation founded by God and His people, contrary to what the secularists in the media and in the educational system would have us believe. Historically we have been a nation that has acknowledged God in our laws, in our courts, in our schools, and in our society. As a result, we live in the greatest nation in the world because of God's blessings.

As history will prove, America was also a nation founded by God's people and by those who wanted the freedom to worship Him in any way they deemed appropriate, without interference from the federal government. These truths will be personally testified to by our founding fathers in the following chapters. However, secularists and socialists in this country have, over a period of 50-plus years, removed these truths from American history books by saying that including these historical truths in government-funded history books would violate the 1st Amendment to the Constitution. We are left with many Americans who have absolutely no idea about their true American heritage and the circumstances surrounding the founding of this great country.

As we will see in the next chapter, for the first 150 years, our American government not only encouraged religion and morality as *an essential pillar of society*, it actively supported it. Then in the 1940s–1960s, the government began to take what it called a position of "neutrality" with regard to religion, and tried to tell the American people that a government divorced from religion was what our founding fathers intended.

After they were able to convince the American public that this was what the founding fathers intended when writing the U.S. Constitution, the federal government, led by the federal judicial system and several left-wing advocacy groups like the ACLU and Americans United for the Separation of Church and State, have for the last 40 years been actively persecuting people of faith in America under the guise of "federal neutrality."

In fewer than 80 years, the federal government has gone from encouraging and actively supporting religion and morality as an essential pillar of society, to being "neutral" on the issue or religion, to openly hostile to religion and the biggest persecutor of people of faith. I believe that if their assault is not stopped and reversed, the persecution will only get worse.

The debate over the Ten Commandments in the United States Supreme Court is just the tip of the iceberg. It is simply getting the attention that *many* other similar cases of religious persecution are not.

For the last 40 years, the federal government has been the biggest persecutor of religious freedom, and the other stories of religious persecution are all but ignored by the secular media.

I believe the American people are growing sick and tired of the minority secular establishment force-feeding its propaganda down the throats of a majority. Many are beginning to rise up in opposition to the secular takeover of our media, courts, and our educational and religious systems.

I received the following in an email that apparently came from the pen of Nick Gholson, a columnist for the *Times Record News* in Wichita Falls, Texas, as a result of the Supreme Court forbidding the Texas tradition of saying a prayer before a high school football game. I believe this quote reflects the opinion of the majority of the American people.

> "I don't believe in Santa Claus, but I'm not going to sue somebody for singing a Ho-Ho-Ho song in December. I don't agree with Darwin, but I didn't go out and hire a lawyer when my high school teacher taught his theory of evolution.

"Life, liberty or your pursuit of happiness will not be endangered because someone says a 30-second prayer before a football game. So what's the big deal? It's not like somebody is up there reading the entire book of Acts. They're just talking to a God they believe in and asking him to grant safety to the players on the field and the fans going home from the game.

"'But it's a Christian prayer,' some will argue. Yes, and this is the United States of America, a country founded on Christian principles. According to our very own phone book, Christian churches outnumber all others better than 200-to-1. So what would you expect—somebody chanting "Hare Krishna"?

"If I went to a football game in Jerusalem, I would expect to hear a Jewish prayer. If I went to a soccer game in Baghdad, I would expect to hear a Muslim prayer. If I went to a ping pong match in China, I would expect to hear someone pray to Buddha. And I wouldn't be offended. It wouldn't bother me one bit. When in Rome.

"'But what about the atheists?' is another argument. What about them? Nobody is asking them to be baptized. We're not going to pass the collection plate. Just humor us for 30 seconds. If that's asking too much, bring a Walkman or a pair of ear plugs. Go to the bathroom. Visit the concession stand! Call your lawyer!

"Unfortunately, one or two will make that call. One or two will tell thousands what they can and cannot do. I don't think a short prayer at a football game is going to shake the world's foundations.

"Christians are just sick and tired of turning the

other cheek while our courts strip us of all our rights. Our parents and grandparents taught us to pray before eating; to pray before we go to sleep. Our Bible tells us to pray without ceasing. Now a handful of people and their lawyers are telling us to cease praying. God, help us.

"And if that last sentence offends you, well... just sue me. The silent majority has been silent too long. It's time we let that one or two who scream loud enough to be heard... that the vast majority don't care what they want. It is time the majority rules! It's time we tell them, you don't have to pray; you don't have to say the Pledge of Allegiance; you don't have to believe in God or attend services that honor Him. That is your right, and we will honor your right. But by golly, you are no longer going to take our rights away. We are fighting back... and we WILL WIN!

"God bless us one and all... especially those who denounce Him. God bless America, despite all her faults. She is still the greatest nation of all. God bless our service men who are fighting to protect our right to pray and worship God. May 2006 be the year the silent majority is heard and we put God back as the foundation of our families and institutions. Keep looking up."

Whether you are a Republican, Democrat or an Independent; a liberal, conservative or a moderate; whether you support the Constitution Party, the Libertarian Party or the Green Party, we are all going to have to come to the realization that our founding fathers created the greatest Constitution that is was possible for mortal man to create, and unless we return to the ideals of our founding fathers when drafting the Constitution, America is headed for disaster.

W.E. Gladstone, who served as Prime Minister of Great Britain on and off from 1868 to 1894, had this to say about the U.S. Constitution:

> [8] "As the British Constitution is the most subtle organism which has proceeded from the womb and long gestation of progressive history, so the American Constitution is, so far as I can see, the most wonderful work ever struck off at a given time by the brain and purpose of man."

Unless we return to the system of government that our founding fathers instituted when drafting and ratifying the American Constitution, America and the American system of government that they created will become, at best, a hollow shell of what it once was.

As we will see throughout this book, the socialization and secularization of America has been historically opposed by both Republicans and Democrats alike, and I believe if we are going to fix the problems in American society, this is where the two parties stand the greatest chance of finding common ground. If not, then maybe it is time for another political party to rise up that will support and defend the Constitution.

Understanding Socialism and Secularism

Before we begin exploring the ideas of our founding fathers concerning the "form of the government" and "social system" that the Constitution guarantees us, it is important that we first understand the terms "secularism" and "socialism." As we will see, these two ideologies are totally contrary to the type of government created by the Constitution.

Secular or secularism can be defined as "being without

God or religion." Therefore, secularization can best be defined as "the removal of God and religion from all aspects of American society and government." Every poll taken in the history of America has shown that the majority of Americans are not secular, nor do they support the secularization of American society. That is, most Americans do not agree with the total and absolute removal of God and religion from every aspect of American society and government.

The total concept of socialism is a little more complex. It is defined as [9] "various economic and political theories advocating collective or governmental ownership and administration of the means of production and distribution of goods."

Socialists and communists all hold to basically the same ideology. Therefore, if a person denies any links to this ideology, you can still identify them by the issues and policies they defend.

Socialism is a very ineffective form of government. For this reason, socialists oftentimes have to change to the "label" that they wear to identify themselves. Today they prefer the term "Progressives." However, there are three common and distinguishing characteristics that we can use to identify these individuals, no matter what "label" they choose the wear. It is essential to be able to identify these left-wing ideologies in order to identify those in America who are attempting to destroy our Constitution and our traditional American way of life. The three identifying features are:

1. Strong centralized government
2. Redistribution of wealth
3. Atheism

These first two ideological beliefs, "strong centralized

government" and the "redistribution of wealth," can clearly be seen in Communist countries, such as China and the former Soviet Union's use of the collective farm system. The collective farm system includes a number of farm households or villages that all work together under state control. These farmers spend all year growing their crops and then, at harvest time, the federal government collects all their produce and then evenly (I use the word "evenly" reluctantly) redistributes it to the people, wherever the government sees fit.

If one farmer decides he is not going to grow any crops and his neighbor busts his tail farming 50 acres of land, the government will come in and take all of the food from the farmer who grew the 50 acres of food and redistribute some of it to the farmer who did not grow anything (after the government has taken its disproportionate share).

Do you understand what type of economy this creates? Why would people want to go out and work hard, just to have the government come along and give what they have worked so hard for to someone who does not work at all? In America this is called the welfare system. One report showed that for every 21 dollars that the American people sends to Washington, 9 dollars of it actually reaches welfare recipients. Socialism is an inefficient system that rewards the lazy and penalizes the faithful and hard-working. In the must-read 1964 book by Billy J. Hargis, *The Far Left*, we read:

> [10] "History records that Hitler and Mussolini were both Socialists. Hitler, the Nazi, chose for his party the name, "The National *Socialist* German Workers Party." He did so because, ideologically, he was a socialist—a fanatical advocate of the government planned economy...
>
> "Mussolini, the fascist dictator, was a dedicated

socialist all of his life. Mussolini was able to retain his power because of his 'promises to the working class...' The appeal of American liberalism today (remember, this was written in 1964) is the same appeal of Hitler's Nazism and Mussolini's Fascism. They all accomplish the same thing:

1. Wage rates were raised regardless of productivity,
2. Higher pensions were decreed and at an earlier age—the nation's capacity to support persons no longer productive bore no relationship to the size of the pensions,
3. The number of people holding soft jobs on the government payroll was built up,
4. Workers were required to become union members as a means of subjecting them to union discipline,
5. Union leaders were brought into the ruler's inner circle...

"In a speech before Congress in 1938, (Martin Dies) said: 'I regard communism and Nazism and Fascism as having one underlying principle— dictatorship. The theory that government should have the right to control the lives, the fortunes, the happiness, the beliefs and every detail of the life of a human being and that man is a pawn of the government rather than the American conception that (government) is created for the benefit of mankind'."

"Strong centralized government" is one of the biggest aspects of socialism and it is in place for one reason and one reason only: **CONTROL**.

In America this is seen when the American people are

forced to send all their tax dollars to Washington, and then Washington legislates what the states have to do to get their money back. They say, "Unless you do this or that, we will not send you your highway money." Or "Unless you teach what the government mandates that you teach, we will withhold your education money." This type of behavior is nothing more than political blackmail in which the federal government "blackmails" the states into adapting its political and social policies, or run the risk of not receiving *their own* tax dollars back.

Now we see a push in this country for more and more government involvement in the everyday lives of Americans. This most recent push comes in the form of a federal healthcare system. While the bleeding heart media hypes up stories about "Aunt Mary's" healthcare cost, they offer as the only solution as a federal healthcare system. (Sound familiar?)

While reading *The Warren Court and its Critics*, I found that 50 years ago, one congressman attacked then Supreme Court Justice Earl Warren, saying:

> [11] "[He] advocated 'socialized medicine' in California and 'this is the first step Communists use in organizing a totalitarian state'."

If you think you have seen inefficiency in the welfare system, wait until the government gets hold of your healthcare.

The absolute last thing that we as Americans should want is the federal government controlling another aspect of out lives. The people of this country are slowly sitting by and watching everything that our founding fathers created being sucked in by the socialist machine.

This is why our founding fathers were so opposed to

a strong centralized government and a Constitution that could be twisted in such a way as to nullify states rights. It all boils down to a matter of power and control. P. J. O'Rourke, humorist and political commentator, once said, "Giving money and power to government is like giving whiskey and car keys to teenage boys."

Thomas Jefferson warned that a "government big enough to supply everything you need is big enough to take everything you have... The course of history shows that as a government grows, liberty decreases."

When the government has the people and the states by the purse strings and tells them that they cannot have *their own money* back unless they do certain things, this is **un-American**, totally opposed to the original intent of our founding fathers, and a violation of the U.S. Constitution.

The third and most important identifying feature often shared by communists and socialists is "atheism" and their hatred of God and religion. This is why they promote secularization and seek to remove all aspects of religion from the public square.

This can be clearly seen in the Constitution of the former Soviet Union. A good friend of mine asked me recently why the majority of Americans believe that *our Constitution* calls for a separation of church and state. I told him that these organizations have learned that if you repeat something enough, by sheer force of repetition people will begin believing the lie, unless the lie is challenged every time it is spoken. I then asked him, "Do you really want to know where the phrase 'separation of church and state is found? It is found in the Constitution of the Soviet Union'."

The Constitution of the United Soviet Socialist Republics of 1936 reads as follows:

[12] ARTICLE 124: "In order to ensure to citizen's freedom of conscience, **the church in the U.S.S.R. is separated from the State,** and the school from the church."

Communist objectives widely publicized in their own literature were briefly summarized by a Congressional committee in 1931, which, I feel, is still the best short definition of communism:

[13] "Hatred of God and all forms of religion. Destruction of private property and inheritance. Promotion of class hatred."

When a handful of bureaucrats in Washington can tell five average people in Montana that they cannot pray over their school lunches or display a banner reading "God Bless our Troops" or "God Bless America" in their classroom, you have just succeeded in destroying the inalienable rights that our founding fathers fought and died for, and have replaced it with a government that resembles communism.

When you combine both secularism and socialism, you are left with a strong centralized government that forbids religious expression under penalty of imprisonment. This reflects the ideals and the principles of Communism more than it does the American Republic that our founding fathers created.

Separation of church and state is a communist and socialist ideology to which our founding fathers did not subscribe. While it is true that you can trace the idea of church–state separation back to the 1600s, when read in its true context, it was always an idea that meant that the government would not have the power to enact laws restricting the religious liberties of its people.

The Constitution of the U.S.S.R. and its "separation of church and state" existed a full generation before the socialist- and secularist-controlled Supreme Court **changed** our Constitution to match it.

We are all familiar with the horrible natural disasters that test our strength and courage. I speak in this book of an *invisible* disaster of the worst kind, one that many of us cannot even recognize, but the devastation of which could stretch into eternity. How may we remove this cloak of invisibility? By exposing our enemies for what and who they are.

America's Rise
1492–1940 A.D.

"The young must be taught, and they must be taught truly if the spring waters of democracy are to be kept untainted. The influence of the scriptures in the early days of the Republic is plainly revealed in the writing and thinking of men who made the nation possible... They found in the scriptures that which shaped their course and determined their actions."

Franklin D. Roosevelt

Chapter 3

The First American Revolution

> [1] *"That to secure these Rights, Governments are instituted among Men, deriving their just Powers from the Consent of the Governed, that whenever any Form of Government becomes destructive of these Ends, it is the Right of the People to alter or to abolish it, and to institute new Government."*
>
> **The Declaration of Independence**

As we look at the Revolutionary War era, and take a deeper and more specific look at the life and faith of the founding fathers, we will soon see that the most influential men during the time of the American Revolution and the writing of the Declaration of Independence and the Constitution were primarily men with deeply held religious beliefs.

The U.S. Constitution is the sole document from which the entire United States federal government derives its power. Therefore, it is absolutely imperative that we properly interpret what the founding fathers intended when authoring these documents.

A brief study of the lives of these men will later aid us in understanding why they felt the need to author these documents in the first place, and what role they intended the Constitution to play in American government and society.

Contrary to what secularists in the mainstream media and educational system may have us believe, most of the men responsible for the Declaration of Independence and the U.S. Constitution were men with firm religious convictions.

Many credible studies of the religious and moral influence of our founding fathers by educated individuals and universities have been largely ignored by the mainstream press and the federal courts. I cite the following conclusion of a study by the University of Houston:

> [2] "Over a ten year period, political science professors at the University of Houston analyzed over 15,000 writings and speeches by the founding fathers to determine the primary source of ideas behind the Constitution. The three most quotes sources were the French philosopher Montesquieu, English jurist William Blackstone, and English philosopher John Locke. *But the bible was quoted more than any of these*: four times more than Montesquieu, six times more often than Locke, and twelve times more than Blackstone. Thirty-four percent of the Founding Father's quotes were quoted either directly or indirectly, from the bible."

I believe the historical revisionists have done this country a great injustice by removing our founding fathers' faith and the influence that it had on their lives and on the founding of our nation from our children's public school history textbooks. However, for the sake of time and space, I would like to focus solely on the lives of three of the Constitution's most influential members: George Washington, Benjamin Franklin and James Madison.

George Washington

No man had a greater influence upon the American Revolution and the United States Constitution than George Washington. His name is so revered, even to this day, that most secular humanists dare not bash his reputation.

George Washington was a national hero and admired by most Americans. Following the American Revolution, he served as President over the Constitutional Convention. Many historians believe that if George Washington had not been there to give his seal of approval, the Constitution would never have been adapted. Needless to say, George Washington was an influential man with regard to the Constitution.

However, as we saw earlier, when writers talk at great lengths about a man but fail to mention the factor that most guided his life (faith), we are left with the illusion that faith had little, if any, influence on his actions.

John Marshall, Chief Justice to the Supreme Court, had the following to say about George Washington:

> [3] "Without making ostentatious professions of religion, he was a sincere believer in the Christian faith, and a truly devout man." Said the Rev.

J.T. Kirkland after Washington's death in 1799, "The virtues of our departed friend were crowned by piety. He is known to have been habitually devout. To Christian institutions we gave the countenance of his example; and no one else could express, more fully, this sense of the providence of God, and the dependence of man."

By almost every contemporary account, George Washington was the greatest man in the colonies—and he was acknowledged so by almost all Americans. In fact, his work and leadership for our country were such that the *World Book* encyclopedia stated in the opening remarks about Washington, [4] "In the history of the world, no man has done more to help any country than Washington did to help the United States."

Yet, it has been all but omitted from modern history textbooks that he was an extremely dedicated Christian. Read what Washington himself had to say to the Delaware Indian chiefs in 1779:

> [5] "You do well to wish to learn our arts and ways of life, and above all, the religion of Jesus Christ. These will make you a greater and happier people than you are. Congress will do everything they can to assist you in this wise intention."

Why would George Washington say, "Congress will assist you in learning the religion of Jesus Christ"? Today's secularists who oppose the ideology established by the founding fathers would call this a violation of separation of church and state. Does this sound like a man who would have wanted God kept out of schools and out of the affairs of government? Allow me to let Mr. Washington speak for himself:

Government: "Above all, the pure light of revelation

has had an influence on mankind, and increased the blessings of society. It is impossible to rightly govern the world without God and the Bible."

Schools: "The future of our country depends upon the Christian training of our youth."

With these two statements from George Washington in mind, how then can we truly believe that he expected religion to be kept out of schools and government?

Many of today's secularists, who are determined to eliminate the Judeo-Christian principles upon which this nation was founded, often claim that our founding fathers were not Christians, but deists. The following quotes from Patrick Henry and John Adams should expose this for the lie that it is. Patrick Henry, who greatly influenced the adoption of the Bill of Rights, which are the first ten amendments to the Constitution, is quoted as saying:

> [6] *"It cannot be emphasized too often or too strongly that this great nation was founded not by religionists but by Christians; not on religions but on the gospel of Jesus Christ. For this very reason peoples of other faiths have been afforded asylum, prosperity, and freedom of worship here."*

President John Adams clearly supports Patrick Henry's claim that America was founded by Christians and not by deists. Upon his election as the Second President of the United States, he had this to say in his inaugural address:

> [7] "I feel it to be my duty to add, if a (respect) for the religion of a people who profess and call themselves Christians, and a fixed resolution to consider a decent respect for Christianity among the best recommendations for the public service…"

President Adams, one of the founding fathers, clearly stated his opinion with regard to a nation living according to biblical precepts:

> [8] "Suppose a nation... should take the Bible for their only law book and every member should regulate his conduct by the precepts their exhibited... What a Utopia, what a paradise would this region be. I have examined all (religions)... and the result is that the Bible is the best book in the world. It contains more of my little Philosophy than all the libraries I have seen. And such parts as I cannot reconcile with my little philosophy, I postpone for future investigation."

Benjamin Franklin

Many secular people and organizations today attempt to portray Benjamin Franklin as a deist who was driven more by principles than by religion. While it is true that Ben Franklin was one of the least orthodox of the founding fathers, to call him a deist contradicts the very definition of the word.

Deists believe that God created the world and then left it to operate without His divine assistance or intervention. Thus, deists also do not believe that the Holy Scriptures are divinely inspired. The evidence shows that that Mr. Franklin believed in no such impersonal deity. In a letter to Ezra Styles, President of Yale University, Franklin defined his religious creed:

> [9] "Here is my creed. I believe in one God, the creator of the universe. That He governs it by His

providence. That He ought to be worshiped. That the most acceptable service we rendered to Him is in doing good to His other children. That the soul of man is immortal, and will be treated with Justice in another life respecting its conduct in this. These I take to be the fundamental points in all sound religion."

Benjamin Franklin's view of God and his belief that God hears the prayers of man is made clear by his statement on the floor of the Constitutional Convention in 1787. During this time, the Constitutional Convention was deadlocked, and some of the delegates from New York had even left. Just when things began to look hopeless that the United States would ever have a federal Constitution, Benjamin Franklin stood and addressed George Washington and the other delegates.

James Madison, the convention's Secretary, recorded for all posterity the words of Benjamin Franklin. What Mr. Franklin said on the floor of the Constitutional Convention is relevant today to counter those who insist that our founding fathers never intended God, prayer or the Bible to influence the affairs of government. Here is a portion of what he said:

> [10] "In the beginning of the contest with Great Britain, when we were sensible of danger, we had daily prayer in this room for our divine protection. Our prayers, Sir, were heard, and they were graciously answered. All of us who were engaged in the struggle must have observed frequent instances of a superintending Providence in our favor. To that kind of Providence, we owe this happy opportunity of consulting in peace on the means of establishing

our future national [happiness]. And have we now forgotten this powerful friend? Or do we imagine we no longer need His assistance? I have lived, Sir, a long time, and the longer I live, the more convincing proofs I see of this truth— that God governs in the affairs of men. And if a sparrow cannot fall to the ground without His notice, is it probable that an empire cannot rise without His aid? We have been assured, Sir, in the sacred writings, that "except the Lord build the house, they labor in vain that build it." I firmly believe this; and I also believe that without His concurring aid, we shall succeed in this political building no better than the builders of Babel... I therefore beg leave to move—that henceforth prayers imploring the assistance of heaven, and its blessing on our deliberations, be held in this assembly every morning before we proceed to business, and that one or more of the clergy of this city be requested to officiate in that service."

When an objective and unbiased individual reads Mr. Franklin's speech on the floor of the Constitutional Convention, one cannot help but acknowledge many truths about Mr. Franklin, his faith and the role he felt that God and Christianity should play in the affairs of government.

1. He felt it was perfectly acceptable for government officials, as part of their official duties, to pray and ask God for divine guidance, direction, favor and protection for their nation.
2. He believed in a personal God who not only heard their prayers, but also answered them.
3. He believed God had personally intervened in the war and had shown favor to the colonists' cause.

4. He asked the questions, "And have we now forgotten this powerful friend? Or do we imagine we no longer need His assistance?" Mr. Franklin was aware of the tendency of man to forget God and think that we no longer need His help once everything begins to look good.
5. He demonstrates his knowledge of the Judeo-Christian Bible by referring to the "sacred writings," and then quoting two scripture passages and referring to another biblical event. This shows that he used the Judeo-Christian Bible as the basis for his religious beliefs.

Anyone who has read the writings of Benjamin Franklin would have to admit that while he may not have been the most orthodox of the founding fathers, he was far from being an atheist, agnostic or a deist. And his thoughts concerning the relationship between religion and government were well known:

> "That wise Men have in all Ages thought Government necessary for the Good of Mankind; and, that wise Governments have always thought Religion necessary for the well ordering and well-being of Society." (Benjamin Franklin, On that Odd Letter of the Drum, April 1730)

James Madison

According to *World Book* encyclopedia [11], "James Madison (1751–1836), the Fourth President of the United States, is often called "The Father of the Constitution." He played a leading role in the Constitutional Convention of 1787, where he helped design the checks and balances that operate among Congress, the President, and the Supreme Court. He also helped create the U.S. federal system, which divides power between the central government and the states."

While most of James Madison's accomplishments are recorded in modern history books and encyclopedias, not surprisingly, his faith has been left out. Madison's views on religion and government should not surprise us, for he held the same beliefs that the rest of America and the founding fathers held. He is quoted as having said:

> [12] "Religion, or the duty we do our creator, and the manner of discharging it, can be directed only by reason and conviction, not by force or violence; and, therefore, *that all men should enjoy the fullest toleration in the exercise of religion* according to the dictates of conscience, unpunished and *unrestrained by the magistrate*, unless under color of religion and a man disturbed the peace, the happiness, or safety of society, and that it is the mutual duty of all to practice Christian forbearance, love, and charity toward each other."

James Madison was indeed a man of faith. As a matter of fact, this was the genesis of what would become the 1st Amendment to the Constitution, which he influenced. In this quote we see that he believed religious activities should be unpunished and unrestrained by the magistrate (judges, government officials, etc.).

What was his view concerning government and religion? Did Madison seek to protect government from religion? *No!* He wanted to protect religion from the federal government. He felt *"that all men should enjoy the fullest toleration in the exercise of religion... unpunished and unrestrained by the magistrate [judges]."*

As we will later see, this was the founder's motivation for drafting the 1st Amendment, and not vice versa, as many today would have us believe.

Thomas Jefferson

You may wonder why, when writing about the three most influential men in the final outcome of our American Constitution, I did not include Thomas Jefferson. The answer is simple. Contrary to what the Supreme Court might lead you to believe, and contrary to what those organizations that oppose God might try to make you think, *Thomas Jefferson had absolutely nothing to do with the writing of the Federal Constitution!*

In one of the primary cases that started the assault on the religious liberties of the American people, the Supreme Court made this statement in *Everson v. Board of Education:*

> [13] "This Court has previously recognized that the provisions of the First Amendment, in the drafting and adoption of which Madison and Jefferson played such leading roles... In the words of Jefferson, the clause against establishment of religion by law was intended to erect "a wall of separation between church and State."

Here again is how secularists will try to fool you. They make historical quotes and hope that nobody will "do their homework" to find out how much truth is in their statements. In the cases where the Supreme Court kicked religion out of America, the Court made this statement: "This Court has previously recognized that the provisions of the 1st Amendment, in the drafting and adoption of which

Madison and Jefferson played such leading roles."

Did this court go on to quote Madison's above statement with regard to the role of religion and government? No! If they had, it would have destroyed their argument. The Supreme Court would have us believe that Thomas Jefferson played a leading role in the drafting and adoption of the 1st Amendment of the Constitution. While it is true that Jefferson played a part in the Virginia Bill for Religious Liberty, he played no role in the drafting of the federal Constitution.

A simple comparison of the timelines between the writing of the Constitution and the whereabouts of Jefferson at the time proves that Jefferson was nowhere around the North American continent when the Constitution was written or adopted.

> [14] "In May 1784, Congress sent Jefferson to France to join John Adams and Benjamin Franklin in negotiating European treaties of commerce. The next year, Franklin resigned as minister to France, and Jefferson succeeded him in Paris... Jefferson had taken his daughter Martha to France with him, and Mary joined them in 1787. Both girls attended a convent school in Paris. Jefferson traveled widely in Europe. He broadened his knowledge of many subjects, especially architecture and farming. He applied for a leave in 1789 and sailed for home in October."

As you see, Thomas Jefferson was acting as the minister to France from May 1784 to October 1789. Now let's compare this to when the United States Constitution was written. According to the [15] Library of Congress Time Line, America During the Age of Revolution, 1776-1789:

> *1787*: "The Constitutional Convention. Every

state but Rhode Island sent delegates to the Constitutional Convention in Philadelphia... the Convention succeeded in completing a rough draft of a Constitution... After carefully reviewing the draft, the Convention approved the Constitution on September 17. After signing it and sending it to Congress, the Convention adjourned... On September 28, Congress agreed to pass the Constitution on to the states, so each could debate it in separate ratifying conventions.

1788: "The Constitution Is Ratified by Nine States. On June 21, New Hampshire became the ninth state to ratify the new Constitution, making its adoption official." "On July 2, Congress announced that the Constitution had been adopted. By September, a committee had prepared for the change in government, naming New York City as the temporary official capital, and setting dates for elections and for the meeting of the first Congress under the new Constitution. Congress completed its business on October 10."

By these timelines, it is easy to see that since Thomas Jefferson was in France during the Constitutional Convention, he could have not been involved in its writing. Now if these dates are not enough to convince you that Jefferson had nothing to do with the writing of the Constitution, then maybe Jefferson himself could better convince you.

A man named Dr. Joseph Priestly sent Jefferson a copy of an article he planned to publish. In that work, Priestly credited Jefferson with being a major influence in the framing of the Constitution. Jefferson knew this claim to be erroneous, and on June 19, 1802, he wrote to Dr. Priestly, instructing him to correct that error:

[16] "One passage in the paper you enclosed me must be corrected. It is the following: 'And all say it was yourself more than any other individual, that planned and established it,' i.e. the Constitution. *I was in Europe when the Constitution was planned, and never saw it till after it was established.'"

Jefferson's own words support the timeline previously cited. He was in Paris when the Constitution was planned, and never saw it till after it was established.

The last piece of proof I would like to present to prove that Jefferson was not present during the writing of the Constitution is an excerpt from the U.S. Supreme Court case *Reynolds v. United States*, which was decided in 1878:

[17] "In a little more than a year after the passage of this statute, the convention met which prepared the Constitution of the United States. Of this convention Mr. Jefferson was not a member, he being then absent as minister to France."

Why then did the Supreme Court in 1962 want to use Jefferson so badly that they would distort history to do so? It is because in a letter between Jefferson and the Danbury Baptist in 1802, almost 14 years *after* the Constitution was ratified, Jefferson used the phrase "wall of separation of church and state" to insist that the federal government was forbidden from involving itself in the religious affairs of the states and the secularist Supreme Court, in its blatant attempt to rewrite the Constitution, wanted to "shoehorn" this statement into its ruling as a means to alter the true intentions of the founding fathers and change the Constitution in order to deny Americans the God-given right to acknowledge God.

The Reasons for War

In the 1950 book *The Causes of the American Revolution*, Bernard Knollenberg cites at least six reasons why the colonies wanted independence:

1. [18] "In 1759, the Privy Council which consisted of a number of distinguished gentlemen selected by the King to advise him on issues relating to the administration of the government forbade the colonies from repealing or amending any acts unless first approved by the council in England. This order struck at the very root of self-government in Virginia."
2. [18] "Issuance in 1761 of general writs of assistance empowering officers of the English customs service in Massachusetts to break into and search homes and stores for supposed smuggled goods."
3. In 1759, the Massachusetts government passes an [19] "act to establish a congregational missionary society for work among the American Indians." The Privy Council disallowed this. Herein lies the root of the 1st Amendment. *The Massachusetts government* wanted to take the Christian faith to the Indians and the English government forbade it."
4. [19] "The sugar act of 1733 imposed a prohibitive (tax) on imports of foreign colonial molasses."
5. In 1764, the English parliament passed the American act which imposed [20] "new restrictions on colonial trade and levying taxes in the colonies to support an enlarged standing

British army in America."
6. The Stamp Act of 1765: [20] "Warned by a resolution of the House of Commons in 1764 and by their agents in London that a bill for such an act would probably be introduced in the next session of Parliament, the legislatures of the leading North American colonies petitioned against the proposed new act only to have their petitions rejected and the act adopted by an overwhelming majority in both houses."

Even the US government has a web site explaining the history behind the Bill of Rights. It shows us that one of the primary reasons the colonists felt the need to declare independence from Great Britain was over property rights. The US State Department has this to say about the reasons for the Revolutionary War:

[21] "The same generation that declared independence from Great Britain and fought the American Revolution also ratified the Constitution; indeed, many of the men who put their signatures to the Declaration in 1776 also signed the Constitution 11 years later. The two documents are not antithetical but complementary; one proclaimed that the country was rebelling because King George III had trampled upon the rights of Englishmen, while the other set up a framework of government to protect those rights, including the fundamental right to own property."

"Today property rights are still important to the American people. The right to own what you have created, built, purchased or even been given as a gift —knowing that the government cannot take it from you except under stringent legal procedures—provides the material security that goes hand in hand with less tangible freedoms, such as speech and privacy. People whose economic rights are threatened are just as much at the mercy of a despotic government as are those who find their freedom of expression or their right to vote curtailed."

When we combine these ideas, we see that the colonies felt the need to secede from British rule for four primary reasons:

1. Britain restricted the colonies' religious liberties
2. Britain imposed oppressive taxation
3. Britain rejected an appeal to allow the colonies' self-government
4. Britain had trampled upon the rights of the people to own property free from government seizure.

It is important to pay close attention to the reasons for the first American Revolution because from many in our own government we, as Americans, are experiencing much of the same tyranny that the founding fathers experienced from the leaders of Britain; a government that restricts religious liberties, nullifies private property rights, enforces oppressive taxation and rejects an appeal by the states for a system of self-government.

The Declaration of Independence

The Declaration of Independence was written by our founding fathers to serve notice to England that they would no longer be recognized as their government. *World Book* encyclopedia explains it like this:

[22] "Declaration of Independence is the historic document in which the American Colonies declared their freedom from the British. The Second Continental Congress, a meeting of delegates from the colonies, adopted the Declaration on July 4, 1776. This date has been celebrated ever since as the birthday of the United States.

The Declaration of Independence eloquently expressed the colonies' reasons for rejecting British rule. Its stirring opening paragraphs stated that the people of every country have the right to change or overthrow any government that violates their essential rights. The remainder listed ways the British government had violated American rights. The ideas expressed so majestically in the Declaration have long inspired the pursuit of freedom and self-government throughout the world."

In the Declaration of Independence, the founding fathers mention either God or His creation four times. As you read this document, keep one thing in mind—if this document had been written by Congress today, many secular organizations would challenge the Declaration of Independence as unconstitutional and the Supreme Court would strike it down as a "government establishment of religion" and a violation of the 1st Amendment to the Constitution. In one of America's first founding documents, our founding fathers expressed many thoughts that some in today's government and media not only deny, but also aggressively persecutes anyone who tries to live according to the convictions of our founders.

In this document, the founding fathers stated that God had given mankind certain rights upon which governments are unable to infringe. Freedom of religion was one of the most important rights that our founding fathers sought to protect. This can be seen by the 1st Amendment in the Bill of Rights. They also stated that all men are "created" equal. If teachers tell a student today that God "created man," they can be fired or jailed for teaching a truth that our founding fathers had absolutely no doubt about.

The founding fathers then go on to appeal to the Creator God (the Supreme Judge of the World) and express "a firm Reliance on the Protection of divine Providence."

The Declaration of Independence also talks about "Laws of Nature and of Nature's God." What did our founding fathers mean when they made this statement? John Quincy Adams explains:

> [23] "The laws of nature and of nature's God... of course presupposes the existence of a God, the moral ruler of the universe, and a rule of right and wrong, of just and unjust, binding upon man, preceding all institutions of human society and of government."

When our founding fathers used the phrases "the laws of nature and of nature's God," they were saying the following:

1. That there is a God.
2. That He is the moral ruler of the universe.
3. That He alone determines what is right and wrong; just and unjust.
4. That His decisions are binding upon mankind.
5. That His decrees supersede all human institutions of societies and government.

After eight years (1775–1783), the Revolutionary War ended with the signing of The Paris Peace Treaty in 1783. Among its signers were John Adams, Benjamin Franklin and

John Jay. The Treaty of Paris begins with the phrase "In the name of the most holy and undivided Trinity..." and continues by stating that the founders believed that it was God's divine will to free America from the tyranny of Britain and its king. "It having pleased the Divine Providence to dispose the hearts of the most serene and most potent Prince George the Third."

These outright declarations of the founders' faith prove that the founders never intended to discard all religion from the affairs of government. The following report from Mr. Machamp in a House Committee of the United States Congress on March 27, 1854, will also show us what our founding fathers would have thought about the secularization of American government:

> [24] "At the time of the adoption of the Constitution and the amendments, the universal sentiment was that Christianity should be encouraged, not any one sect [denomination]. Any attempt to level and discard all religion would have been viewed with universal indignation. The object was... to prevent rivalry among the [Christian] sects to the exclusion of others."

If we as Americans wish our society and our government to return to the type of system that our founding fathers created, we again must understand these truths and apply them to our way of life. In order to do so, we must learn the truth about our Constitution.

Chapter 4

The U.S. Constitution

[1] *"As the British Constitution is the most subtle organism which has proceeded from the womb and long gestation of progressive history, so the American Constitution is, so far as I can see, the most wonderful work ever struck off at a given time by the brain and purpose of man."*

**W.E. Gladstone
Prime Minister of Great Britain 1868-1894**

Once the Revolutionary War with Britain had been won, our founding fathers began the process of establishing a federal government for the newly independent states. The first attempt at this was an agreement between the states called "the Articles of Confederation."

However, these Articles were found lacking in that they did not give enough power to the federal government to solve national problems, especially with regard to trade.

By 1786, James Madison and Alexander Hamilton realized that these Articles of Confederation would not suffice and the two men began to call for a convention to address these shortcomings. Once the convention had commenced, the delegates agreed that the Articles of Confederation would have to be abandoned and another document had to be created, which would give the federal government enough power to better address the growing nation's problems. This took the form of what we now know as the U.S. Constitution. The Constitution's preamble explains its purpose:

> "We the people of the United States, in order to form a more perfect Union, establish justice, insure domestic tranquility, provide for the common defense, promote the general welfare, and secure the blessings of liberty to ourselves and our posterity, do ordain and establish this Constitution for the United States of America."

Our founding fathers wrote several documents ensuring that future generations would retain certain "rights." The Declaration of Independence states that we are "endowed by our Creator with certain unalienable rights." The word "unalienable" means "rights that cannot be surrendered." The United States Constitution and the Bill of Rights were established to protect those "unalienable" rights. It established America's fundamental laws by which the federal government is to operate, and it set parameters that told the federal government, "Your power goes this far and no farther."

The Constitution itself does not contain the word "right" or "rights." This is why our founding fathers insisted on amendments attached to the Constitution ensuring the rights of every citizen. These first ten amendments, also known as the *Bill of Rights*, were written with the intention of guaranteeing certain rights to the citizens of the United States, should the federal government ever be taken over by tyrants.

Samuel Adams expressed this thought well as to why the Bill of Rights was needed:

> [2] "I mean... to let you know how deeply I am impressed with a sense of the importance of Amendments; that the good people may clearly see the distinction—for there is a distinction—*between the federal powers vested in Congress and the sovereign authority belonging to the several states*, which is the [protection] of the private and personal rights of the citizens."

Many Americans fail to realize that the American Constitution was almost never ratified. Our founding fathers were well aware of the atrocities committed by the federal government in England. For this reason, they were determined not to give the newly created federal government the power that England commanded over every aspect of society, including religion. Many of our founding fathers were against a Federal Constitution for fear that this new U.S. government would become so large and powerful that it would oppress the rights and freedoms of the people, as was perpetrated in England.

To truly understand the Constitution and your constitutional rights, you must first understand what our founding fathers intended with regard to the role of the federal government and its relation to the state governments. To fully comprehend this, basic knowledge of the debate that took place over these topics is essential.

Thomas Jefferson tells us that if we want to understand why the Constitution was constructed the way it was, we need to go back to that time, *recollect the spirit of the debate*, so that we might better understand what was meant when it was passed.

> [3] "On every question of construction, carry ourselves back to the time when the constitution was adopted, recollect the spirit manifested in the debates, and instead of trying what meaning may be squeezed out of the text, or invented against it, conform to the probable one in which it was passed."

In order to "carry ourselves back to the time when the constitution was adopted" and "recollect the spirit manifested in the debates," I first had to acquire several documents: The Declaration of Independence, the Constitution, a copy of the *Journal of the Constitutional Convention* written in 1840, the Federalist Papers and the Anti-Federalist Papers. All of these sources should be required reading for public school American history classes and as "LAW 101" in every law school.

The *Journal of the Constitutional Convention* was printed in 1840 under the direction of the United States government, from the original documents written by James Madison during the Constitutional Convention.

Through these and other resources, we will piece together "the spirit of the debate" between those who wanted a federal government and those who did not, and why. By doing this, we will have a more accurate interpretation so that we do not, as Jefferson put it, "squeeze something out of the text" or "invent" an interpretation of the Constitution that the founders never meant.

Anti-Federalists such as Thomas Jefferson, Patrick Henry and George Mason initially opposed the ratification of the Constitution because they believed *it endangered the rights of individuals and states.* Federalism was one of the prevailing fears in the colonies at the time.

Our founding fathers, knowing what happens to people when they get into power, foresaw the day in which tyrants would attempt to gain total authority over both individual and states' rights.

In the Declaration of Independence, the colonists expressed the belief that their civil rights came from the hand of God and not from the government. They firmly believed that government was to receive its power from the consent of the people. In order to guarantee these principles, the challenge that the founding fathers had before them while drafting the Constitution was to create a federal government that was given enough power to operate efficiently, yet be restricted enough that it would never trample the God-given rights of the American people.

The Constitution was instituted as a "rule book" telling the federal government what it could and could not do and to list the God-given rights that the federal government would be forever forbidden to infringe upon. However, over the last 60 years, the Supreme Court has turned the Constitution on the American people and has now ruled that the Constitution was written as a "rule book" to govern the lives of the American people.

The Constitution, along with the Bill of Rights, was originally written to guarantee and protect the rights and freedoms of the American people. Now the Bill of Rights is frequently, illegally and unconstitutionally used by the Supreme Court to deny us those very rights that the founding fathers went out of their way to protect. Patrick Henry, one of the leaders of the Anti-Federalist movement is quoted as saying,

> [4] "The Constitution is not an instrument for government to restrain the people; it is an instrument for the people to restrain the government—lest it come to dominate our lives and our interests."

Our founding fathers would never have created a federal government had they known that the government would grow so large and so powerful that it would interfere with the private and personal rights of the states and its citizens. Again, Samuel Adams expressed this thought well from the floor of the Constitution Convention:

> [5] "I mean... to let you know how deeply I am impressed with a sense of the importance of Amendments; that the good people may clearly see the distinction—for there is a distinction—*between the federal powers vested in Congress and the sovereign authority belonging to the several states*, which is the [protection] of the private and personal rights of the citizens."

Unless the Constitution delegates a certain power to the federal government, or unless the Constitution prohibits the states from certain powers, then the people and the states should be the final voice in what they would do in any given situation, especially when it came to issues of morality. Thomas Jefferson, in correspondence with Supreme Court Justice William Johnson, reminded him of this fact:

> [6] "Taking from the States the moral rule of their citizens, and subordinating it to the (Federal Government)... would... break up the foundations of the

Union... The States can best govern our home concerns and the general government our foreign ones. I wish, therefore... never to see all offices transferred to Washington, where, further withdrawn from the eyes of the people, they may more secretly be bought and sold at market."

This statement best sums up the spirit of the debate at the Constitutional Convention. The states were given complete control over the internal and moral affairs of its citizens, while the federal government was tasked with primarily foreign affairs.

Anyone who has objectively studied the Constitution and how it was developed understands that the U.S. Constitution was a *federal* document, intended to establish the scope of powers that the newly-formed federal government would possess. It is clear from Thomas Jefferson's letter that Constitution was established to restrain the federal government from denying the states their freedoms.

Federalism vs. Anti-Federalism

There were two schools of thought during the Constitutional Convention. One group, known as the Federalists, wanted to form a federal government, while the other group, the Anti-Federalists, feared that a federal government would grow so powerful that it would ultimately restrict the freedoms and liberties of its citizens.

Before many of our founding fathers would sign the Constitution, the framers insisted that the Constitution contained in the Bill of Rights a specific clause now known as the 10th Amendment. This amendment restricted the federal government from usurping the rights of the states and of the people. It reads:

Amendment 10 - The powers not delegated to the United States by the Constitution, nor prohibited by it to the states, are reserved to the states respectively, or to the people.

World Book encyclopedia explains the original intent of the Constitution's framers when adopting the 10th Amendment:

> [7] "This amendment was adopted to reassure people that the national government would not swallow up the states. It confirms that the states or the people retain all powers *not given to the national government.*"

The Constitution lists the powers that are granted to the federal government and prohibited to the states. Section 8 of the Constitution enumerates the specific powers that have been granted to the Congress by the founding fathers. They consist of things such as borrowing money on the credit of the United States, regulating commerce with foreign nations, the right to coin money and to establish post offices.

Section 10 of the Constitution enumerates the specific powers that are forbidden to the states. They consist of things such as forbidding states from entering into any treaty, alliance, or confederation, to coin money, enter into any agreement or compact with another state, or with a foreign power, or engage in war.

Any "power grab" in which the federal government attempts to govern beyond what the Constitution allows in section 8 is known as *Usurpation*. In order for the American people to know and understand if their constitutional rights have been violated, they must first know two things:

1. What the term *usurpation* means

2. How much power the federal government was granted by our founding fathers when they authored the Constitution

Webster's *1828 Dictionary* defines "usurpation" as "to seize power without right." A more complete and exhaustive definition of the word "usurpation" would be as follows:

[8] "*Usurpation* is the exercise of powers by an *agent* which have not been delegated to him by the *principal*. In a *constitutional republic* like the United States of America, *acts by officials are legitimate only if they are consistent with and based on a constitution.*"

James Madison stated that the reason for having a Constitutional Convention in the first place was to combine [9] "a federal form (of government) with the forms of individual republics, as may enable each to supply *the defects of the other and obtain the advantages of both.*"

Our founding fathers, having great political insight of the history of governments in ages past, politically speaking, were light years ahead of us with regard to effective government, and they knew that the involvement of the people was critical. Their only motivation was the well-being of the people and of the nation and the securing of individual and state liberties.

Our founding fathers knew that both federal and state governments have defects, and that both have advantages. Their goal was to minimize the defects while maximizing the advantages. They knew that large federal governments could not micro-manage the society of an entire nation from one central location, and that is why the internal affairs of the nation were left up to the individual state governments.

State governments, on the other hand, could organize and govern their respective societies far better than the federal government, but were weak in areas such as national defense, war, and foreign commerce. This is why the Constitution was written so that individual states were allowed to govern the internal affairs of their own lives and societies as they saw fit, and why the federal government was given limited power and left to deal with foreign issues such as war, peace, and foreign commerce. James Madison said the following in support of the Constitution:

> [10] "The powers delegated by the proposed Constitution to the federal government are *few and defined*. Those [powers] which are to remain in the state governments are *numerous and indefinite*. The former [federal government] will be exercised principally on external objects such as war, peace, negotiation, and foreign commerce... The powers reserved to the several states will extend to all the objects which, in the ordinary course of affairs, concern the lives, liberties, and properties of the people, and the internal order, improvements and prosperity of the states."

Patrick Henry (an Anti-Federalist) objected to creating a federal government. He knew that while this all sounded good, once the American people lost sight of why this country had been founded, the federal government would eventually, over an extended period of time, begin to swallow up the power given to the states and destroy our civil liberties. Knowing the history of world governments of the past and using history as his guide, he is quoted as saying:

> [11] "If consolidation proves to be as mischievous to this country as it has been to other countries... this government... will destroy the state govern-

ments and swallow the liberties of the people, without giving previous notice."

It seems that Patrick Henry's words were prophetic. As we look at America in the 21st century, this is exactly what the federal government has done. Throughout the Constitutional Convention, we see this debate played out over and over. The Anti-Federalists feared a federal government would swallow our states' rights and states' liberties while the Federalists, led by Madison and others, insisted it would never happen. The debate continues: Francis Corbin, one of the ablest political students of his time, then joined Madison in soothing the growing fear that the federal government might one day absorb the state governments. He said:

> [12] "The powers of the general government are only of a general nature, and their object is to protect, defend, and strengthen the United States; *but the internal administration of governments is left to the state legislatures*, who exclusively retain such powers as will give the states the advantages of small republics, without the danger commonly attendant on the weakness of such governments."

Madison could not understand how anyone could possibly believe that years down the road, anyone in the federal government could use the Constitution to justify interference in the internal affairs of the state governments. He is quoted as saying:

> [13] "The proposed federal government extends to the general purposes of the union. It *does not intermeddle with the local, particular states*... I wonder how any gentleman, reflecting on the subject, could conceive an idea of the possibility of the latter...

'Henry conceived it. He conceived it very clearly. The proposed Constitution, he felt, was "extremely (destructive, unwise) and dangerous... If you make the citizens of this country agree to become the subject of one great consolidated empire of America, your government will not have sufficient energy to keep them together. Such a government is incompatible with the genius of Republicanism."'

As we have seen from the debates, neither the Federalists nor the Anti-Federalists wanted to created a federal government that would infringe on the sovereignty of the states. Their task was quite challenging. They wanted to create [14] "a system that would avoid the inefficacy of a mere confederacy, without passing into the opposite extreme of a *consolidated* government." Many of these constitutional debates often hinged over one word in a sentence. In one argument, the delegates argued whether the new "American" government would be a *federal* government or a *national/supreme* government.

Today, we may not actually see the difference, especially since our federal government has become a national or supreme government, but the delegates knew too well that the word they chose to describe the new government would ultimately determine the extent of power that later generations would perceive the new "American" government to have been given. The word "federal" is defined as:

> [15] "A compact between parties, particularly and chiefly between states... founded on alliance by contract or mutual agreement; as a federal government, such as that of the United States."

From the floor of the convention, [16] "Mr. Gouverneur Morris explained the distinction between a *Federal* and a *National or Supreme* government; the [Federal government] being a mere compact resting on the good faith of the parties; the [national or supreme government] having a complete and compulsive operation."

To the delegates of the Constitutional Convention, the difference between the words "federal" and "national" was quite substantial. To them, a federal government would be a compact between sovereign states that would enjoy all the benefits of a federal government, such as defense, trade, economics, etc., whereas a national government would mean just that—a government that would rule the people from a federal level and control the everyday lives of its citizens from a central location.

From the floor of the Constitutional Convention, Mr. William Patterson had this to say about the will of the people with regard to a national government, as opposed to a federal one:

> [17] "The idea of a national government, as contradistinguished from a federal one, never entered into the mind of [the American public]; and to the public mind we must accommodate ourselves. *We have no power to go beyond the federal scheme*; and if we had, the people are not ripe for any other. We must follow the people; the people will not follow us."

Delegates to the convention knew and articulated well that the American people did not want a national government to rule their lives from one central location. This would reflect the system of socialism, as opposed to Republicanism. They wanted a federal government in which the everyday lives of its citizens were to be determined by themselves and their state legislatures. So strongly did they feel this way, that on June 16th, Mr. Patterson had this to say:

[18] "New York would never have concurred in sending deputies to the [Constitutional] convention, if she had supposed the deliberations were to turn on a consolidation of the states, and a *national* government."

Everyone at the convention realized one common truth—they knew that if this convention were to deliberately turn America into a strong centralized government, in which a national government would make laws to govern the lives of the individual states, none of the delegates would have even considered attending the Constitutional Convention.

While writing the Federalist Papers No. 39 in January 1788, James Madison said the following with regard to the states retaining their sovereignty under the proposed Constitution:

"Each State, in ratifying the Constitution, is considered as a sovereign body, independent of all others, and only to be bound by its own voluntary act. In this relation, then, the new Constitution will, if established, be a FEDERAL, and not a NATIONAL constitution."

Likewise, in the Federalist Papers No. 32 written on January 3, 1788, Alexander Hamilton promises the people of the state of New York that the ratification of the Constitution would not in any way do away with their sovereignty.

"But as the plan of the convention aims only at a partial union or consolidation, the State governments would clearly retain all the rights of sovereignty which they before had, and which were not, by that act, EXCLUSIVELY delegated to the United States."

The Federalists assured them that the federal government would never be allowed to interfere in the internal affairs of the states. The 10th Amendment to the Constitution made it illegal for them to do so. Still, the Anti-Federalists were adamant about the fact that the federal government would eventually sweep away individual rights and the rights of the states to handle their own internal affairs. Many of them refused to sign the new American Constitution because of these fears.

Those who shared this fear of a "large, out-of-control federal government" agreed to support the Constitution only after it was agreed to add certain amendments to the Constitution, known as the Bill of Rights. If the Constitution had not been amended to include the Bill of Rights, the delegates would never have signed it and the states would never have ratified it. The ten amendments to the Bill of Rights were put in place *to protect the people and the states from the federal government.*

Republic vs. Democracy

One of the biggest misconceptions among the American people is regarding which type of government America was founded as. If 100 Americans were asked, "What type of government is the United States?", I would venture to say that over 95 out of 100 would say that America is a democracy. Our founding fathers did not create this government as such.

Upon leaving one of the many sessions of the Constitutional Convention held in Philadelphia in 1787, Benjamin Franklin, one of the delegates, was asked what type of government they had created for America. "A *Republic*, if you can keep it," was his reply.

America was founded as a *Constitutional Republic*. This can clearly be seen in *the Pledge of Allegiance*.

> "I pledge allegiance to the flag of the United States of America, *and to the Republic for which it stands*, one nation, under God, indivisible, with liberty and justice for all."

The Pledge of Allegiance brings out a profound truth. The pledge does not say "and to the *democracy* for which it stands"; it says "and to the *Republic* for which it stands." Therefore it is imperative to understand the difference between a democracy and a republic. If we wish to interpret the thinking of the founding fathers, we must go back many years to avoid the historical revisionism. Here are the definitions of "democracy" and "republic," as found in the 1828 *Webster's* dictionary:

> [19] REPUBLIC: A commonwealth; a state in which the exercise of the sovereign power is lodged in representatives elected by the people.
>
> [19] DEMOCRACY: Government by the people; a form of government, in which the supreme power is lodged in the hands of the people collectively, or in which the people exercise the powers of legislation. *Such was the government of Athens.*

It is clear by the 1828 *Webster's* dictionary that the founding fathers did not consider the American nation a democracy. If they did, then the definition of the word "democracy" in the 1828 *Webster Dictionary* would have said, "Such is the government of *America*," and not "Such was the government of *Athens*."

Nowhere in the Declaration of Independence or the U.S. Constitution will you find any variation of the word "democracy." However, Article 4 Section 4 of the Constitutions guarantees the Americans states a republican form of government.

> "The United States shall guarantee to every state in this Union a republican form of government."

Why then did our founding fathers set up a republic, as opposed to a democracy? What are the fundamental differences? They created a republic over a democracy to establish a government that would be stable and could not be changed every time popular sentiment or the moral condition of the nation changed.

In reality, a democracy is nothing more than "mob rules," in which if the morality of the "mob" changes, so does the system of government. This is why democracies are so unstable. A republic, on the other hand, is a government *based upon law*. Our American Republic was to be established based upon both Constitutional and Common law.

In the American Republic, no law can be passed that would violate either the Constitution or the common law. *Common law* is defined in the 1828 *Webster's* dictionary as: [18] "That body of rules, principles and customs which have been received from our ancestors, and by which courts have been governed in their judicial decisions."

The common law in America has historically been based upon Christianity and the concept that if God had already ruled on an issue, the issue was forever settled; the Supreme Court often used the Bible to aid them in their rulings.

In the 1892 Supreme Court case *The Church of the Holy Trinity v United States*, the high Court verifies this for us by stating: "Christianity, general Christianity, is, and has always been, a part of the common law."

Noah Webster, one of America's founding fathers, made

it clear that the *American Republic* was created to be governed by biblical principles:

> [20] "Our citizens should early understand that the genuine source of correct republican principles is the Bible, particularly the New Testament, or the Christian religion."

A common theme you'll find running through most of the founding fathers' statements and early Supreme Court rulings is that they all agreed on the fact that if God had already ruled on an issue, the issue was forever settled. Remember, one of the principles of the Declaration of Independence was that *God's laws are binding upon all institutions of human society and of government.*

However, if God had not ruled on an issue (i.e. trade with China), our elected representatives would then be free to rule the issue in such a way that would best benefit the nation.

Here, then, we see the fundamental difference between a republic and a democracy. In both types of governments, final authority and power is in the hands of the people. In the American Republic, supreme power was lodged in the hands of a people whose lives were governed by the *principles of the Bible, particularly the New Testament, or the Christian religion*, whereas in a democracy, the supreme power is in the hands of the people who are unguided and unrestrained by nothing but their own sense of right and wrong.

In the following illustration, allow me to show you our founding fathers' understanding regarding the difference between a democracy and a republic, to illustrate why democracies are unstable and constitutional republics are firm.

Let us say that a fishing party consisting of five men and three women are shipwrecked on a remote island, where there is no chance of being rescued. Realizing that they will be there forever, they decide to form a government. They discard all forms of government but two: a democracy and a republic. Here is how life would play out under these two governments.

In a democracy, majority rules no matter what is morally right or wrong. In a constitutional republic, their leaders are elected and decisions are made based upon a majority; however, no law can be passed that violates the Constitution or the common law, which is based upon Judeo-Christian principles.

One day, one of the men proposes a law that states "a man can have his way with any woman any time he chooses, regardless of whether or not she consents." Now under a democracy, if the five men vote yes to this law, you have a government where forcible rape is now legalized. However, under a republic, such a law would not be permitted because it violates the common law, wherein rape is forbidden by God. This same scenario could be used with murder, theft, etc.

Our founding fathers knew exactly what they were doing when they formed our government. And for that reason, they *rejected* democracy as the new nation's form of government. Thomas Jefferson once said: "Democracy is nothing more than mob rule, where fifty-one percent of the people may take away the rights of the other forty-nine."

Americans have a tendency to believe that America is the first and only country at this point in history to institute democracy as its form of government. But as we saw by the definition of the word, Athens had also been a democracy, and it failed. Again, using history as their guide, listen to what John Adams and many of the other founding fathers had to say about the history of democracies: [21] "Remember,

Democracy never lasts long. It soon wastes, exhausts, and murders itself. There never was a democracy yet that did not commit suicide." Benjamin Rush, who signed the Declaration of Independence, said: [22] "A simple democracy... is one of the greatest of evils." Noah Webster is quoted as saying: [23] "In democracy... there are common tumults and disorders... Therefore a pure democracy is generally a very bad government. It is often the most tyrannical government on earth." John Quincy Adams said: [24] "The experience of all former ages has shown that of all human governments, democracy was the most unstable, fluctuating, and short lived." In Federalist No. 10, James Madison said, "Democracies... have, in general, been as short in their lives as they have been violent in their deaths."

The U.S. Constitution was a revolutionary document. Never before in the history of the world had a government attempted such an aggressive experiment. As a matter of fact, the Constitution was so revolutionary that it was often called the "Great American Experiment." The eyes of the entire world were upon this newly formed republic to see if this form of government would last. As one man stated: [25] "We must consider that we shall be as a city upon a hill; *the eyes of all people are upon us.*"

What made the new U.S. Constitution so revolutionary? Why was it considered an experiment never before tried in the history of civilization? For the first time in history, a government was founded that would be a fusion of government and the Judeo-Christian worldview. This was what made it so revolutionary.

In his early 1800s book, *Democracy in America*, the French observer Alexis de Tocqueville was one of the first foreigners to explore the relationship between religion and the newly founded American Republic.

"The Americans combine the notions of Christianity and of liberty so intimately in their minds, that it is impossible to make them conceive the one without the other... In France I had almost always seen the spirit of religion and the spirit of freedom marching in opposite directions. But in America I found they were intimately united and that they reigned in common over the same country."

John Quincy Adams, the Sixth President of the United States, also bears witness to this fact:

[26] "The highest glory of the American Revolution was this: *that it connected in one indissoluble bond civil government with the principles of Christianity.*"

The people living under an American Republic were to be guided by two constitutions: a *civil* constitution and a *moral* constitution. Therefore, to understand how our government and society was designed to function by our founding fathers, we must recognize the difference between a civil constitution and a moral constitution. A constitution is defined as [27] "the system of fundamental laws and principles of a government, state, society, corporation, etc., written or unwritten."

The civil constitution that was created to govern the federal government is what we know today as the U.S. Constitution, which includes the Bill of Rights. The civil constitution established in writing what the federal government was and was not permitted to do and established the extent of its powers.

However, to understand the definition of America's *moral constitution*, as viewed by the founding fathers, we must once again go back into the books of last century to see the mindset of the American people in the 1800s. *The Webster's*

Dictionary of 1828 defines the word "Constitution" as:

[28] "A system of fundamental principles for the government of rational and social beings. *The New Testament is the moral constitution of modern society.*"

As we see from the *Webster's Dictionary* of 1828, the morals of modern society were governed by the New Testament. The moral constitution (the Bible) established in writing what the people were and were not permitted to do.

The New Testament was the moral constitution of American society before 1950. Just as the U.S. Constitution was written to establish guidelines by which the federal government was to operate, the moral constitution, which governed the individual lives of the American people, was the New Testament.

The new American Republican government was nicknamed the "Great American Experiment" because these two great documents (the U.S. Constitution and the New Testament) complimented each other in governing the lives of the American people. Noah Webster, one of the first individuals to call for a Constitutional Convention, had this to say about those who wrote the Constitution:

[29] "The brief exposition of the Constitution of the United States will unfold to young persons the *principles of republican government*; and it is the sincere desire of the writers [of the Constitution] that our citizens should early understand *that the genuine source of correct republican principles is the Bible, particularly the New Testament or the Christian religion.*"

Our founding fathers did not place the future of the newly-formed American government in the hands of the government or political institutions, but rather upon the moral constitution, which was the Judeo-Christian worldview. James Madison, whom many consider the Father of the Constitution, is quoted as saying the following while speaking in 1778 to the General Assembly of the State of Virginia:

> [30] "We have staked the whole future of American civilization, not upon the power of government, *far from it.* We have staked the future of all of our political institutions upon the capacity of mankind of self-government; *upon the capacity of each and all of us to govern ourselves, to control ourselves, to sustain ourselves according to the Ten Commandments of God.*"

At the time of the Revolutionary War, 98% of the people in this country professed to be Protestant Christians. Roman Catholics made up 1.8%; and 0.2% were Jewish believers. Combining these figures shows that America at the time of the Revolutionary War was made up of 99.8% of people who held the Judeo-Christian worldview.

The founders of the American Republic created a government with two requirements in order to operate properly. First, it required that the federal government adhere to, and not exceed, the powers granted to it by the Constitution (which it has not). Secondly, it intended the American people to be responsible enough to adhere to the precepts of Christianity, which as a society we have failed to do in the last generation. If these two conditions had been met and adhered to, then the American people could enjoy lives of freedom, peace, prosperity, liberty and happiness.

This type of government ensures two things. First, if the American people agree to live their lives according to the precepts of Christianity, in which we are taught to love God and love our neighbor as ourselves, then we will not be plagued with issues such as high crime rates and an overpopulated prison system. If the American people agreed to live their lives in this manner, the government would have nothing to do, because the people would be regulating their conduct according to God's law.

Unfortunately, since our civil constitution (the U.S. Constitution) has been all but rewritten by a socialist-controlled Supreme Court, and the moral constitution (the New Testament) has been deemed "unconstitutional" by the same Supreme Court, America is in the midst of social upheaval, moral decay and dwindling civil rights.

The American form of government under which we presently live is a far cry from the ideals set forth by our founding fathers and, as a result, our society is crumbling under our feet.

I was recently watching the movie *The Patriot*, starring Mel Gibson. The character he plays says a line in the movie that I believe best sums up the feelings of many in colonial America during the time that the new American government was being proposed. His words were almost prophetic:

> [31] "Please tell me why I should trade one tyrant 3,000 miles away for 3,000 tyrants one mile away? An elected legislature can trample a man's rights as easily as a King can!"

This is why of the 55 delegates who attended the Constitutional Convention, only 39 signed the document. Tyranny was the greatest fear of many of our founding fathers. Thus our founding fathers created a Constitution in which the federal government had no power to interfere in the internal or moral affairs of the individual states. However, within less than fifteen years, the federal government would begin to loosen the restraints imposed upon itself by the Constitution.

Chapter 5

The Second American Revolution

[1] *"The opinion which gives to the judges the right to decide what laws are constitutional and what are not... would make the judiciary a despotic branch. To consider the judges as the ultimate arbiters of all constitutional questions is a very dangerous doctrine indeed, and one which would place us under the despotism (absolute power) of an oligarchy (form of government in which the supreme power is placed in a few hands)... The Constitution has erected no such single tribunal.'"*

Thomas Jefferson

On September 17, 1787, the newly created U.S. Constitution passed the Constitutional Convention with a vote of 39—16, with the Federalists coming out victorious. Despite their warnings, the Anti-Federalists were unable to convince their fellow delegates that the creation of a federal government would ultimately swallow individual and states' rights. The Anti-Federalists had lost the battle, but had yet to lose the war.

The newly created U.S. Constitution would not become a binding federal document until ratified by the individual states. Therefore, there began a great political debate in the states between the Federalists and the Anti-Federalists, with each seeking to convince the American people why they should or should not ratify the Constitution. These debates took the form of what we now know as the Federalist and Anti-Federalist Papers.

The Federalist Papers were a series of articles printed primarily in New York newspapers, written by Alexander Hamilton, John Jay and James Madison, seeking to gain support for the Constitution's ratification. They argued that if America was to become a military and economic superpower, it could not do so as a mere confederacy.

The Anti-Federalist Papers were a compilation of articles written by Robert Yates and speeches given by Patrick Henry. They argued that throughout the history of the world, when government consolidated its power in one central location, those who had been granted power ultimately became tyrants. Patrick Henry warned:

> [2] "If consolidation proves to be as mischievous to this country as it has been to other countries... this government... will destroy the state governments and swallow the liberties of the people, with-

out giving previous notice."

By May 29, 1790, the Federalists had apparently presented a more convincing argument to the American people, and the Constitution was ratified by all thirteen states. The "New World" would no longer be a confederation of totally sovereign states, as it had been under the Articles of Confederation since 1781, but would now be a "United States" under the banner of "America."

The Federalists would carry this political momentum into the upcoming election and dominate the federal government for the next twelve years.

[3] "After George Washington became President in 1789, a political division appeared between those who favored a strong federal government and those who opposed it. The Federalist Party was developed under the leadership of Alexander Hamilton, Washington's Secretary of the Treasury. Hamilton believed that the Constitution should be loosely interpreted to build federal power. He favored the interests of commerce and manufacturing over agriculture. Hamilton also wanted the new government to be on a sound financial basis. He proposed tax increases and the establishment of a national bank.

"Thomas Jefferson and James Madison opposed Hamilton. Their followers became known as Democratic-Republicans. They believed that the Constitution should be strictly interpreted, and that the states and citizens should retain as many of their powers and rights as possible. John Adams, a Federalist, succeeded Washington as President in 1797."

However, by the time the next elections occurred, the Federalist Party would lose the presidency, the Senate and the House of Representatives. For the first time since the creation of the American Republic, the Federalists would lose total control of the federal government, and within fourteen years, they would cease to exist as a political party. Fearing that Anti-Federalist forces would now totally dominate the entire federal government, John Adams sought to strengthen the one remaining branch of government that the Federalists still controlled -- the Supreme Court.

Since the Federalists controlled the federal government for the first twelve years of its existence, all Supreme Court judges were appointed for life by Federalists. If the Federalists were to retain any power in the newly created American Republic, they would have to strengthen the power given to the weakest arm of the federal government—the Supreme Court.

[4] "Adams acted quickly, using what little time he had left, to shore up Federalist control of the federal courts. First, on January 20, 1801, Adams appointed his Secretary of State, John Marshall, to the position of Chief Justice. Marshall was confirmed on January 27 and sworn in on February 4, 1801, at the beginning of the Supreme Court's first term in Washington. Then, also in February 1801, the outgoing Federalist Congress passed several judiciary acts... Jefferson saw clearly that all this legislation was a Federalist ploy to enable Adams to entrench a Federalist judiciary and to protect the Supreme Court from any quick changes through appointment by the new President... However, after Jefferson became President on March 4, 1801, the new Congress acted to undo as much as it could of Adams' manipulation of the judiciary... These Machinations provide the

crucible in which Chief Justice John Marshall managed to form a strong and independent Supreme Court. The process began with the most celebrated case in American constitutional history, *Marbury v. Madison*."

The historic 1803 case of *Marbury v. Madison* became the Second American Revolution, in that it resulted in a revolutionary departure from the system of government that the founding fathers created, because it resulted in the decision in which the Supreme Court would *give itself* the power of judicial review.

The doctrine of judicial review created by Chief Justice John Marshall led to the flawed decision that has given the Supreme Court the power to review federal laws enacted by the elected representatives of the people and declare such laws unconstitutional.

Nowhere in the Constitution did the founding fathers give the Supreme Court the power to veto legislation enacted by the American people. During the Constitutional Convention, the delegates debated whether or not the Supreme Court should be given the power to veto federal legislation, and the notion was rejected. Instead, the power to veto legislation was given to the President. The constitutional delegates had an opportunity to give the Supreme Court this power; it decided against it.

In the historic 1803 case of *Marbury v. Madison*, [5] "(Chief Justice Marshall) used the supremacy clause to reason that if the Constitution is supreme, then any law repugnant to the Constitution is invalid. However, this argument begs the question, Who has the power to decide whether or not a particular law is repugnant to the Constitution? Marshall also reasoned that the justices should have the power of judicial review because they had taken an oath to support and defend the

Constitution. It would be difficult to understand, he argued, how the justices could be compelled to take such an oath and not be empowered to invalidate the laws that are repugnant to that which they have sworn to support. But this so-called argument is flawed... [T]his oath is not particular to judges but is taken indiscriminately by every officer of government. It no more proves that the power of judicial review resides in the Court than it proves that it resides in the President... The language of the Constitution does not preclude the Court from exercising the power of judicial review, but neither does it grant that power. Marshall never managed to explain why such an important power was granted by implication rather than by flat statement."

For the first time in America's short history, the power to determine which federal laws were to be enacted had been taken from the hands of the American people and their elected representatives and subjected to a majority on the Supreme Court. The Marshall-led court had now determined for itself that it would be the final arbitrating authority on what is legal and illegal in American society. Thomas Jefferson, a strict Anti-Federalist, had this to say about the Supreme Court's decision:

> [6] "This member of the government (the Supreme Court) was at first considered as the most harmless and helpless of all its organs. But it has proved that the power of declaring what the law is... by sapping and mining slyly and without alarm the foundations of the Constitution, can do what open force would dare not attempt."
>
> [7] "The opinion which gives to the judges the right to decide what laws are constitutional and what are not... would make the judiciary a despotic

branch. To consider the judges as the ultimate arbiters of all constitutional questions is a very dangerous doctrine indeed, and one which would place us under the despotism (absolute power) of an oligarchy (form of government in which the supreme power is placed in a few hands)... The Constitution has erected no such single tribunal."

The founding fathers did not set up the Supreme Court to reign over the other branches of government and, ultimately, over the people. The Supreme Court was created to be the weakest of the federal government's branches, never to be granted power over the other two departments (i.e. the Congress and the President).

The historic case of *Marbury v. Madison* resulted in a revolution, in which the Supreme Court did what an army would never have attempted and the people, had they known what was taking place, would never have consented to. The Court had established itself as the ultimate and unchallengeable rulers over the American people. America would now be ruled not by the consent of the people, but by a majority on the Supreme Court.

While this was a revolutionary departure from the system of government that our founding fathers created, the initial impact of this case was relatively minor because the American people had no idea how this decision would later be used to alter the Constitution and seize our civil rights. This Court decision impacted only the judicial review of laws enacted by the U.S. Congress, and the Supreme Court would be unable to find any constitutional justification to strike down states' laws and state Constitutions. It would take nearly 150 years for the Supreme Court to illegally cross that line.

Thomas Jefferson knew that the doctrine of judicial review was unconstitutional and that if this ruling was not corrected, the Constitution would become, as Jefferson said, "a mere thing of wax in the hands of the judiciary which they may twist and shape into any form they please."

The Federalists—who had created a federal government in order to make America a military and economic superpower, while still giving the American people the power to rule and govern their individual states and societies as they saw fit—had inadvertently sown the seeds of tyranny. Modern-day tyrants have used this case over the last generation to wield absolute and total dictatorial control over the American people so that we are no longer a government "of the people and by the people," but rather a government "of the Court and by the Court."

When one studies the Constitutional convention, it is clear that neither the Federalists nor the Anti-Federalists ever intended to give the Supreme Court the power to decide which state laws would and would not go into effect, nor did they give the Court the power to invalidate state Constitutions.

James Madison, the chief architect of the U.S Constitution, was also the chief architect of the Virginia Constitution of 1776. He makes the spirit and intent of the founding fathers clear with regard to whether or not they felt that the will of the people should ever be overruled:

> [8] "All power to suspend laws, or the execution of laws, by any authority, without the consent of the representatives of the people, is injurious to their rights, and ought not to be exercised."

Clearly, James Madison, the Father of the Constitution, believed, as the Declaration of Independence says, "that government derives its power from the consent of the people." The Father of the Constitution did not feel that the Supreme

Court should have the power to override the will of the American people and suspend laws, or the execution of laws, without the consent of the representatives of the people.

Separation of Powers

In setting up America's fundamental government, our founding fathers established the three branches of government: the judicial, legislative and executive branches, with specific powers granted to each. The legislative branch would make the laws; the executive branch would enforce the laws; and the judicial branch would interpret the law. In constitutional terminology, this is known as the "separation of powers." However, one common misconception among the American people is that the Constitution created a "balance of power," as opposed to a "separation of powers." The difference is quite substantial.

The phrase "separation of powers" means that each branch of the federal government has specific and limited powers granted to it, and that each branch has the authority to check the power of the other branches of government should one of the other branches exceed its jurisdiction and begin to rule the American people with an iron fist.

"Balance of power," on the other hand, *implies* that each branch of government would share equal amounts of power. For example, the President would have one-third of the power, the Congress would have one-third, and the Supreme Court would have the remaining third. This would be an inaccurate perception of the amount of power that the Constitution's framers sought to put in place when creating the federal government.

The only "balance of power" created by the Constitution was the balance of power between the federal and state governments. Alexander Hamilton explained this concept in a speech to the New York Ratifying Convention, June 17, 1788:

> "This balance between the National and State governments ought to be dwelt on with peculiar attention, as it is of the utmost importance. It forms a double security to the people. If one encroaches on their rights they will find a powerful protection in the other. Indeed, they will both be prevented from overpassing their constitutional limits by a certain rivalship, which will ever subsist between them."

If we study the journal of the Constitutional Convention and the Federalist papers, the two books that reveal to us the true intent of the framers, we see that this is not the type of government that our founding fathers enacted. While writing the Federalist papers, which sought to sway the American people into ratifying the Federal Constitution, Federalist Alexander Hamilton, signatory of the Constitution, had this to say about the power granted to the Supreme Court:

> [9] "We now proceed to an examination of the judiciary department of the proposed government... The Judiciary is beyond comparison the weakest of the three departments of power... it can never attack, with success, either of the other two... It may be truly said to have neither Force nor Will, but merely judgment; and must ultimately depend on the aid of the executive arm for the efficacy of its judgments"

If we were to put the amount of power granted to each branch of the federal government in percentage form, it would look more like 40% to the President, 60% to the Congress and 20% to the Supreme Court. According to Alexander Hamilton, the Supreme Court was clearly regarded as the "weakest" of the federal branches, the reasoning of which is consistent with the ideology behind a Constitutional Republic.

The Presidents and the Congress are elected and accountable to the American people; therefore their power is kept in check by the people. If either of these branches makes a law or a decision that is repugnant to the majority of the American people, they can be removed from office by either vote or impeachment. Therefore, power is left in the hands of the American people.

The Supreme Court, on the other hand, is not elected by the people and is appointed for life. It is inconsistent with the principles of a Constitutional Republic to place too much power in the hands of an unelected and unaccountable handful of judges, which puts America right back into the grip of a handful of tyrants if these judges were to abuse their Constitutional power.

In the Federalist papers, Alexander Hamilton stated that the Supreme Court had no power to force its will on the American people, but rather had to "depend on the aid of the executive arm for the efficacy of its judgments." This constitutional principle was understood for the first century and a half of American history.

The Supreme Court was never granted the constitutional authority to overturn or override the will of the people. This is why Supreme Court rulings begin with "In the opinion of the court..." When a court case is decided; there is a "majority opinion" and a "dissenting opinion."

Our founding fathers created the Supreme Court to review laws made by the federal legislature and to give its *opinion* as to whether or not the laws were in violation of the Constitution. However, these rulings were intended to be only "an opinion" and not a legal mandate to be forced on the people. When the Supreme Court rendered its "decision," our elected representatives could consult that decision but were not legally bound to abide by it.

In the Federalist Papers No. 81, Alexander Hamilton assured the American people that the proposed Constitution would not give the federal courts the power to *interpret* laws.

> "In the first place, there is not a syllable in the plan under consideration which directly empowers the national courts to [interpret] the laws according to the spirit of the Constitution, or which gives them any greater latitude in this respect than may be claimed by the courts of every State."

The Constitution has not given the Supreme Court authority or any other means of enforcing its decisions, nor can it punish Americans for disregarding its decisions. In the 1857 law book, *The Historical and Legal Examination of That Part of the Decision of the Supreme Court of the United States in the Dred Scott Case*, we see that it is permissible to disregard the "opinion" of the Supreme Court because it was not given the constitutional power to exert its will upon the American people.

> [10] "The power of the [Supreme] Court is judicial—so declared in the Constitution; and so held in theory, if not in practice. [The Supreme Court] is limited to cases 'in law and equity,' and though sometimes encroaching upon political subjects, it is without right, without authority, and without the means of enforcing its decisions. It can issue no mandamus to Congress, or the people, nor punish them for disregarding its decisions, or even attacking them."

While the power of judicial review was discussed and suggested by several of the Constitutional delegates, nowhere in the Constitution did the founding fathers give the Supreme Court the power to veto legislation enacted by the American people. The framers realized that if they were to give veto power to the Supreme Court, it would have been inconsistent with the type of government that they were trying to create, because it would have placed a disproportionate amount of power into the hands of an unelected and unaccountable handful of judges. This was one of the major reasons that they fought the war of independence with Britain.

Instead of granting veto power to the Supreme Court, the delegates decided to give veto power to the President. Had the constitutional delegates wanted to give the Supreme Court this power, it had an opportunity to do so and decided against it.

However, this balance of power would soon be upset by the historic 1803 case of *Marbury vs. Madison*, in which the Supreme Court would grant itself the power of judicial review.

> [11] "The central issue in judicial review was not the act of the review but whether the resulting judicial decision usurped power from the people or the other branches [of government]. The judiciary was permitted to examine and review laws, and to give its *opinion* on them; and the other branches were free to consult and include that opinion if they thought it appropriate... However, a ruling by the judiciary on any legislative act *was only an opinion and carried no force of law*; judicial review was never permitted to serve as a conveyance for the expansion of judicial power. As Thomas Jefferson later explained:

'The opinion which gives to the judges the right to decide what laws are constitutional and what are not... *would make the judiciary a despotic branch.* To consider the judges as the ultimate arbiters of all constitutional questions is a very dangerous doctrine indeed, and one which would place us under the despotism of an oligarchy... And their power the more dangerous as they are in office for life and not responsible, as the other functionaries are, to the elective control... *The Constitution has erected no such single tribunal.'"*

As we see from Thomas Jefferson himself, the Constitution did not designate the Supreme Court to be the final and absolute judge on what would be and what would not be constitutional. That was always to be left in the hands of the people and their elected representatives.

There were two reasons why Jefferson felt that the doctrine of judicial review was so dangerous. First, it would put the absolute and supreme power of the American government into the hands of a few judges. Secondly, he knew that since federal judges were appointed to office for life, they would have to be accountable to no one. This in itself shows that the doctrine of judicial review by which the Supreme Court has the power to suspend laws, or the execution of laws that have been enacted by the American people, is inconsistent with the checks and balances that the founding fathers put into the Constitution, for there would be no one to check the Supreme Court if and when it abused its constitutional power.

Today, many Americans are unaware of the provisions of the Constitution and, as a result, have been deceived into thinking that the Constitution created a "Supreme" Court, with the power of final arbitration in all constitutional matters. Again, Thomas Jefferson himself quite clearly stated, *"The Constitution has erected no such single tribunal."*

Forty years after the Constitution was ratified, those in American government still understood that the other branches of government (i.e. Congress and the President) were not compelled by the Constitution to obey an order by the Supreme Court as if the Court were the master of the American people.

"For example, when the Supreme Court ruled that President Andrew Jackson was to take certain actions, he ignored the Court's order. On what grounds? Jackson explained:

> [12] 'Each public officer who takes an oath to support the Constitution swears that he will support it as he understands it, and not as it is understood by others... The opinion of the judges has no more authority over the Congress than the opinion of the Congress has over the judges, and on that point, the President is independent of both. The authority of the Supreme Court must not, therefore, be permitted to control the Congress or the Executive.'"

In the Dred Scott case, the Supreme Court ruled that the federal government did not have the Constitutional authority to ban slavery, thus leaving African-Americans in chains. If the Supreme Court's opinions were intended to carry the force of law that was binding upon all other Americans, then Abraham Lincoln broke the law by issuing the Emancipation Proclamation that freed the slaves.

There has been much controversy and debate, even between the Federalists and the Anti-Federalists, as to whether or not the Constitution granted the Supreme Court the power of judicial review. Even though the Federalists and Anti-Federalists disagreed whether or not the Court had the power to declare acts of the federal Congress unconstitutional, one thing *is* undeniable: the Supreme Court was never given the power to declare *state laws or state constitutions unconstitutional,* and such a doctrine had never even existed until 150 years later, when the Supreme Court illegally and unconstitutionally incorporated states' rights under the 14th Amendment—a decision it had no authority to make and the American people are under no obligation to follow.

Regardless of whether or not you believe the founding fathers gave the Supreme Court the power to declare acts of the *federal* Congress unconstitutional, neither the Federalists nor the Anti-Federalists, while drafting and ratifying the Constitution, had any idea that state laws or state constitutions would one day be dragged before a federal court and declared unconstitutional.

> [13] "It was (Chief Justice of the Supreme Court) John Marshall... who undertook to allay (Mason's) fears now... Marshall saw no danger to the states from decrees of the Supreme Court: "I hope that no gentleman will think *that a state will be called at the bar of the federal court... It is not rational to suppose that a sovereign power should be dragged before a [federal] court.* The debate was long and detailed... but after several days they went on to other aspects of the Constitution. The prospect of judicial (absolutism and dictatorship) was recognized by the few and denied by the many."

This argument from the floor of the Constitutional Convention sums up the amount of power that both the Federalists and the Anti-Federalists felt should be granted to the federal courts. Neither party felt that a sovereign state *would ever* be called to give account before a federal court for the laws that it has passed, or the provisions of its Constitution.

This was the original intent of the founders of this nation. The doctrine of judicial review, in which the Supreme Court decides the constitutionality of laws enacted by the American people and their respective states, is a power never granted in the Constitution. This power was exclusively reserved for the state courts and the Supreme Courts of the individual states.

Chapter 6

The American Civil War

[1] *"My paramount object in this struggle is to save the Union, and it is not either to save or destroy slavery, If I could save the Union without freeing any slave, I would do it, and if I could save it by freeing all the slaves, I would do it; and if I could save it by freeing some and leaving others alone I would also do that."*

Abraham Lincoln

The events surrounding the Civil War and the era following it played an important role in the Constitutional history of America, especially with regard to states' rights. During this era, the Third American Revolution occurred. Many differing opinions abound about the Civil War. From my research, there seems to be enough blame to go around. My intent is not to take a side or assign blame, but simply to address the cause and the results that the war and subsequent Constitutional amendments have had on our modern government and society.

Like most people, I was taught to believe that the Civil War was fought solely over the issue of slavery. When only slavery is emphasized in schools as the main cause of the war, a distortion of 1860s American views of the issue occurs. Under such circumstances, it is easy to believe that everyone in the South wanted slavery and everyone in the North opposed it, thus leading our country into a Civil War. This limited perspective of the historical facts misrepresents the truth and blurs the picture as a whole.

While watching the History Channel one afternoon, I came across a show called "April 1865—the Month that Saved America." This program presented the final days of the Civil War. The Northern, or Union, army was, of course, led by General Ulysses S. Grant, while the Southern or Confederate army was commanded by General Robert E. Lee. After General Lee's surrender at Appomattox Court House on April 9, 1865, he was quoted as saying: [2] "I am rejoiced that slavery is abolished... The best men of the South have long been anxious to do away with this institution... Slavery is forever dead."

As you can imagine, this statement from the Confederate General is confusing. If General Lee was so pleased that slavery was now dead and that many of the best men in the South had long been anxious to do away with the institution of slavery, why was he leading the Confederate army against the North if not to defend slavery? The primary reason for the Civil War was not as much over defending slavery as it was over the defense and protection of *states' rights*.

We must remember that the Civil War was fought only

70 years after the ratification of the Constitution. Those involved in the issues surrounding the Civil War were the children and grandchildren of those very men who had drafted the Constitution, who therefore knew *exactly* what the founding fathers meant when the Constitution was created.

Not only was the sovereignty of the states and a out-of-control federal government a concern of our founding fathers when the Constitution was drafted and ratified, it remained a major concern for their grandchildren prior to the start of the Civil War. The subject of slavery happened to be the issue that brought the Anti-Federalists' worst fears to fruition. In the book *The Civil War and Reconstruction*, we read:

> [3] "The Union created in the Constitution was not a consolidated national state. Americans profoundly feared centralized power and the coercive authority of a national government that had the legal and political means of directly exerting its will over them. Consequently, the new federal government issued no national currency; barely levied any taxes (and most of these were in the form of tariff duties on imports)... The broad powers granted to the federal government involved the areas of commerce, coinage, foreign policy, and military affairs. Other powers were reserved to the states, which still retained their sovereign capacity to govern the daily lives of their citizens."

While it is true that those with the most power and money in the South (the plantation owners) wanted to retain slavery for financial and economic reasons, most of the common people in the South were fighting primarily to retain *states' rights* rather than to retain the institution of slavery.

This is clearly indicated in the statements of General Robert E. Lee. Most southerners did not have a problem with doing away with slavery as much as with what they saw to be an unconstitutional seizing of power by the federal government. In the book *Final Freedom—The Civil War; the Abolition of Slavery and the 13th Amendment,* the author tells us:

> [4] "Most white Southerners accepted the ultimate destruction of slavery. Those who opposed the emancipation amendment generally did so not because they hoped to preserve [slavery], but because they saw the amendment, particularly its enforcement clause, as a *revolutionary* device surrendering their states to the control of federal authorities."

As a result of the Civil War, three new constitutional amendments were passed:
- 13th Amendment (Abolition of Slavery, 1865)
- 14th Amendment (Privileges and Immunities, Due Process, Equal Protection, Apportionment of Representatives, Civil War Disqualification and Debt, 1868)
- 15th Amendment (Rights Not to Be Denied on Account of Race, 1870)

Briefly stated, the 13th Amendment freed the slaves, the 14th Amendment gave them citizenship, and the 15th gave them the right to vote—further evidence that the Civil War was more over the rights of states than the issue of slavery.

Article 5 of the Constitution states that in order for the Constitution of the United States to be amended, three-fourths of the states had to ratify the amendments. Herein lies a major problem. If the Civil War was truly fought primarily over the issue of slavery, and if most of the people in the

South wanted to retain slavery, these constitutional amendments would never have passed the ratification process.

In 1865, the U.S. consisted of 36 states. That meant that 27 of the 36 states would be required to ratify the Constitution. Since Abraham Lincoln only carried 22 states in the 1864 election, he would be required to get at least five more, including some Southern slave states, to ratify the Constitution. If slavery was to be abolished by constitutional amendment, it could not do so without the approval of some of the Confederate states.

At first, many in the North argued that since the South had "seceded" from the Union, that only three-fourths of the "loyal" states were required to ratify the Constitution. President Lincoln knew that if that were the case, the ratification may not be deemed legitimate, so he *demanded* that the Southern states be included in the process. In his mind, this was essential for the nation to begin to heal.

The 13th Amendment was rejected and was not ratified by the state of Mississippi until 1995. One might think that Mississippi initially failed to ratify the amendment because the state wanted to retain slavery. However, In the book Final Freedom—The Civil War; the Abolition of Slavery and the 13th Amendment, the author tells us, [5] "When the Mississippi legislature convened, it rejected ratification, stating that the amendment's enforcement clause was a dangerous grant of power... which, by construction, might admit federal legislation in respect to persons, (citizens), and inhabitants of the state."

States' rights, not slavery, was the core issue under contention between the North and the South. Amazingly, Canadians seem to know more about our history and the purpose of the Civil War than many American professors. The following was taken from a Canadian history website:

[6] "The American Civil War was not fought over slavery as some history professors would have you believe. The fundamental cause was that the confederate states felt that they had a constitutional right to own slaves and that no Yankee or federal government had the right to tell them otherwise.

The US Constitution had put so much power into the hands of the individual states that the states decided that they answered to no one except themselves. And they went to war against their brothers and sisters to underscore that belief."

Those alive at the time of the Civil War understood that the federal government was not granted the authority by the U.S. Constitution to interfere in the affairs of the states, unless the power was specifically granted to it by the Constitution. Remember, the 10th Amendment states, "The powers not delegated to the United States by the Constitution, nor prohibited by it to the states, are reserved to the states respectively, or to the people."

Constitutionally, those in the South were absolutely right in their assertion that since the Constitution did not give the federal government the power to outlaw slavery, and since the Constitution did not forbid the South from retaining it, the federal government had no constitutional right to pass any law declaring slavery either legal or illegal. Constitutionally, it was none of the federal government's business.

For the first time in American history, the United States federal government turned on its own citizens to dictate what the states could and could not do. In the eyes of many, this was clearly a violation of the U.S. Constitution and a usurpation of states' rights.

The two sides disagreed for almost 40 years, until the

matter was settled by the Supreme Court. Those in the South eventually had their position validated by the U.S. Supreme Court case of *Dred Scott v. Sandford*.

Over the last hundred years, there has been much misinformation and misunderstanding concerning the Supreme Court case of *Dred Scott v. Sandford*. Many have been led to believe that the Dred Scott case decided whether or not slavery should continue in America—it did not. The Supreme Court case of *Dred Scott v. Sandford* was to determine whether or not the federal government had the constitutional right to determine which states would enter the union as free states, and which would enter as slave states.

Over the previous 40 years, members of Congress had been at odds over the issue of slavery. This resulted in years of compromises, in which every time a state amassed sufficient population to warrant statehood, the federal Congress would "compromise" by allowing one state to enter as a free state and the next to enter as a slave state. At the heart of the Dred Scott case was the "Missouri Compromise," in which federal politicians "compromised" by allowing Maine to enter as a Free State and Missouri as a slave state that would maintain the balance of power at the federal level between slave states and free states.

The next major compromise was the Nebraska-Kansas Act, which divided the Nebraska Territory into two separate states. Nebraska would enter as a free state and Kansas would enter as a slave state. This outraged the settlers of both states because they did not feel that the federal government had the constitutional authority to determine whether or not a state remained free or slave. There were many in Kansas who abhorred slavery as immoral and barbaric, yet they had had slavery *forced upon them* by federal politicians. They felt that this violated the 10th Amendment to the Constitution, which intended to leave this determination in the hands of the people of the states and not in the hands of federal politicians.

From these debates came a doctrine known as "popular sovereignty." Simply stated, this doctrine meant that once a state was granted statehood, it was no longer under federal control and oversight. It was then up to the people of that state to determine by popular vote whether or not the newly created state would remain free or slave.

This doctrine was consistent with the 10th Amendment to the Constitution. However, this doctrine threatened the power of the slave states because they knew that as a result of the book *Uncle Tom's Cabin*, which revealed the horrors of slavery to the American people, the institution of slavery was becoming more and more unpopular, and that if the determination with regard to which states would enter as free and which would enter as slave states were to be left up to the American people, it was highly unlikely that any state would enter as a slave state. Those in power in the Southern states saw the writing on the wall. Eventually, the free states would greatly outnumber the slave states, and slavery could be brought to an end by constitutional amendment.

All of these disagreements played out in the Dred Scott case. The central issue before the Supreme Court was not whether or not slavery was moral or immoral—the central issue was *federal jurisdiction*. That is, did the Constitution give the federal Congress the power to determine whether or not a sovereign state would enter the union as a free state or as a slave state, or did the founding fathers and the states at the time that the Constitution was ratified intend to leave this decision in the hands of the states?

The U.S. Supreme Court of the 1800s was a just, honorable and unbiased court that differs greatly from the court of the last generation or so. In the Supreme Court case of *Dred Scott v. Sandford*, the Supreme Court Justices set aside their personal opinions toward the institution of slavery and ruled on this case in a purely constitutional manner. They were honorable men who ruled on the original intent of the framers of the Constitution and did not allow their own personal feelings, opinions or agendas to interfere with the task of constitutional interpretation.

Their job was to give a clear and unbiased opinion of what the founders meant when they authored the text, without "twisting" the Constitution to say what they wanted it to say. Here are the Court's own words regarding their duties as judges in this case:

> [7] "It is not in the province of the court to decide upon the justice or the injustice, the policy or impolicy, of these laws. The decision of that question belonged to the political or law-making power; to those who formed the sovereignty and framed the constitution. The duty of the court is to interpret the instrument (constitution) they have framed, with the best light we can obtain on the subject, and to administer it as we find it, *according to its true intent and meaning when it was adopted.*"

The Supreme Court's basic approach was: "Look, if you want the morality or the immorality or the justice or injustice of slavery decided on, that was the responsibility of the people and their representatives. If you want *us* to rule on this case, we can only go so far as the Constitution allows us. We cannot rule on whether or not slavery is right or wrong; all we can do is to decide whether or not Congress had the constitutional right to pass any laws telling the individual sovereign states that they would enter as free states or slaves states." With this foundation in mind, let us continue to read the Court's ruling:

> [8] "The government of the United States had no right to interfere... leaving it altogether with the several states to deal with this race, whether emancipated or not... *The states evidently intended to reserve this power exclusively to themselves...* And the... inquiry is whether Congress was authorized to pass this law under any of the power granted to it by the Constitution, for if the authority is not given by that instrument (the Constitution) it is the duty of this court to declare it void and inoperative."

The U.S. Supreme Court, staying within the bounds of the Constitution and not allowing personal feelings to decide this case, ruled in the only practical way by telling Congress that the framers gave the federal government no constitutional right to require the individual states to be free or slave. When the people of each state ratified the Constitution, the states evidently intended to reserve this power and these decisions exclusively for themselves.

Although it is true that while the states remained territories, they were under the control of the federal government, once the states were granted statehood, this issue of slavery was then to be turned over to the people of the states and not mandated by the federal government.

Sure, the Supreme Court Justices could have become judicial activists, but they did not. Since most of the judges on the Supreme Court at the time had publicly declared the institution of slavery to be immoral, the Justices could have determined beforehand to deem slavery unconstitutional and then twisted the Constitution in such a way as to reach that decision, but it did not.

To further verify that the members of the Supreme Court did not allow their personal feelings to influence their decision, consider the make-up of the Supreme Court at the time. The Court was comprised of five Northern judges and four Southern judges. The Dred Scott decision was seven-two in favor of the Southern states. This means that all four of the Southern judges voted in favor of the South's position. Three of the Northern judges (Chief Justice Taney of Maryland, Justice Nelson of New York and Justice Grier of Pennsylvania) also favored the South's privilege to retain sovereign rights for running the affairs of its own governments. I find it amazing that all three of the Northern Supreme Court Judges were *adamantly opposed to slavery*, yet they still voted that the federal government had no constitutional right to tell the states otherwise.

Take Chief Justice Taney, for example. He was a stanch opponent of slavery and considered the institution immoral: [9] "Taney not only emancipated his own slaves, but gave pensions to those who were too old to work. In 1819 he defended a Methodist minister who had been indicted for inciting slave insurrections by denouncing slavery in a camp meeting. In his opening argument in that case Taney condemned slavery as 'a blot on our national character'."

In his second inaugural address given during the Civil War, President Lincoln also acknowledged that the federal government had no constitutional authority to tell the Southern states what they could do with regard to slavery. The Constitution had not granted the federal government the power to legislate to the states, and as of 1857 this remained a firm and absolute truth.

Again, many Southerners stood up against the federal government in the Civil War not to preserve slavery, but to prevent the federal government from interfering in the internal affairs of the states. The Supreme Court agreed with the South on constitutional principle, while disagreeing with them concerning the immorality of slavery.

A Moral, Not a Constitutional Failure

Now that we see and understand what the perceived role of government was among those living in America preceding the Civil War, we may determine that the Civil War was not a constitutional failure, but a moral failure.

The civil (U.S.) Constitution was created to define and limit the power granted to the newly-formed federal government, and was not created to dictate *moral* policy. That was the responsibility of the *moral constitution*—the New Testament. The argument over slavery was a moral issue more than a political issue, even though it ultimately boiled over into the political arena.

Remember, President John Adams said: [10] "Our Constitution was made only for a moral and religious people. *It is wholly inadequate to the government of any other.*"

Here lies the one weakness with the "Great American Experiment." If the American people were ever to disdain biblical principles as the guide to their lives and societies, the nation would begin to crumble. The book *Religion in American Politics* tells us that the founders of this nation believed [11] "the greatest threat to Republican government was not population expanse, war, or runaway inflation, but infidelity."

"Infidelity" is defined as the [12] "disbelief of the inspiration of the Scriptures, or Unfaithfulness." The founders of this nation believed that the worst thing that could happen to this nation was the unfaithfulness of the people to govern themselves according to biblical principle.

Americans must understand that our founding fathers intended the moral constitution to uphold the civil constitution. The federal Constitution was not set up to deal with issues of morality, like slavery. All issues of morality were the states' and the people's responsibility. As the Supreme Court clearly stated, "The decision of that question belonged to the political or law-making power." In other words, the determination as to whether or not slavery was moral belonged in the hands of the people and not of the court.

When you remove the moral constitution from the equation, the civil constitution begins to fall apart because the U.S. Constitution was created to govern a moral and religious people. Even George Washington knew and understood that morality and religion supports government, and not vice versa.

> [13] "Of all the dispositions and habits which lead to political prosperity, *religion and morality are indispensable supports.*"

Washington declared that religion and morality are indispensable supports to *political* prosperity. The country was thrust into a Civil War due to the failure of the people to consult and allow their lives to be governed by the *moral constitution* to determine whether or not slavery was moral.

When the teachings of the Bible were not voluntarily adhered to by those in power in the South, many in the federal government felt that they had a moral obligation to step in and, for the first time in American history, tell the states what they would and would not do.

If the truths and precepts of the Bible had been taught in the South and the people of the South had allowed these principles to govern their decision about slavery, the Civil War could have been averted and the 13th, 14th, and 15th

Amendments would never have been written.

To summarize, the U.S. Constitution was created to go hand in hand with the moral truths found in the Bible. When the American public chooses to ignore or reject the biblical truths found in the moral constitution, the federal government is left in a no-win situation. Due to a failure of the Southern states to *self-regulate* their lives and societies according to the moral constitution, and voluntarily abolish slavery because it profoundly distorts Christian morality, the federal government was left with two options:

1. The Federal government could remain true to the U.S. Constitution and not interfere in states' rights, allowing the morally corrupt institution of slavery to continue...

-or-

2. For the first time in American history, the federal government could interfere in the affairs of the states to enforce the moral constitution and abolish slavery which would have (and did) violate the mandate of the 10th Amendment to the U.S. Constitution.

Ultimately here we had a case in which both sides were right and both sides were wrong. At this point, America was in a no-win situation. Constitutionally, the South was absolutely right in its assertion that the federal government had no legal or constitutional right to demand that the South abolish slavery. As we have already seen, the Supreme Court, in the Dred Scott case, agreed with that position. In his first inaugural address, President Lincoln also states that the federal government had no legal or constitutional right to interfere with the rights of the sovereign southern states:

> "I have no purpose, directly or indirectly, to interfere with the institution of slavery in the States where it exists. I believe I have no lawful right to do so, and I have no inclination to do so.
>
> Those who nominated and elected me did so with full knowledge that I had made this and many similar declarations and had never recanted them; and more than this, they placed in the platform for my acceptance, and as a law to themselves and to me, the clear and emphatic resolution which I now read:
>
> Resolved, that the maintenance inviolate of the rights of the States, and especially the right of each State to order and control its own domestic institutions according to its own judgment exclusively, is essential to that balance of power on which the perfection and endurance of our political fabric depend."

However, while the South was constitutionally right, those in power in the South were morally wrong to continue defending the institution of slavery.

As is often the case, I imagine that there were those in the South who were not defending slavery, but were not going out of their way to denounce it, either. By sitting idle and not being the salt and the light, their societies paid dearly. This should serve as an object lesson to us today of what happens when the believers do not take an active stand on the moral and immoral issues of the day. Those who fail to learn from the past are doomed to repeat it.

So, if a careful study of the moral constitution found in the sacred texts could have prevented the Civil War and ultimately avoided that which would eventually lead to the forfeiture of the states' rights, why then was the Bible not consulted? If Christianity was so pervasive in the American culture of the 1830s, as reported by French observer Alexis de Tocqueville, why then did the Christian church of the South not deal with the issue and instruct the people what the Bible taught about slavery, thus settling the issue once and for all and not forcing the federal government to intervene in the states' business and eventually alter the Constitution?

The Christian church was, in fact, very vocal about the issue of slavery on both sides of the debate. However, like today, Christians cannot all agree on what the Bible teaches, because some Christians do not like the answers that the Bible gives.

Chapter 7

The Third American Revolution

[1] "In affirming this judgment the Court largely overlooks the *revolution* initiated by the adoption of the Fourteenth Amendment. That revolution involved the imposition of new and far-reaching constitutional restraints on the States. Nationalization of many civil liberties has been the consequence of the Fourteenth Amendment, reversing the historic position that the foundations of those liberties rested largely in state law."

Justice William Douglas in
Walz v. Tax Commission 1970

Why was it was so important to avoid amending the Constitution? How does the ratification of the 14th Amendment classify as a revolution? We must be reminded of what the word "revolution" means. It means to [2] "Overthrow a government, form of government, or social system... with another government or system taking its place."

This time in American history perfectly fits a prescribed "revolution." The social system by those governed was being *gradually replaced* by another system of government.

The founding fathers established a form of government in which the federal government handled foreign affairs, and the local states controlled practically every other aspect of life. While it was not created as such, the 14th Amendment was the beginning of a gradual change that would eventually turn the states right on their heads. James Madison warned the American people from the floor of the Constitutional Convention that this has always been the way in which individual freedoms are taken — *gradually*.

> [3] "Since the general civilization of mankind, I believe there are more instances of the abridgement of the freedom of the people by *gradual and silent encroachments of those in power*, than by violent and sudden usurpations."

Likewise, George Washington, in his Farewell Address of September 19, 1796, explained how free governments are destroyed:

> [4] "Usurpation... is the customary weapon by which free governments are destroyed."

Our founding fathers did not set up a government in which the federal government could interfere in the lives of its citizens. Once the Constitution was amended in the mid-1860s, it was a significant departure from the constitutional government that had originally been established.

When the 14th Amendment was ratified by the states, they understood it to be a constitutional amendment that would guarantee "life, liberty, or property" to those slaves who had been freed by the 13th Amendment. The due process clause of the 14th Amendment gave the federal government the power to enforce these provisions should the southern states refuse to grant them their rights.

This revolution would run its course over the next hundred years. Even though the ideals in these amendments were admirable (the abolishment of slavery and granting the former slaves the same unalienable rights), the social system which our founding fathers had created was gradually being changed into a new type of government, in which the federal government, *if only minutely at the time*, would begin taking a more active and ultimately destructive role in the lives of its citizens.

Many in government, both past and present, have recognized that during this time a constitutional revolution was taking place. During the ratification of these amendments, one Senator even went as far as accusing another Senator of trying to [5] *"revolutionize* all the laws of the states everywhere."

In the book *Final Freedom—The Civil War; the Abolition of Slavery and the 13th Amendment,* Michael Vorenberg tells us that during the ratification of these amendments, "[6] Democrats read from Madison's writings of the necessity of a 'mixed' government to make the case that *any federal usurpation of states power.... would lead to the complete destruction of a Constitutional democracy.* Upset the delicate balance between state and federal power, claimed the amendments' opponents, and the federal government would assume all powers over religion, local election laws, and the marital rights of husbands."

Now, in the 21st century, we clearly see that those deepest fears have been realized. The federal government, led primarily by the Supreme Court, has assumed all power over religion, election laws and marital rights.

In the Supreme Court case of *Walz v. Tax Commission of City of New York* in 1970, we see that Supreme Court Justice Douglas himself acknowledges that a constitutional revolution had indeed taken place:

> [7] "In affirming this judgment, the Court largely overlooks the *revolution* initiated by the adoption of the Fourteenth Amendment. That *revolution* involved the imposition of new and far-reaching constitutional restraints on the States. Nationalization of many civil liberties has been the consequence of the Fourteenth Amendment, *reversing the historic position that the foundations of those liberties rested largely in state law.*"

Those present during the ratification debate knew all too well what would happen as a result of the dangerous precedent of taking away states' rights. They knew that once the federal government got its foot in the door and was allowed to dictate policy to the states, this power grab would never cease. Michael Vorenberg continues:

> [8] "Congressman John V.S.L. Pruyn of New York warned that 'If one right can be taken away, several can be—all can be.' His concern was genuine. As he explained to a visitor from England, the authors of the Constitution intended the states to have author-

ity on 'Domestic matters' whereas the federal government was to be supreme in 'That which concerns the outer world.' Pruyn argued that [9] 'The right to amend [the Constitution] is not a right to extend and enlarge the powers granted under the Constitution.' Some Democrats at the time argued that [10] 'the very process of Constitutional revision could itself be illegitimate'."

Many at the time saw the writing on the wall. If the federal government were allowed to begin to dictate policy to the states, then all rights included in the Bill of Rights, from possession of firearms to religious liberty, could be challenged and incorporated under federal jurisdiction—a revolutionary departure from the intent of the founding fathers. This is obvious in most subsequent amendments.

In the original Constitution authored by our founding fathers, the following phrase was never seen:

> "The Congress shall have power to enforce, by appropriate legislation, the provisions of this article."

Our founding fathers never gave the federal government the right to interfere in the affairs of the states. Such was the intent of the 10th Amendment. Since the ratification of the 13th Amendment, the phrase "The Congress shall have power to enforce, by appropriate legislation, the provisions of this article" has been used in eight of the Constitutional amendments—the 13th, 14th, 15th, 18th, 19th, 23rd, 24th, and 26th Amendments.

Although the federal government had, for the first time in history, turned on its people and on the individual states, infringement of most states' rights, including the religious liberties of the people, had not yet occurred. Contrary to what most modern history books would have you believe, religion in general, and Christianity in particular, was still the most significant influences during the 1800s. In his book *God in the White House*, Richard G. Hutcheson explains what the religious and political system was like during this time:

> [11] "Disparagers of religious influence in national history like to point to the relatively small percentage of Americans as church members in earlier periods. By some estimates less than ten percent had their names on church roles in 1800. Historian Patricia U. Bonomi has, however, laid to rest in a definitive way the myth that low membership meant little influence. Her carefully researched and extensively documented study of eighteenth-century America depicts a pervasive level of religious influence; on political as well as social and cultural life, which is perhaps hard for 20th-century secularists to imagine. It fits well, however, with Tocqueville's portrait of nearly 19th-century in which he said: 'There is no country in the whole world in which the Christian religion retains a greater influence over the soul of men then America...'"
>
> [12] "The spirit of the times may be summed up in a quotation from Philip Schaaf, writing for the American Historical Society in 1888: 'Christianity is the most powerful factor in our society and the pillar of our institutions. It regulates the family and enjoys private and public virtue; it builds up moral character; it teaches us to love God supremely, and our neighbors as ourselves; it makes good men and useful citizens; it denounces every vice; it encourages every virtue; it promotes and serves the public

welfare; it upholds peace and order. Christianity is the only possible religion for the American people, and with Christianity are bound up all our hopes for the future'."

Since we have now filled in the historical holes that the socialists, secular humanists and atheists have created in our United States history, how did the United States Supreme Court ever get the idea that our founding fathers intended Judeo-Christian morality or tradition to be totally eliminated from the public and government arena?

A handful of ungodly secularists (which the 1907 school textbook *The American Nation: a History* called [13] "militant professional atheists") have hijacked America from the hands of the people by rewriting the Constitution, and have taken authority upon themselves never granted to them by our founding fathers or by the Constitution.

America's Fall
1920–Present

"Since the general civilization of mankind, I believe there are more instances of the abridgement of the freedom of the people by gradual and silent encroachments of those in power, than by violent and sudden usurpations."

James Madison

Chapter 8

The Fourth American Revolution

[1] *"The court had opened the door to adoption of the rest of the Bill of Rights. Plainly this was judicial rewriting of the Constitution in the teeth of the founders' rejection of application of the Bill of Rights to the states."*

The Fourth American Revolution was the most radical and far-reaching of any since the original American Revolution itself. In less than 150 years, America would go from a government in which the American people were ruled by a tyrannical king and his magistrates (judges); to a constitutional Republic, in which the government operated by the consent of the people; back to a tyrannical government, in which the American people are once again governed by a handful of tyrannical judges. During this era, the Supreme Court would complete its coup d'état of the federal and state governments. Coup d'état means the [2] "overthrow of a... government... by a small group of people already having some political or military authority."

The Supreme Court is a branch of the federal government given limited authority and jurisdiction by the Constitution. However, in the span of 25 years, the Court would expand and enlarge its power, authority and jurisdiction without the consent of the people until they became the supreme rulers of the American people. In 1959, long-time Democrat and Republican Senator Strom Thurman had this to say about this unconstitutional seizure of power by the third branch of government:

> [3] "The [Supreme] Court has consistently moved to expand its power, till it threatens to be the dominating power of the government. The time has come for action by the Congress to call halt to this unconstitutional seizure of power by the third branch of government."
>
> [4] "Sen. Richard Russell (D. Ga.) noted that 'if the people really value their freedom, they will demand that the Congress curtail and limit the jurisdiction being exercised by [the Supreme Court] before it's too late'."

Prior to 1935, state governments retained most of the sovereign power over their respective states and societies, as guaranteed in the Constitution. Not long thereafter, this would change dramatically. The main architect of this transformation would be Franklin D. Roosevelt (FDR), the 32nd President of the United States. The tool that he used to expand the federal government's power would be the Supreme Court.

FDR was elected in 1933 in the wake of the Great Depression. His goal was to establish the "New Deal," which was a series of legislations intended to pull the United States out of the Great Depression. Roosevelt's initial strategy was to alter the composition of the Supreme Court by adding six new Supreme Court justices to the bench, bringing the total to fifteen and thus giving him majority control of the Court. Since all of these "new" Justices would be appointed by FDR, they would share his political ideology and aid him in forcing his socialist agenda on the American people. Therefore, he could shift the balance of power in his favor. In the must-read book *The Supreme Court Reborn: The Constitutional Revolution in the Age of Roosevelt*, we read:

> [5] "On February 5, 1937, [Roosevelt] dropped a bombshell. Instead of calling for new social legislation, he caught the nation, his Congressional leaders, and his closest friends by surprise with a bold, quite unexpected proposal—to alter the composition of the United States Supreme Court... Roosevelt's proposal to pack the Supreme Court in 1937 bore the mark of a proud sovereign who after suffering many provocations had just received a new conformation of power. In November 1936, the President had won the biggest electoral victory in the annals of the two party system, but his sense of triumph was flawed by the realization that it was incomplete. Even though he controlled the Executive Office and could expect to have his way with Congress... the third branch, the Supreme Court, seemed (not as easily manipulated.)"

Roosevelt, with control of two of the three branches of government, sought to expand the power and authority of the federal government by enacting a series of federal legislation. However, the Supreme Court consistently ruled that much of Roosevelt's legislation was an unconstitutional expansion of the power of the federal government, which violated the 10th Amendment. Roosevelt's only recourse was to get control of the Supreme Court by appointing judges who would ignore the Constitution and 150 years of constitutional and judicial precedent, and side with his radical political agenda.

> [6] "This emphasis appealed to FDR's New Deal supporters, but others bristled at any attempt to tamper with an institution established by the Founding Fathers... one writer encountered an elderly lady who protested, 'If nine Justices were enough for George Washington, they should be enough for President Roosevelt'."

The fact that President Roosevelt wanted to tamper with the Constitution exposed his real motive. He reasoned that: [7] "The [Supreme] Court was dominated by conservative Justices who were making it impossible for the national government to function."

What he was really saying was that the Supreme Court was made up of strict constructionist Justices who would not allow him to expand the scope and power of the federal government beyond what the founding fathers had intended. If Roosevelt was to gain absolute control of the federal government, he would have to get political control of the only obstacle stopping him—the Supreme Court. Once he achieved that, he could then set out to destroy the 10th Amendment to the Constitution, a prerequisite to destroying the rest of our freedoms and liberties enumerated in the Bill of Rights.

However, Roosevelt's "Court-packing plan" would not have to go into effect. With the unexpected resignation of Justice Willis Van Devanter, the balance of power on the Court shifted in Roosevelt's favor, which would give him a 5–4 advantage on the Court once he appointed a new Supreme Court Justice who sided with his political and ideological agenda. He appointed former Ku Klux Klan member Hugo Black to the position.

Now that Roosevelt had seized political control of the Supreme Court, he had the leverage to move the United States government in a totally new direction. This unholy alliance between the three branches of the federal government brought to fruition the worst fears of the framers of the Constitution, as expressed by Alexander Hamilton in the Federalist Papers No. 78:

> "And it proves, in the last place, that liberty can have nothing to fear from the judiciary alone, but would have everything to fear from its union with either of the other departments."

The Court would start approving Roosevelt's "New Deal" legislation, which it had just recently deemed an "unconstitutional expansion of government power." The Supreme Court began to overturn many of *its own rulings*, some made a mere 10 months earlier. Detroit *News* correspondent Jay Hayden wrote that Roosevelt's usurpation of power would:

> [8] "Constitute a *revolutionary* change in the American form of government... From 1937 on, the relationship among the branches of government shifted dramatically, as an era of judicial supremacy... Until

the age of Roosevelt, the court had never found an act of congress unconstitutional for delegating legislative power to the executive, but starting in 1935 it did so three times in a little more than a year."

From this point on, the Supreme Court would evolve from a branch of government that interpreted existing law and relied on long-established legal precedents, to a political body used as a political tool to strong-arm the American people and the state governments and ultimately lead America down the road to socialism. FDR would turn what had historically been the judicial branch of the federal government, whose purpose was constitutional interpretation, into another political branch of the government no longer bound by strict constitutional precedents, which could mold and shape the Constitution in any way it choose, regardless of the historical problems its rulings created or how many judicial precedents it had to ignore.

Now that FDR had political control of all three branches of the federal government, he would enlarge the government's power far beyond what even the federalists had ever imagined or consented to:

> [9] "In the spring of 1937... the Court began to execute an astonishing about-face.... That same afternoon, the Court approved three acts of Congress extending federal power... 'What a day!' Robert H. Jackson later wrote... The Court was on the move... These rulings marked a historic change in constitutional doctrine. The Court was now stating that local and national governments had a whole range of powers that the same tribunal had been saying for the past two years these governments did not have."

Voiding the 10th Amendment

In order for the FDR-controlled federal government to gain total control of the state governments, it would have to judicially do away with the 10th Amendment to the Constitution, which had placed almost all power in the hands of the American people and into the hands of the sovereign individual states.

Since the founding of this nation, no Supreme Court had ever ruled that the federal government could constitutionally exercise control over the lives of the American people and their sovereign right to rule their respective state governments. If FDR was going to alter the balance of power from state control to federal control, he would have to judicially rewrite the Constitution and insist that the federal government be granted power that neither the founding fathers nor the American people had granted it.

Before the Supreme Court could begin to restrict the civil rights of the American people, it had to first find a way to justify sticking its nose into the states' business, especially with regard to the Bill of Rights. It would have to find Constitutional justification to nationalize the Bill of Rights under federal control—a power the founding fathers never granted them in the Constitution. This would totally revolutionize the American system of government. This was accomplished by distorting the original intent of the 14th Amendment.

As we have discussed, the 14th Amendment to the Constitution, along with the 13th and 15th Amendments, were written directly after the Civil War as civil rights legislation. These amendments ended slavery (13th), gave former slaves the rights as citizens (14th), and gave them the right to vote (15th).

When adopting the 14th Amendment, the only purpose and intent of those who drafted and ratified the amendment was to ensure "life, liberty, and property" to those slaves who had been freed by the 13th Amendment, and they did not intend to give the federal government unlimited power to dictate policy to the states—especially with regard to the Bill of Rights. This would totally reverse the type of government that our founding fathers established.

Before the 14th Amendment was added to the Constitution, lawyers had unsuccessfully attempted to incorporate all of the original Bill of Rights under the due process clause of the 5th Amendment. In 1833, just over 40 years after the Constitution was created, the Supreme Court ruled in the case of *Barron v. Baltimore* that the Bill of Rights applies only to actions *of the federal government*, and not to the local or state governments. Therefore the Supreme Court felt it would have been in error to apply them to the states.

> [10] "In almost every convention by which the Constitution was adopted, amendments to guard against the abuse of [federal] power were recommended. These amendments demanded security against the apprehended encroachments of the [federal] government—not against those of the local governments. In compliance with a sentiment thus generally expressed, to quiet fears extensively entertained, amendments were proposed by the required majority in Congress and adopted by the states. *These amendments contain no expression indicating an intention to apply them to the state governments. This court cannot so apply them.*"

After the ratification of the 14th Amendment, lawyers unsuccessfully attempting to incorporate all of the original

Bill of Rights under the due process clause of the 14th Amendment. The first attempt was the 1884 case of *Hurtado vs. California*.

In this case, the Supreme Court ruled that those who ratified the 14th Amendment intended it to apply only to the newly freed slaves; that it was never intended to absorb the rest of the Bill of Rights; and that the founders had originally intended to leave these rights in the hands of the states and the people. Again in 1900, lawyers attempted to say that the 14th Amendment [11] "imposed national standards on the states. The Supreme Court... went out of its way to say that the Fourteenth Amendment had effected no new curbs on behavior of the states."

Even though two judicial precedents had been established, lawyers still tried unsuccessfully to federalize states rights. In the case of *Twining vs. New Jersey*, which was decided in 1908, [12] "[Supreme Court] Justice William H. Moody declared... that the question whether the Bill of Rights applied to the states via the privileges and immunities clause 'Is no longer open to this Court'."

It is apparent by his statement that the Supreme Court Justices were tired of lawyers attempting to incorporate the Bill of Rights under federal jurisdiction and control. Justice William H. Moody tried to settle the question once and for all by stating, "that the issue was no longer open to this court."

The law school textbook, *American Constitutional Law*, which is nothing more than a law textbook filled with many of the most historic Supreme Court cases in American history, illustrates that the early Supreme Court refused to rule against state legislation. After citing three previous Supreme Court cases (*The Slaughterhouse cases of 1873, Davidson v. New Orleans 1878 and Hurtado v. California*), the book shows that,

[13] "The [federal Supreme Court] Justices were not yet willing to become censors of state legislation. Judge Matthews argued that, since the Fifth Amendment contained a due process clause as one of many safeguards in the Bill of Rights, the same provision in the Fourteenth Amendment *could not logically be held to include its other specific guarantees.*

[14] "The country had now gone through the 1870s, 1880s, 1890s, and would go through the first two decades of this century and more, with the situation regarding the nationalization of civil liberties essentially unchanged from what it had been before the Civil War."

Since the ratification of the Constitution, the right of self-rule remained in the hands of the people and the individual sovereign states. However, in 1925, that would all change. America was about to experience the most radical and far-reaching change in its system of government since the American Revolution.

The Fourth American Revolution began with the case of *Gitlow vs. New York*, when the Supreme Court ignored both history and judicial precedent. For the first time it would reverse all of the Supreme Court's previous decisions and say that the 14th Amendment *had* adopted the rest of the Bill of Rights under federal jurisdiction.

Legally, the Supreme Court should never have been allowed to decide this case again. When a case that sought to nationalize states rights appeared before the Court, it should have ruled that it would not even take the case, since the issue had already been decided over and over again by Court. The precedent was already set. The fact that it took the case to begin with showed its willingness to ignore judicial precedent and rewrite the Constitution.

The law school textbook, *American Constitutional Law*, states, [15] "One of the most spectacular developments in American constitutional law has been the Supreme Court's expansion of the due process clause in the Bill of Rights to include the Bill-of-Rights 'guarantees'."

What this book calls a "spectacular development," many Americans see as a tyrannical usurpation of power, in which the federal government began to turn on its citizens and restrict the civil liberties and freedoms granted to them by their founding fathers. It is clear that the Supreme Court did not care about the original intent of the Constitution and of the founding fathers. Had they cared, they would have done several things differently.

First, the Court should have done what Thomas Jefferson encouraged all constitutional judges and lawyers to do, that being:

> [16] "On every question of construction, carry ourselves back to the time when the constitution was adopted, recollect the spirit manifested in the debates, and instead of trying what meaning may be squeezed out of the text, or invented against it, conform to the probable one in which it was passed."

If we truly want to know if our founding fathers thought it appropriate for individuals and sovereign states to be dragged before a federal court, we must do what Thomas Jefferson said: go back and recollect the spirit manifested in the debates. To do that we must consult the writings of the day.

During the Constitutional Convention and its subsequent ratification by the states, a debate raged between its members as to the amount of power given to the Supreme Court. At the point of the provision "the judicial power shall extend to all cases, in law and equity, arising under this Constitution," a major disagreement occurred between members as to how this provision would later be interpreted. I will allow the participants to speak for themselves:

> [17] "Grayson agreed: 'The jurisdiction of all cases arising under the Constitution and the laws of the Union is of stupendous magnitude. It is impossible for human nature to trace its extent. It is so vaguely and indefinitely expressed that its latitude cannot be ascertained'."
>
> [18] "True, said Mason: The court's jurisdiction 'may be said to be unlimited.' *He was profoundly disturbed by the prospect.* The greater part of the powers given to the court, he felt, 'are unnecessary, and dangerous, as tending to impair, *and ultimately destroy the state judiciaries*, and, by the same principle, the legislation of the state governments'."

Oh, if these men had only known how prophetic their words were. What they feared most has come to pass. The state judiciaries, constitutions and legislative bodies of the state governments have been destroyed by the power-usurping Supreme Court. No longer does it matter in America what the majority of the American people want, nor does it matter what the state courts, state constitutions or state legislatures say. If the U.S. Supreme Court does not agree with a decision made by the American people, such as state laws banning flag burning, it simply calls the states to the judicial bar and manipulates the Constitution, regardless of whether or not it has the authority to do so. (Again the word is *usurpation!*)

What did our founding fathers have to say during the Constitution's ratification about the prospect that a sovereign state would someday be called before the federal court? Their debate continues:

> [19] "It was (Chief Justice of the Supreme court) John Marshall... who undertook to allay (Mason's) fears now. The federal government, he insisted, certainly would not have the power 'to make laws on every subject.'
>
> Marshall saw no danger to the states from decrees of the Supreme Court: "I hope that no gentleman will think *that a state will be called at the bar of the federal court.... It is not rational to suppose that a sovereign power should be dragged before a (federal) court.* The debate was long and detailed... but after several days they went on to other aspects of the Constitution. The prospect of judicial [tyranny] was recognized by the few and denied by the many."

A few of the delegates foresaw what has ultimately happened to our inalienable rights, but most denied that the Supreme Court would ever have the power to override state laws, state constitutions and state court decisions and restrict the inalienable rights of its citizens. Many of our founding fathers believed the Constitution was so well written that the Supreme Court would never be permitted to usurp power not delegated to it by the Constitution. Oh, how wrong they were!

After the 1925 *Gitlow* case, Charles Warren prophesied the next year (1926) that by enlarging the 14th Amendment to include states rights,

> [20] "The court had opened the door to adoption of the rest of the Bill of Rights. Plainly this was judicial *rewriting of the Constitution* in the teeth of the founders rejection of application of the Bill of Rights to the states."

Charles Warren argued that by expanding the due process clause 14th Amendment, the federal government could apply the same control to any provisions of the Bill of Rights, and violate everything our founding fathers stood for. He called this a *"judicial rewriting of the Constitution."*

Charles Warren was right. The Supreme Court had just rewritten the Constitution without the consent of the people, and the Roosevelt administration would later be more than happy to expand the power of the federal government now that it had a fallacious judicial precedent on which to build.

This is how the Supreme Court would operate from there on. The Court would ignore history and long-established judicial precedents, make a new historic and precedent-setting decision, and treat that decision as if it were the original intent of the founding fathers.

The Supreme Court had now swallowed up the states' right to rule themselves and their respective societies without the approval of anyone in the nation. FDR would spend nearly four terms in office and would appoint a total of eight Supreme Court Justices to the bench, most of whom would be involved in the most historical precedent-setting cases in American history. By the time Roosevelt and his conspirators on the Supreme Court were done, the constitutional Republic that our founding fathers had created would be destroyed and America would be returned to a tyrannical government, in which the American people were once again governed by a handful of tyrannical judges.

It was during the Roosevelt era that the Supreme Court would complete its *coup d'état* of the federal and state governments. The Supreme Court cases of *Cantwell vs. Connecticut* in 1940, *Murdock vs. Pennsylvania* in 1943 and *Everson vs. Board of Education* in 1947 (all decided by Roosevelt's appointees) had essentially destroyed the 10th Amendment and swallowed up the rights of the states to rule themselves. If only the Federalists had heeded the warnings of the Anti-Federalists during the ratification of the Constitution:

> [21] "If consolidation proves to be as mischievous to this country as it has been to other countries... this government... will destroy the state governments and swallow the liberties of the people, without giving previous notice."

It would take only 137 years for the prophetic warnings of the Anti-Federalists, such as Patrick Henry, to come to pass. America has now become a socialist-totalitarian state ruled by an out-of-control judiciary. The body (the Supreme Court), which the founding fathers created to protect the Constitution, has turned the Constitution against us.

The Supreme Court, having abolished the 10th Amendment by judicial decree, has nullified the fundamental freedom of self-government and replaced it with government controlled largely by the judiciary under the power of socialist and secularists. However, this was not the end, but only the beginning. The Supreme Court would use these cases as its foundation in the future social engineering of American society, culture and government.

Chapter 9

The Fifth American Revolution

> [1] *Revolution: To overthrow a government, form of government, or social system by those governed... with another government or system taking its place."*
>
> **Webster's New World Dictionary**

In the previous chapters, we explored the events surrounding the creation of the American Republic. When we look at the Constitution and the government it created, we must understand what our founding fathers knew all too well. The American Constitution was created to govern the lives of a Judeo-Christian people—a people who would have enough self-discipline and self-restraint to self-govern their lives according to biblical principles.

In 1888 Philip Schaaf, a writer for the American Historical Society, is quoted as saying, [2] "Christianity is the most powerful factor in our society and the *pillar* of our institutions." Schaaf expresses a fundamental truth that we must not fail to understand. Webster's 1828 *Dictionary* defines a pillar as [3] "that which sustains or upholds; that on which some superstructure rests."

Over 150 years after the Constitution was written, our government and our society were still operating the way in which it was designed to operate, with Judeo-Christian morality serving as the pillar that upholds and supports our society.

What happens when you remove a pillar from a building? The structure falls! When an architect designs and builds a house, he builds it to be structurally secure. In order to support the weight of a structure, an architect may place a pillar in its foundation. This pillar is responsible for bearing the weight of the rest of the structure. Now, you may buy and move into the house and decide that you do not like this pillar in the middle of your basement. However, if you removed the pillar, your house would collapse.

As we have seen, our government was intentionally designed around Judeo-Christian principles. Religion and religious principles were the pillars that supported our government and our society. However, in the last 60 years, our government has been infiltrated by socialists and secularists who do not want to see Judeo-Christian principles as a pillar for our American society, and have sought to have it removed. Unfortunately, when you remove a pillar specifically designed to support something, once removed, that which it was supporting begins to fall.

Eighty-plus years ago, America's enemies understood that America was too strong militarily and economically to ever be destroyed from the outside. If they wanted America taken down, it needed to be done from within. What, then, was the strategy? Remove the pillar that was supporting American society—*Christianity*. This was accomplished by attacking and rewriting our Constitution.

As a matter of fact, the founding fathers so wanted to protect the pillar from being removed or otherwise tampered with by the federal government that they made it unconstitutional for anyone to mess with the pillar. The first amendment to the Constitution was designed to keep the government from interfering with this pillar. It reads:

> "Congress shall make no law respecting an establishment of religion or prohibiting the free exercise thereof."

The religious clauses of the 1st Amendment of the Constitution have two parts, which the Supreme Court has consistently forgotten about. They are:

1. Congress shall make no law respecting an establishment of religion
2. Congress shall make no law prohibiting the free exercise of religion.

In legal terminology, these two clauses are called the 1) "Establishment clause" and the 2) "Free exercise clause."

The provision stating that *Congress shall make no law respecting an establishment of religion* did not mean that Judeo-Christian morality, tradition and symbols were meant to be excluded from all aspects of public life.

The original intent of the First Amendment of the Constitution was that *Congress* could pass no law telling people (the states) what to believe, what and when to pray, or make it mandatory (by law) for a person to be a member of any church or any denomination. What our founding fathers did not want was another Church of England, in which the federal government determined what Christians would believe, and what church they had to attend, and they would have the power of the government to impose a legal penalty (i.e. jail) on anyone who disobeyed.

The founders did not want the federal government to be given so much power that common, everyday citizens could be arrested, jailed and even put to death because they did not attend government-sanctioned churches or believe what the government-sanctioned church told them to believe.

Considering the faith and intent of our founding fathers, how could the Supreme Court find *historical justification* for removing the pillar from our government and our society? Who gave them the authority to outlaw religion and religious expression in the first place? With the history of the American republic in mind, how did we allow our courts to remove all acknowledgments of God from the classrooms and from government?

Remember, in 1925 the teaching of creation was common practice and the teaching of evolution was illegal in many states. Eighty years later, we find the exact opposite to be true. Evolution is taught in every public school in the nation and the teaching of the biblical account of creation to explain the origin of man and of the universe is illegal. This alone proves that America has experienced a "bloodless coup d'état."

The unlawful and unconstitutional nationalizing of states' rights that resulted in the removal of Judeo-Christian principles from all aspects of American society and government was the Fifth American Revolution.

The Supreme Court did not have the *historical justification* to throw God, prayer, and the bible out of the classrooms and out of government; nor did it have the *legal or constitutional authority* to do so. This only happened because the American people of a generation ago, being ignorant of their constitutional rights, sat back and allowed it to happen.

Kicking God out of American Life

It is clear by the writings of all our founding fathers that the Bill of Rights was written in order to protect religion from the government, and not vice-versa. However, the secular establishment in America has so perverted the original intent of the Constitution that now that which is moral has been outlawed, and that which is vile and perverse has been called "constitutional rights." At this point in history our government no longer honors God with its laws and rulings. Our government blatantly and deliberately violates His precepts under the guise of "civil liberties" and a "constitutional separation of church and state."

How could a majority of Americans actually think that our founding fathers intended there to be a separation of church and state, as is forced upon us today? How did we allow ourselves be convinced that the pillar (religion) that the founding fathers deliberately installed to uphold society and government should be excluded from its affairs?

Two major reasons explain the widespread belief that the Constitution demands a separation of church and state. The first is that the American people have been fooled because the secular media and educational institutions has been keeping them ignorant of the faith of the founding fathers. Therefore, the re-education of the American people is the key to taking our country back.

Separation of the historical setting from the text of the Constitution itself perverts the original intent of the founding fathers. James Madison warned us about separating the text of the Constitution from its historical text:

> [4] "Do not separate text from historical background. If you do, you will have perverted and subverted the Constitution, which can only end in a distorted, bastardized form of illegitimate government."

This is why Christianity was one of the first institutions attacked by those who wished to pervert our Constitution. When the secularists succeeded in separating the text of the Constitution from its historical Judeo-Christian background, they succeeded in perverting and subverting the Constitution. This has resulted in a bastardized form of illegitimate government that now persecutes religious freedom, rather than encourages it as a pillar for a civilized society.

The other deception for a separation of church and state is keeping the American people ignorant of the U.S. Constitution. Even America's most prominent law schools no longer require their students to read the Constitution, the Journal of the Constitutional convention, the Federalist Papers or the Anti-Federalist Papers. One prominent lawyer had this to say about his time in law school:

> [5] "I spent three years getting my law degree at Yale Law School. From the moment I enrolled, I was assigned huge, leather-bound editions of legal cases to study and discuss. I read what lawyers and judges, professors and historians said about the Constitution. But not once was I assigned the task of reading the Constitution itself... Over the last decade, however, I have become a student of the Constitution, searching each line for its meaning and intent... It is

amazing how much more you will learn when you quit studying *about* [the Constitution] and pick it up and *read it for yourself.*"

It is akin to a minister going through a four-year seminary, reading theological textbooks to see what other theologians have to say about the Bible and never once being required to read the Bible itself. How could this be? The answer is clear. When the American people (and even lawyers and judges) are ignorant of their Constitution and the powers granted to the federal government, usurpation of power becomes far easier to achieve. If we fail to read the Constitution for ourselves and understand the historical context in which it was written, then we are easily deceived.

In the early 1900s, socialists and secularists failed to gain the power they wanted because attempted passage of laws to restrict the civil rights of the American public were ruled unconstitutional by the courts, thus thwarting their agenda.

When they attacked the Judeo-Christian values that supported and stabilized our society, the state and federal Constitutions were there to protect our rights and our way of life. The 1st Amendment did exactly what it was designed to do; that is, serving as protection for the pillar that supported and stabilized our society.

These individuals finally realized that no matter how hard they tried to suppress American's civil and states' rights, the Courts would strike down these arguments. The Constitution was so well written that their only option then would be to gain control of the Supreme Court and, by intentional misinterpretation of the original intent of the founding fathers, alter our Constitution. This is known as "judicial rewriting of the Constitution."

Many in America's Congress and on the courts today

understand that if the Constitution were interpreted the way it was originally intended, the federal government would not be involved in the daily affairs of the American people.

This is how their agenda works. First they convince you that they have the Constitutional right to micro-manage your life from Washington, and then once you believe this lie, they begin to seize your civil rights.

How then did the United States Supreme Court find the legal or historical justification to strike down the religious freedoms that our founding fathers had guaranteed? In the case of *Abington v. Schempp*, activist judges intentionally perverted our great Constitution by linking the 1st Amendment to the 14th Amendment.

> "First, this Court has decisively settled that the First Amendment's mandate that Congress shall make no law respecting an establishment of religion, or prohibiting the free exercise thereof has been made wholly applicable to the states by the Fourteenth Amendment.... The Fourteenth Amendment has rendered the legislatures of the states as incompetent as Congress to enact such laws."

The 14th Amendment to the Constitution, along with the 13th and 15th Amendments, were written directly after the Civil War as civil rights legislation. These amendments ended slavery (13th), gave former slaves the rights of citizens (14th), and gave them the right to vote (15th).

Before the Supreme Court could restrict the civil rights of the American people, it had to first find a way in which the federal government could justify sticking its nose into the states' business. As we saw in the last chapter, this was accomplished in 1925, 1940, 1943 and 1947.

Previous Supreme Court rulings (*Gitlow v. New York*

1925, *Cantwell v. Connecticut* in 1940, *Murdock v. Pennsylvania* in 1943 and *Everson v. Board of Education* in 1947) had so twisted and bastardized the original intent of the 14th Amendment that it became no longer just a constitutional amendment that granted citizenship to the newly freed slaves, but had been *misinterpreted* as an amendment to the Constitution that gave the federal government, particularly the Supreme Court, the power to dictate to the states federal policy with regard to all our civil rights.

Since the federal government got away with telling the Southern states what they could do with the civil rights of former slaves, this court began to say that the 14th Amendment also afforded them the authority to dictate policy with regard to *all* Americans' civil rights, including the 1st Amendment.

The Bill of Rights was adopted to limit the federal government from suppressing the civil rights of the people of the individual states. The provisions contained in the Bill of Rights did not apply to the states; that is, the bill of rights was not created to tell the states what they could and could not do—*it was created to tell the federal government what it could and could not do*. Supreme Court Justice Potter Stewart made this clear in his dissenting opinion in the case of *Abington School District v. Schempp*:

> "As a matter of history, the First Amendment was adopted solely as a limitation upon the newly created National Government."

Once we understand that the federal Constitution was a federal document created to *restrict the power of the federal government* and not a national document created to *restrict the rights and freedoms of the states or the general public*, we are much closer to understanding our Constitution than our own Supreme Court. As Patrick Henry, one of the leaders of the Anti-Federalist movement is quoted as saying, "The Constitution is not an instrument for government to restrain the people; it is an instrument for the people to restrain the government—lest it come to dominate our lives and our interests."

Even in 1959, four years before the Supreme Court incorporated the 1st Amendment into the 14th Amendment, Supreme Court Justice Frankfurter had this to say in the case of *Bartkus v. Illinois* about applying the Bill of Rights to the states:

> [6] "We have held *from the beginning and uniformly* (1884, 1900, 1908) that the due process clause of the Fourteenth Amendment does not apply to the states any of the provisions of the first ten amendments as such... The relevant historical materials demonstrate conclusively the Congress and the members of the legislatures of the ratifying states, did not contemplate that the Fourteenth Amendment was a shorthand incorporation of the first eight amendments making them applicable as explicit restrictions upon the states."

In 1959, the Supreme Court still understood that the 14th Amendment had not been ratified by the states in order to give the federal government the authority to incorporate the Bill of Rights under federal jurisdiction.

In the Supreme Court case of *Walz v. Tax Commission* in 1970, Justice William Douglas stated that by linking these two Amendments (the 1st and the 14th), the Supreme Court had created *an American Revolution* that began to take away the articles of the Bill of Rights from the states, which was clearly not the intent of the Constitution's framers.

[7] "Governments have not always been tolerant of religious activity, and hostility toward religion has taken many shapes and forms—economic, political, and sometimes harshly oppressive... The limits of permissible state accommodation to religion are by no means co-extensive with the noninterference mandated by the Free Exercise Clause. *To equate the two would be to deny a national heritage with roots in the Revolution itself...*

"In affirming this judgment the Court largely overlooks the *revolution initiated by the adoption of the Fourteenth Amendment. That revolution involved the imposition of new and far-reaching constitutional restraints on the States.* Nationalization of many civil liberties has been the consequence of the Fourteenth Amendment, *reversing* the historic position that the foundations of those liberties rested largely in state law... *And so the revolution occasioned by the Fourteenth Amendment has progressed as Article after Article in the Bill of Rights has been incorporated in it and made applicable to the States.*"

The U.S. Supreme Court was created by our founding fathers as a board of judicial review whose only authority was to give *their opinion* upon the constitutionality of laws passed by the U.S. Congress and was not permitted to strike down federal laws, state Constitutions or the laws passed by the states' legislatures. In the landmark case of *Abington v. Schempp*, these socialist activist judges intentionally perverted our great Constitution by linking the 1st Amendment with the 14th Amendment:

[8] "First, this Court has *decisively settled* that the First Amendment's mandate that "Congress shall

make no law respecting an establishment of religion, or prohibiting the free exercise thereof" has been made wholly applicable to the states by the Fourteenth Amendment... The Fourteenth Amendment has rendered the legislatures of the states as incompetent as Congress to enact such laws."

According to the Supreme Court, the 14th Amendment to the Constitution has given the federal government the power to tell the states what they can and cannot do, even going as far as restricting the freedoms that the 1st Amendment and subsequent amendments so guaranteed.

Was this the intent of our founding fathers? Absolutely not! Thomas Jefferson made this perfectly clear in the year 1808. He received a letter from a Rev. Millar, who asked President Jefferson to declare a day of prayer and fasting. On January 23, 1808, Thomas Jefferson responded to the letter of Rev. Millar, in which Jefferson states:

> [9] "I have duly received your favor of the eighteenth, and am thankful to you for having written it, because it is more agreeable to prevent than to refuse what I do not think myself authorized to comply with. I consider the government of the United States as indicated by the Constitution from intermeddling with religious institutions, their doctrines, disciplines, or exercises. This results not with religion, only from the provision that no law shall be made respecting the establishment or free exercise of religion, but from that, also, which reserves to the states the powers not delegated to the United States.
>
> "Certainly, no power to prescribe any religious exercise, or to assume authority in religious discipline, has been delegated to the [federal] government.

It must, then, rest with the States... and this right can never be safer than in their own hands, where the Constitution has deposited it.

"I am aware that the practice of my predecessors may be quoted. But I have ever believed that the example of state executives led to the assumption that authority by the general government, without due examination, which would have discovered that what might be a right in a state government, was a violation of that right when assumed by another."

Thomas Jefferson said that even though his predecessors George Washington and John Adams had called for days of prayer and fasting, and even though the Continental Congress 30 years earlier had purchased 20,000 bibles and called for the first day of prayer in 1778, Thomas Jefferson refused to recommend a day of prayer and fasting, not because he felt that it was a violation of the 1st Amendment, but because he believed that doing so would violate the states' rights to call for such a day on their own.

He reminded Rev. Millar that his own approval was not necessary to sanction the day of prayer and fasting because *the Constitution had placed those rights into the hands of the people* and that he, as President, felt that he would, in principle, be violating the authority granted to the states to make such a decree for themselves.

Of course the Supreme Court failed to take this letter into consideration when insisting that Thomas Jefferson demanded that the 1st Amendment to the Constitution had erected a "wall of separation between of church and state" and that the states did not have the authority to allow religion in the government or in the schools.

Chapter 10

The Battle Behind the Battle

> [1] *"I apprehend no danger to our country from a foreign foe. The prospect of a war with any powerful nation is too remote to be a matter of calculation. Besides, there is no nation on earth powerful enough to accomplish our overthrow. Our destruction, should it come at all, will be from another quarter..."*
>
> **Daniel Webster**

Now that we have proven that our Constitution has been hijacked and that the right of self-government that is guaranteed by the 10th Amendment has been nullified, we need to ask, "Who then is responsible for this socialization and secularization of America?"

Why then has the Supreme Court, from 1940 to the

present, completely reversed what their predecessors on the Supreme Court had held to be true since the founding of this nation? I do not believe that these rulings were simply bad decisions made by incompetent or uninformed judges. The truth is far more sinister and much more chilling. To identify those in the American government today who hold the same beliefs as those who stripped us of our Constitutional rights to self-government and the freedom of religion, we must understand and identify their ideology.

Socialists support the confirmation of activist judges who will twist and alter the Constitution until it fits their agenda. They appoint judges who do not rule according to the law, previous Supreme Court precedents or the original intent of the founding fathers. Instead, they push their secularist and socialist agendas, often ruling against what previous Supreme Courts have decided and contrary to what the majority of Americans desire. Our government of the people and by the people has become a government of the few. Present-day America is far closer to a socialist state than to a Constitutional Republic.

For the past 80 years, a battle has raged for the very soul of the American Republic. The United States of America and the Soviet Union have had two totally different ideologies that have been warring against each other since the Soviet revolution of 1917. These two governments, societies and ideologies could not have been more diametrically opposed.

America is a capitalistic society whose form of government was created as a Constitutional Republic, while the government of the former Soviet Union was Communist.

America was a nation founded by the people of God and, without question, we have been the most prosperous, blessed and freest people in the history of the world.

The USSR, on the other hand, was a communist nation whose official state religion was, and is, *atheistic*. America was created as a nation whose federal government was given little power and control over the lives of its people. The power of the American federal government was limited to defense, trade, foreign affairs etc.

Communism and socialism, however, are exactly the opposite. In a communist society, all power is given to the centralized government. This national government rules all aspects of society, including religious freedom from one centralized location.

Communists and socialists and progressives hold to basically the same ideology. Therefore, if a person denies any links to these three ideologies, this person may still be identified by the issues and policies he/she defends. (Socialism and liberalism are America's version of communism). As we have previously discussed, the three common, distinguishing characteristics identify these individuals, no matter what "label" they choose to wear. They are:

1. Strong centralized government

2. Redistribution of wealth

3. Atheism (or secularism)

The most important identifying feature that communists and socialists often share is "atheism" and their hatred of God and religion. [2] Communist objectives, widely publicized in their own literature, were briefly summarized by a Congressional committee in 1931, which, I feel, is still the best short definition of communism:

> "Hatred of God and all forms of religion. Destruction of private property and inheritance. Promotion of

class hatred. (This is from report 2290, U.S. House of Representatives—1931.)"

They are opposed to any religious influence over a society, and one of the first things that they seek to do when they take over a government is to work tirelessly to secularize that society. This is why they seek to remove all aspects of religion from the public square. This ideology is clearly seen in the Constitution of the former Soviet Union, which reads as follows:

> [3] ARTICLE 124: "In order to ensure to citizen's freedom of conscience, *the church in the U.S.S.R. is separated from the State,* and the school from the church."

The type of government that has been forced upon Americans for the last 60 years is far from the Constitutional Republic that our founding fathers created. The federal government, as it operates today, is far closer to socialism than to a constitutional Republic. Separation of church and state is a *communist and socialist ideology* to which our founding fathers did not subscribe.

The Constitution of the U.S.S.R. and its "separation of church and state" existed for nearly a generation before the socialist-overrun Supreme Court *changed* our Constitution to match it. Most of our elected representatives, who are secretly opposed to the type of government our founding fathers created, would never publicly admit to their hostility toward religion or states' rights, because doing so would be extremely unpopular. However, one must only look at the policies they support to see through their deception.

While the Supreme Court did not actually rewrite the Constitution, its activist rulings have had exactly the same effect. America is now a country in which separation of church and state is the governing maxim, not because the Constitution demands it, nor because the American people want it or because our founding fathers prescribed it, but because the activist, socialist, Supreme Court has ruled it to be so, and the American people are blindly following its rulings.

Once the American people learn the facts surrounding our founding fathers and the true intent of the Constitution, they must demand that our nation be returned to the type of system that we are guaranteed in the Constitution. The steady decline of everything good and moral in American society and the rise of everything evil may be traced back to the actions of these godless people who infiltrated our society at every level, from politics to the media to the church to education and to the courts.

Democratic Senator Robert Byrd, in his book *Child of the Appalachian Coalfields* repeatedly blames "liberal judges" and "activist judges" for many of the nation's problems:

> "The high court's share of the responsibility for our increasing lawlessness lies in two areas—its zeal for bringing about precipitous social change, and its over-concern for the rights of criminals and its under-concern for the rights and safety of society. I urged President Nixon to appoint conservative jurists to the court. I said that such a return to a conservative philosophy would be 'the greatest single service President Nixon could perform for his country.' I said that the court had hurt the United States with its rulings on school prayer and in criminal cases, and had given aid and comfort to subversives by refusing to bar communists from schools and defense plants."

Due to the nature of America's free society (freedom of speech, freedom of press, etc.), socialists, secular humanists and communists engaged in a "subversive war" with the American way of life since well before the "Cold War" began in 1945 and well after its supposed end in 1991. Call them communists, call them socialists, call them atheists, call them secular humanists, call them liberals, or call them progressives - they have but one objective—the destruction of the American way of life. *And they are accomplishing it from within!*

This tactic is known as *subversion.* These socialists and secular humanists (the term "communists" seems almost like a term from another era) represent a small section of American society, yet they are responsible for many of America's policies.

For so few in number, they hold enormous power, having control of many of the educational, judicial and political positions, not to mention control of the mainstream media and press and even many Christian denominations. They do not like to be linked with Communists because for the last generation and a half, communism has been seen as the ideological and military enemy of America. However, communists themselves know that socialism is nothing more than America's version of communism.

Shortly after World War I, the Communists realized that the USA was too strong militarily and economically to ever be destroyed from the outside. So what did they do? *They found a way to use our own Constitution against us.* As Clifford M. Lytle tells us in his book, *The Warren Court and Its Critics*:

> [4] "This was known as *Soviet Principle 10.* It was a plan to break America's resistance without resorting to war."

Our founding fathers intended Judeo-Christian values

to be the pillar holding up and stabilizing or society; therefore, the best way to destabilize American society was to remove the pillar that our founding fathers felt was essential to support it.

Hundreds of years ago, Daniel Webster, lawyer and member of the House of Representatives, warned the American people that since America was so powerful that we would never be defeated from outside, *if America were to be destroyed, it would come from within.*

> [5] "I apprehend no danger to our country from a foreign foe. The prospect of a war with any powerful nation is too remote to be a matter of calculation. Besides, there is no nation on earth powerful enough to accomplish our overthrow. Our destruction, should it come at all, will be from another quarter; from the inattention of the people to the concerns of their government, from their carelessness and negligence."

Daniel Webster knew what just about every government in the world knew and understood about America's might: that "no nation on earth was powerful enough to accomplish our overthrow." America would have to be destroyed from within.

How could this be accomplished? By removing that which made America great in the first place—its dependence upon God and the modeling of American society after His laws.

Alexis de Tocqueville, after visiting America and studying its institutions, said that it was Christianity that had made America great. In his final campaign address in Boston, Massachusetts, on November 3, 1952, Dwight D. Eisenhower quoted Alexis de Tocqueville with regard to the secret of America's success:

[6] "I sought for the greatness and genius of America in her commodious harbors and in her ample rivers, and it was not there. I sought for the greatness and genius of America in her fertile fields and boundless forests, and it was not there. I sought for the greatness and genius of America in her rich mines and her vast world commerce, and it was not there. I sought for the greatness and genius of America in her public school system and her institutions of learning, and it was not there. I sought for the genius and greatness of America in her democratic congress and her matchless constitution, and it was not there. Not until I went into the churches of America and heard her pulpits flame with righteousness did I understand the secret of her genius and power. America is great because America is good, and if America ever ceases to be good, America will cease to be great."

What then did Daniel Webster mean when he said "Our destruction... will be... from the inattention of the people to the concerns of their government, from their carelessness and negligence?" He was referring to a country ignorant of its own Constitution, a country that had lost its spiritual heritage. He referred to a people too lazy or too indifferent to a stand for what is important; a country that had forsaken God and the bible and the faith that our founding fathers held so dear.

Thanks in part to the many recent historical revisionists, it may be difficult to fathom that those in government felt so strongly about religion. However, before the 1960s, many Americans, including the U.S. court system, knew that if the Judeo-Christian principles that formed our government were to be removed or abolished, America would be in deep trouble. In the 1846 Case of *Charleston v. Benjamin*, this Supreme Court itself ruled:

> [7] "What constitutes the standard of good morals? Is it not Christianity? There certainly is no other. The day of moral virtue in which we live would, in an instant, if that standard were abolished, lapse into the dark and murky night of pagan immorality... Christianity has reference to the principles of right and wrong... it is the foundation of those morals and manners upon which our society is formed; it is their basis. Remove this and they would fall."

Enemies of the American Republic clearly understand what this 1800s Supreme Court meant. Remove the foundational pillar of Christianity and our society would fall. Therefore, it is imperative that we identify the enemy that has succeeded in destroying the pillar.

Chapter 11

America's Enemies

[1] "Those who are endeavoring to eradicate the principles of religion and virtue, by discarding Christianity, however extensive the benevolence may be which they profess, are our worst enemies."

Samuel Taggart, U.S. Congressmen 1803–1817

As a military veteran, I took an oath to "support and defend the Constitution of the United States against all enemies, foreign and domestic... So help me God." And as far as I am concerned, that oath did not end with the end of my military service.

So many times we focus only on America's foreign enemies while forgetting that America also has "domestic" enemies.

Who are these enemies of the Constitution? Are there foreign enemies who would destroy our Constitution? Does Al-Qaeda have the power to seize our civil and Constitutional rights? No. Our overseas enemies cannot take our freedoms and civil liberties away from us. It is only America's "domestic" enemies who could pull off such a feat. This is something that had to be accomplished internally.

For the last 60 years, a battle has raged for the soul of America. We need to understand who it is that we are up against. To do so, we must first identify the enemies of the American Republic.

The socialists and secularists in the government understand the battle taking place in America. Robert Reich, former labor secretary under Bill Clinton and author of the book *Reason: Why Liberals Will Win the Battle For America*, had this to say when referring to evangelical Christians, Catholics and orthodox Jews:

> [2] "The underlying battle of the 21st century will be between modern civilization and anti-modernist fanatics, between those who believe in the primacy of the individual and those who believe that human beings owe blind allegiance to a higher authority, between those who give priority to life in this world and those who believe that human life is no more than preparation for an existence beyond life, between those who believe that truth is believed solely through scripture and religious dogma and those who rely primarily on science, reason and logic."

Men like George Washington believed that the future of our country depended upon the Christian training of our youth. However, these secularists try to instill fear in the American public by saying things like, "Christians just want to take us back to the Dark Ages!"

During the debate over the Ten Commandments monument in the Alabama courthouse, one individual writes the following:

[3] "We are seeing the birth of a new Dark Ages. [Judge] Roy Moore's followers are clearly growing in number and also undoubtedly growing stronger... The Dark Ages are coming..."

Recently, Maureen Dowd of the *New York Times* accused Christians of taking America into [4] "another Dark Age, where we replace science with religion and facts with faith."

Allow me to explain why they would make such a statement. Even though most would probably not admit it, in many of their minds, God is nothing more than myth and fable. One atheist who is waging a self-proclaimed "War on Faith" is quoted as saying:

[5] "We have the ACLU to fight our battles in the courtroom, but we have to fight our own battles in our everyday lives. It's time to remove the myths surrounding faith and the faithful. Surely we will never be able to rid society of this blight called religion, but at least we can remove the misleading cloak of respectability that the masses have wrapped it in."

For many Americans, if a person were to venture into a rain forest and find a tribe worshipping a tree trunk, these people would be perceived as primitive. Similarly, in the minds of America's enemies, anyone who believes in God is just as primitive, holding on to some outdated myth. They see the fact that God and the Bible have been removed from our schools and our government as necessary for our continued evolution. In their minds, if America were to return to its Judeo-Christian roots, it would be a giant step backward in the evolutionary process—hence, a return to the Dark Ages.

During the same time, the *New York Times* ran an op. ed. piece by Gary Wills, who questioned whether a people who believe in the Virgin Birth of Jesus can be called an enlightened nation. These secularists in the media do not want God to have anything to do with society or government, and they will distort and misrepresent the truth to keep it that way. Sadly, they have convinced much of the American public that our founding fathers demanded that religion be kept separate from our schools and government, but as we continue to see from quotes of our founding fathers, this is decidedly untrue.

Benjamin Rush, a signer of the Declaration of Independence who was influential in ratifying the federal Constitution in Pennsylvania, said:

> [6] "The great enemy of the salvation of man, in my opinion, never invented a more effectual means of [extinguishing] Christianity from the world than by persuading mankind *that it was improper to read the bible at schools.*"

Secularists have been effective at spewing this type of rhetoric. They have successfully convinced a portion of the American public that our founding fathers felt it was *"improper to read the bible at schools."* They can be convincing until their statements are compared to the facts.

Our Worst Enemies

Many socialist and secular lobbying groups are waging an all-out war against the traditional America created by our founding fathers. These organizations usually take on patriotic names to promote themselves as "American" champions of "liberty and freedom" when, in reality, these organizations support a government and a society that is the polar opposite of the American Republic our founding fathers created.

In the book *Religion in American Politics* we see that the founders of this nation believed

> [7] "the greatest threat to Republican government was not population expanse, war, or runaway inflation, but infidelity—bad faith... Samuel Taggart (U.S. Congressman, 1803–1817) warned, 'A nation habitually irreligious cannot long be free. Those who are endeavoring to eradicate the principles of religion and virtue, by discarding Christianity, however extensive the benevolence may be which they profess, are our worst enemies.'"

Samuel Taggart tells us that no matter how patriotic a person or organization may try to appear, anyone who attempts to eradicate the principles of religion and virtue is America's worst enemy.

Listen to what two of our founding fathers had to say about these types of people. George Washington said the following in his Farewell Address:

> [8] "Of all of the dispositions and habits which lead to political prosperity, religion and morality are indispensable supports. In vain would that man claim the tribute of patriotism who should labor to subvert these great pillars of human happiness."

Jeremiah Smith (1759–1842), a Revolutionary soldier, judge, U.S. Congressman and Governor of New Hampshire, is quoted as saying:

> [9] "Cherish and Promote the interest of *Knowledge, virtue and religion*. They are indispensable to the support of any free government... Let it never be forgotten

that there can be no genuine freedom where there is no morality, and no sound morality where there is no religion... Hesitate not a moment to believe that the man who labors to destroy these two great pillars of human happiness.... *is neither a good patriot nor a good man."*

In the opinion of George Washington and Jeremiah Smith, it would be foolish for a man or an organization to claim to be a patriot while also trying to subvert the religion and morality that are absolutely necessary to ensure political prosperity and genuine freedom. Any person or organization who subverts religion and morality is nothing more than a wolf in sheep clothing. Jesus taught that we would know people by their fruit, not by their words. People today are often more swayed by words than by actions when, in fact, it is the *actions* that most need to be watched.

Three of the biggest enemies to the Republican form of government are the America United for the Separation of Church and State (AU) and the American Civil Liberties Union (ACLU) and the People for the American Way (PFAW).

These American imposters have given themselves patriotic "American" names in order to deceive people into believing that they stand for traditional "American" government, when in fact they stand for a system of government exactly opposite to the one our founding fathers created. George Washington, in his Farewell Address given on September 19, 1796, warned us to "guard against the impostures of pretended patriotism."

Taking on patriotic names is a clever way to deceive the American people—after all, who would support them if their names were to reflect their true ideology. If these organizations had named themselves according to their true ideology, they would be named the "Anti-Christian Lawyers' Union" or "American Communist Lawyers Union" (ACLU), Communists United for the Separation of Church and State" (AU), and the "People for the Socialist Way" (PFAW).

Are the actions of these organizations preserving the traditional American way of life as they claim or are they, in fact, destroying it? You decide.

The ACLU announced its latest cause: protecting the rights of child molesters. Alleging that "important" 1st Amendment (free speech, free association) rights were at stake, the ACLU proudly announced its intent to defend the North American Man-Boy Love Association (NAMBLA), NAMBLA, whose motto is "After eight, is too late," and advocates sexually oriented adult male/young boy relationships and officially claims that its goal is to "speak out against societal oppression and celebrates the joys of men and boys in love." Saying (obviously tongue-in-cheek, based upon its selective past representation) that "the Constitution is for everybody," the ACLU (Boston chapter) voted proudly and "overwhelmingly" to represent these advocates of child molestation.

Arguing that "under the first Amendment, there are no illegal ideas," the ACLU will use its extensive legal and financial resources to support NAMBLA, which advocates *real acts* of child molestation, not just ideas. Harvey Silvergate, an ACLU member, acknowledged that NAMBLA argues for "changes in society's views about consensual sex between adults and minors and a lowering of the age of consent," but goes on to state that the NAMBLA actually does not advocate illegal acts of child molestation... but even if NAMBLA does, such would be protected by the First Amendment. Unbelievable? No. This is actually going on in our country.

In 1994, Megan Kanka was abducted from her suburban New Jersey neighborhood, raped and murdered. A twice-convicted child molester who lived across the street from her subsequently confessed to the crime and was convicted. The New Jersey legislature then passed the first "Megan's Law," which required information on the whereabouts of previously convicted child molesters to be made publicly available. In prompt order, all other state legislatures and Congress adopted their own versions of "Megan's Law." Critics of these laws, including the ACLU, claim that they violate the "constitutional right of privacy" of the convicted molesters, after they have been released from prison.

The ACLU is against freedom of speech. They claim to stand for free speech, yet demand the right to approve public speech. In the ACLU's view, pornography—even child porn—is protected free speech, but public prayer is to be forbidden.

The American people must wake up and recognize that these organizations (the ACLU and the Americans United for the Separation of Church and State, and People for the American Way) are subversive socialist organizations that, under the guise of "civil liberties" and "constitutional rights," are partially responsible for the moral decay of American society.

When the ACLU defends child molestation and declares it a "constitutional right," whose children do you think they are advocating molesting? Their own? Is that even legal? Doesn't Children's Services take children out of the homes of people who molest their own children? If these perverts are advocating molesting children under the age of eight, where do you think these children are coming from? *I'll give you a hint—look on a milk carton!*

On a web site titled "Revealing FACTS on the ACLU from its own writings" by Diane Dew, we can see what these so-called "patriotic organizations" are really all about:

[10] "Ever notice how the American Civil Liberties Union (ACLU) seems to take on only cases that are anti-Christian—pro-sodomy, pro-abortion, anti-family, pro-pornography, pro-prostitution, pro-euthanasia, pro-homosexual, pro-infanticide, pro-crime, pro-humanism, anti-God—and, except for atheism, anti-religion?

"It calls itself the American Civil Liberties Union, but the ACLU *is not American*; it is *un*civil; and it knows nothing of *true liberty*, which can only be found in Jesus Christ, when one is set free from the bondage of all the sin this evil organization promotes!

"The following are stated goals of the ACLU, from its own published Policy Issues:
- The legalization of prostitution (Policy 211);
- The defense of all pornography, including *child porn*, as "free speech" (Policy 4);
- The decriminalization and legalization of all drugs (Policy 210);
- The promotion of homosexuality (Policy 264);
- The opposition of rating of music and movies (Policy 18);
- Opposition against parental consent of minors seeking abortion (Policy 262);
- Opposition of informed consent preceding abortion procedures (Policy 263);
- Opposition of spousal consent preceding abortion (Policy 262);
- Opposition of parental choice in children's education (Policy 80)

"Not to mention the defense and promotion of euthanasia, polygamy, government control of church institutions, gun control, tax-funded abortion, birth limitation, etc. (Policies 263, 133, 402, 47, 261, 323, 271, 91, 85).

"Following is a case in point from David Barton's *America: To Pray or Not to Pray*. In 1988, California considered adopting legislation on sex education for public schools requiring that course material and instruction should stress that monogamous heterosexual intercourse within marriage is a traditional American value. The Senator promoting the bill received a letter of protest from the ACLU dated April 18, 1988 stating: 'It is our position that monogamous, heterosexual intercourse within marriage as a traditional American value is an unconstitutional establishment of religious doctrine in public schools... We believe [this bill] violates the First Amendment.'

Secularists are unwilling to simply let others be, but rather seek to force and impose their ungodliness upon a historically Christian nation. It is their *mission* to pervert the freedoms of others. The ACLU does not run to the defense of those who are harmed; it aggressively seeks out opportunities to corrupt pure freedoms."

In the preceding chapters I have disclosed how much of our government has been taken over by socialist and secularists determined to destroy our Constitution and the traditional American way of life. While the American people are beginning to wake up and remove these individuals from political office, many of the judges whom they have appointed remain on the bench *for life*.

The stick with which these secularists have beaten traditionalists for years is the new and distorted First and Fourteenth Amendments to the Constitution. Everything that our founding fathers believed would help and edify society, they call a "violation of a separation of church and state," and everything that our founding fathers felt was destructive to the moral fabric of America, they call "civil liberties."

This battle is raging today, led by organizations such as the ACLU. Diane Dew continues:

> [11] "The ACLU is destructive to the fabric of our society. Christians must recognize Satan as the source—the instigator—when the end results of an organization's efforts are only 'to kill, to steal, and to destroy.' All we need do is examine the rotten fruit. However, we must understand that the battle is more spiritual in nature than political. While this battle has manifested itself in the political area, we must understand its root. We must also understand that many liberal beliefs are the results of deception, and Satan is the source."

While organizations such as Americans United for Separation of Church and State (AU) and the America Civil Liberties Union (ACLU) and the People for the American Way (PFAW) have set themselves up as the physical or earthly opponents to the type of government enacted by our founding fathers, they themselves are not the true enemy, because they themselves are being deceived. We are engulfed in a war that has existed from before time itself and a war that will continue until time itself ends. It is a war between good and evil; God and Satan; Christ and anti-Christ.

A Return to the Dark Ages?

Many of these organizations try to instill fear in the American public by saying that Christians want to return America to the Dark Ages. Let us compare the America of our grandparents' day to modern society. A generation or two ago, our parents and grandparents could sleep with all their windows and doors wide open without fear for their lives or their safety. When people left their houses, they did not even lock them up, because they did not worry about people breaking in and stealing all of their belongings. When people drove, they did not lock their cars, because they did not worry about being carjacked or abducted. Young children were given free reign of their local neighborhoods because their parents were not worried about their children being kidnapped, molested or killed by some pervert addicted to child pornography.

In today's society, many people do not even feel safe with their doors and windows locked. When Christianity was the dominant influence in society and in the government, we had much more freedom and security than now.

Why do you lock your doors and windows? Because you are afraid to wake up with a Christian sitting on your chest and pointing a gun at your head, demanding that you pray with him or because you fear for the safety of yourself and your family?

Why do you lock your car when you are driving down the road? Is it because you fear being carjacked by a Christian and forced to drive him to church? Or is it because you fear someone finding your body dead on the side of the road?

Why do you lock and alarm your car when you go into the store? Is it because you are afraid that a Christian will break into your car and leave a Bible on your seat, or is it because you are afraid some thief will steal something that you have worked so hard for?

Why do the police advise people to take great precautions when walking alone? Is it because they're afraid that a Christian will jump out of the bushes and force you to read the New Testament?

Why do you not allow your children out of your sight when they are playing? Is it because you are afraid that some Christian may tell your child about Jesus, or because you have seen the recent string of child abductions, rapes and murders of children on television?

Jewish medical educator David C. Stolinsky laments the loss of Christian values that dominated America in the 1950s:

> [12] "The reason we fear to go out after dark is not that we may be set upon by bands of evangelicals and forced to read the New Testament, but that we may be set upon by gangs of [wild and violent] young people who have been taught that nothing is superior to their own needs or feelings."

Forty years ago, we did not live in a society in which high school massacres were commonplace and the kidnapping, rape and murder of our children from our own homes was something that you read about every other month. Forty years ago we were not plagued with a string of cases of our teachers molesting our children. If they had, the media certainly would not have referred to such molestations as "relationships."

When scripture, which governed American life, school and government from the early 1600s until the early 1960s, was exchanged for "situation ethics"—otherwise known as "relativism"—all hell broke loose.

Our founding fathers lived in a primitive time as far as technology goes, but morally and socially they were a nation of light. Daniel Webster, lawyer and member of the House of Representatives in 1812, practically prophesied what would happen to American society if the Bible were ever removed from a place of prominence and influence in American society:

> [13] "If religious books are not widely circulated among the masses in this country, I do not know what is going to become of us as a nation. If truth be not diffused, error will be; If God and His Word are not known and received, the devil and his works will gain the ascendancy. If the evangelical volume does not reach every hamlet, the pages of a corrupt and licentious literature will. If the power of the Gospel is not felt throughout the length and breadth of the land, anarchy and misrule, degradation and misery, corruption and darkness will reign without mitigation or end."

Our founding fathers understood that nature abhors a vacuum. If you remove something from a given space, that space will not remain empty. *Something* will come in and fill the void. Daniel Webster felt that if the gospel of Christ were ever removed from this land, darkness would reign. He felt that if God and His word were removed, the devil and his works would fill the void. This is what has happened in America over the last generation. The light has been removed and darkness has filled the void.

What happens when you walk into a room at night, close the door and turn off the light? It gets dark! Why did it get dark? Is it because you invited in the darkness or because you removed the light? There is no such thing as a "dark switch." A person or a nation sick and tired of being in the dark cannot say, "Hey, someone turn off the dark!" Darkness is the state or result of being "devoid of light." Passing more restrictive laws that steal our civil liberties will not restrain the darkness. It is often more effective to turn on the light than it is to sit and curse the darkness.

America, for the last 40 years, has been trying to remove the darkness that permeates our society, but it has done so by passing more and more restrictive laws, resulting in the elimination of many of our civil liberties instead of bringing the light back in. The Bible teaches that the word of God and Jesus Christ are light, and by forcing God, the Bible and Christianity out of our schools and our government, we have ushered darkness into our society. It is not that we have voluntarily said "bring in the darkness"; darkness is the ultimate result of the "absence of light."

The unconstitutional rulings concerning the mythical separation of church and state had a devastating effect upon the moral and social fabric of our society. The National Center for Policy Analysis, a non-profit, non-partisan public policy research organization, confirms this. It has reported that an unprecedented rise in crime coincided with the Supreme Court rulings of a generation ago. It says:

> [14] "The serious crime rate exploded during the 1960s and 1970s... The crime rates for murder, rape, robbery and serious assaults and burglary rose slightly during the 1950s and then exploded during the 1960s and 1970s, increasing the serious crime rate fourfold."

Could this have been a result of removing biblical morality from our schools? If there are gangs of wild and violent young people who have been taught that nothing is superior to their own needs or feelings, then where do you think they learned such things?

Secularists want Americans to believe "Christians just want to take us back to the Dark Ages," when, in reality, it is organizations such as the ACLU, Americans United for the Separation of Church and State and other secular humanist organizations that are responsible for bringing America into the Dark Ages.

Our Constitution has granted every American citizen certain "rights." However, these rights were intended for a moral and religious people. If the supervising oversight of Judeo-Christian morality in the lives of the American people is removed, the Constitution might as well be thrown out the window. When the American people have thrown off biblical restraint, the government has been forced to step in and restrict our civil rights in order to keep lawlessness at bay.

Before the supervising aspect of Christianity was removed as the moral standard in America, our founding fathers saw fit to give the American people the right to keep and bear arms. Why? Because average American citizens of faith would never use firearms as an instrument to perpetrate violence against his neighbor, and poses no threat to society.

However, once these firearms are put into the hands of citizens who are void of faith, they become a menace to society. The cry for gun control laws only became prominent in America once people started using weapons against their innocent neighbors.

The secularists in this country want you to believe that it is the *number* of firearms in America that causes firearm violence, rather than the actual cause: our nation is unbridled by morality and religion.

Darrell Scott, father of Rachel Scott, a victim of the Columbine High School shootings in Littleton, Colorado, was invited to address the House Judiciary Committee's subcommittee. What he said to our national leaders during this special session of Congress was painfully true. They were unprepared for what he said, and it wasn't received well. Every parent, teacher, politician, sociologist, judge and psychologist should heed his words. The following is a portion of the transcript:

> [15] "Since the dawn of creation there has been both good and evil in the hearts of men and women. We all contain the seeds of kindness or the seeds of violence. The death of my wonderful daughter, Rachel Joy Scott, and the deaths of that heroic teacher, and the other eleven children who died must not be in vain. "Their blood cries out for answers.

"The first recorded act of violence was when Cain slew his brother Abel out in the field. The villain was not the club he used. Neither was it the NCA, the National Club Association. The true killer was Cain, and the reason for the murder could only be found in Cain's heart.

"In the days that followed the Columbine tragedy, I was amazed at how quickly fingers began to be pointed at groups such as the NRA. I am not a member of the NRA. I am not a hunter. I do not even own a gun. I am not here to represent or defend the NRA because I don't believe that they are responsible for my daughter's death. Therefore I do not believe that they need to be defended. If I believed they had anything to do with Rachel's murder I would be their strongest opponent.

"I am here today to declare that Columbine was not just a tragedy—it was a spiritual event that should be forcing us to look at where the real blame lies. Much of the blame lies here in this room. Much of the blame lies behind the pointing fingers of the accusers themselves. I wrote a poem just four nights ago that expresses my feelings best. This was written way before I knew I would be speaking here today:

> *Your laws ignore our deepest needs;*
> *your words are empty air.*
> *You've stripped away our heritage,*
> *you've outlawed simple prayer.*
> *Now gunshots fill our classrooms,*
> *and precious children die.*
> *You seek for answers everywhere,*
> *and ask the question "Why?"*
> *You regulate restrictive laws,*
> *through legislative creed.*
> *And yet you fail to understand,*
> *That God is what we need!*

"Men and women are three-part beings. We all consist of body, soul, and spirit. When we refuse to acknowledge a third part of our make-up, we create a void that allows evil, prejudice, and hatred to rush in and wreak havoc. Spiritual presences were present within our educational systems for most of our nation's history. Many of our major colleges began as theological seminaries. This is a historical fact.

"What has happened to us as a nation? We have refused to honor God, and in so doing, we open the doors to hatred and violence. And when something as terrible as Columbine's tragedy occurs, politicians immediately look for a scapegoat such as the NRA. They immediately seek to pass more restrictive laws that continue to erode away our personal and private liberties. We do not need more restrictive laws.

"Eric and Dylan would not have been stopped by metal detectors. No amount of gun laws can stop someone who spends months planning this type of massacre. The real villain lies within our own hearts. Political posturing and restrictive legislation are not the answers. The young people of our nation hold the key. There is a spiritual awakening taking place that will not be squelched! We do not need more religion. We do not need more gaudy television evangelists spewing out verbal religious garbage. We do not need more million-dollar church buildings built while people with basic needs are being ignored. We do need a change of heart and a humble acknowledgment that this nation was founded on the principle of simple trust in God!

"As my son Craig lay under that table in the school library and saw his two friends murdered before his very eyes, he did not hesitate to pray in school. I defy any law or politician to deny him that right! I challenge every young person in America, and around the world, to realize that on April 20, 1999, at Columbine High School, prayer was brought back to our schools.

"Do not let the many prayers offered by those students be in vain. Dare to move into the new millennium with a sacred disregard for legislation that violates your God-given right to communicate with Him. To those of you who would point your finger at the NRA, I give to you a sincere challenge. Dare to examine your own heart before casting the first stone. My daughter's death will not be in vain. The young people of this country will not allow that to happen."

Darrell Scott did not blame the NRA or the gun that killed his daughter—he blamed those in government who outlawed God and prayer in the schools. He blamed those responsible for removing "love your neighbor as yourself" and "do not murder" from the classroom.

This is not just the opinion of some radical right-wing conservatives, unless you consider our founding fathers as such. President John Adams is quoted as saying:

> [16] "We have no government armed with power capable of contending with human passions unbridled by morality and religion."

Our founding fathers understood that the only thing the government could do is prosecute people after they have committed a crime. Religion and morality may arrest the crime within the heart of man before it happens. This is why our founding fathers felt religion to be an indispensable support to America and its form of government.

Our founders knew and understood that the heart of man is desperately wicked, and that if the heart of man is not changed and guided by a sense of something greater than himself, there is no limit to the evil of which we are capable.

More restrictive laws will never solve this problem. Let us say, for argument's sake, that all the guns in America disappeared tomorrow. What or who are they going to blame for murder once all the guns are abolished? Do you think people will quit killing each other? People have killed each other long before firearms arrived on the world scene. What will be banned next? What if people start killing each other with knives, steel pipes or rocks? Will these items also be banned?

A generation ago, if anyone in this nation had blamed murders on firearms instead of the individuals who committed the crime, they would have been laughed off the street. Guns do not kill people; *evil people* kill people.

When civil and moral individual responsibilities were

taught in the classroom and in society and people were held accountable for their actions, these crimes were not blamed upon "inanimate objects." We have become a society in which everything we do is someone else's fault, and we are unwilling to be held accountable for our own actions.

Government is unable to stop crime. Government can only track down and punish those who commit crime after the fact. Religion and morality, on the other hand, has the power to stop crime before it starts by arresting it in the hearts of man before it becomes a problem. Our founding fathers understood this truth all too well.

James Madison, whom many consider the Father of the Constitution, is quoted as saying:

> [17] "We have staked the whole future of American civilization, not upon the power of government, far from it. We have staked the future of all of our *political institutions* upon the capacity of mankind of self-government; upon the capacity of each and all of us to govern ourselves, to control ourselves, to sustain ourselves according to the Ten Commandments of God."

John Adams also understood that government was powerless to restrain human behavior. He felt that the only way a civil American society could exist was if morality and religion continued to influence society.

> [18] "We have no government armed with power capable of contending with human passions unbridled by morality and religion. Avarice, ambition, revenge, or gallantry would break the strongest cords of our Constitution as a whale goes through a net. *Our Constitution was made only for a moral and reli-*

gious people. It is wholly inadequate to the government of any other."

Until this nation accepts that *wickedness in men's hearts*, unbridled by religion or morality, is causing all of our social disorders, we will continue to run in circles looking for an answer to society's problems, when the solution is literally staring us in the face. Actually, the answer is 40 years *behind* us. Our media and government simply refuse to accept it.

Chapter 12

The Warren Court

[1] *"Communism and socialism are almost one and the same, and that the whole Supreme Court is a nest of socialists and even worse."*

Robert Welch, of the John Birch Society

[2] *The Warren Court had a tendency to permit (the Constitution's) living phrases to be distorted and twisted to meet the immediate needs of those whose dedicated purpose is to destroy it and replace it with the Constitution of the Soviet Union."*

Representative Donald Jackson (R. Cal.) commenting on the string of Supreme Court decisions handed down by the Warren Court

The United States Supreme Court of the late '50s and early '60s was a socialist, activist renegade court. Many Americans today are not old enough to remember the controversy that rocked this nation in the '40s, '50s and early '60s, so here is a brief recap.

Before 1920, almost no one in America was considered a socialist or a secularist. The following quote from Alexis de Tocqueville shows this to be true:

> [3] "I am certain that [Americans] hold [religion] to be indispensable to the maintenance of Republican institutions. *This opinion is not particular to a class of citizen or to a party, but it belongs to the whole nation, into every rank of society.*"

Prior to 1920, all Americans, regardless of party affiliation, held "religion to be indispensable to the maintenance of Republican institutions." Unfortunately this holds true no longer. Therefore, when the American Communist Party and other left-wing political groups began to infiltrate the United States, everyone from Republican and Democratic Senators to the media and many in the courts began to get concerned. The people of the United States saw this as an attack on the very fabric of American society. Just as we are learning 80 years later, the fact that America is an open society tends to allow those who do not have the best interests of the American people into the country. The same problem existed in the 1920s to 1940s.

> [4] "After the ground swell against communism in 1920, from 1921–1924 members of the communist party sought to avoid arrest by operating underground. But when the Wartime Emergency Acts were repealed, the communist leaders came to the

surface again and continued their campaign openly for a revolution to overthrow the United States Government.

"Unable to make substantial advances among the masses, the communists turned to the so-called intellectuals in the early 1930's. The appeal of communism to the sophisticated intellectuals coincided with the age of daring debunking. This was a time when men and woman began to question the existence of God. Litigations were being filed in courts across the land trying to outlaw any recognition of God in the public schools and government life. This was the age of evolution, when the seeds of doubt were first planted in America's educational system concerning the creation of the world by a merciful Father...

"The unbelievable extent to which Americans participated in Russian-directed espionage against the United States during the Depression and World War II has only recently (1964) become generally recognized. Many complete books have been written which summarize the evidence unearthed by the FBI, the courts, and the Congress. It is fitting to remember at this point that Whitaker Chambers, one of the top communists in the United States... broke with communism in the late 1930's and because of his sensational testimony before the House Committee on Un-American Activities, exposed Alger Hiss. No greater volume is available anywhere on the communist conspiracy in the United States than Chambers' autobiography, *Witness*.

"(Former spy) Elizabeth Bentley said the Soviet underground tapped in Washington, D.C., during the times she served as the Russian Secret Police paymaster and courier in the nation's capitol. Miss Bentley worked doggedly for the Soviets until 1944. After becoming disillusioned with communism in 1944, she walked into FBI Headquarters in Washington, D.C., stating she was willing and ready to reveal all that she knew about the communist conspiracy in the nation's capitol and to make amends to her native country. After her sensational break with communism, the...liberal press of the United States began to accuse her of being everything from a degenerate to a psychopathic liar or a victim of insanity. She found herself like Whitaker Chambers, after his break with communism, cast away and alone.

"Volume after volume of Congressional reports of the communist conspiracy internally are printed at the taxpayer's expense, but their message goes unread and unheeded by the majority of America's liberal leaders in politics, education, and religion, and by the American people as a whole. Only small vocal anti-communist militants known as 'conservatives' have shown any interest in recent years in the Congressional reports on the communist conspiracy internally."

The following is but a short excerpt from the book *Treason* by Ann Coulter. This book is a must-read for all who consider themselves patriots and who want to defend the traditional American way of life:

[5] "The Soviets used a code that was, in theory, unbreakable. But by the war's end, the Americans had cracked it. And when the Venona [project] cryp-

tographers read the Soviet cables they discovered something far more sinister than Stalin's war plans: The Roosevelt administration was teeming with paid agents of Moscow. Stalin's handmaidens held strategic positions at the White House, the State Department, the War Department, the Office of Strategic Services, and the Treasury Department.

"Only a small number of intercepted Soviet cables have been decoded. But even that much proves [Joseph] McCarthy was absolutely right in his paramount charges: The U.S. government had a major Communist infestation problem... It can now be said that McCarthy's gravest error was in underestimating the problem of Soviet subversion.

"The scale of the conspiracy was unprecedented. Hundreds of Soviet spies honeycombed the U.S. government throughout the forties and fifties. America had been invaded by a civilian army loyal to a hostile power. There was no room for denying it...

"McCarthy was accused of labeling 'anyone with liberal views' a Communist. As we now know, that wouldn't have been a half-bad system."

From the book *The Far Left*, written in 1964 in an attempt to warn Americans to take action against the socialist and secular forces that were increasingly gaining influence in America, we learn:

"America is being led today, for the most part, by a strange breed of individuals who have formed an intellectual, sophisticated cult bent on the destruction of Constitutional government and orthodox Christianity, [about this] there can be little doubt... These simple minded souls would have you believe that this foreign directed conspiracy, which has already enslaved approximately one-third of the people of the earth, and is resolutely working night and day to bring us to our knees, is a myth."

May we go so far as to consider that a conspiracy has been perpetrated to alter our government? The word *conspiracy* is defined as [6] "a planning and acting together secretly, esp. for an unlawful or harmful purpose."

In a court of law, one must only prove a case "beyond a reasonable doubt." Therefore, let us consider the facts:

1. Our founding fathers created a government in which they deemed religion essential to maintaining a civilized society. Therefore, the 1st Amendment to the U.S. Constitution forbids the federal government to interfere with the religious liberties of the American people. The idea of church and state separation simply meant the government would not have the power to legislate and criminalize religious conduct.
2. Article 124 of the Constitution of the Soviet Union adopted in December of 1936 reads: "In order to ensure to citizens freedom of conscience, the church in the U.S.S.R. is separated from the state, and the school from the church."
3. In 1958, during debate over the Jenner bill (S. 2646, appendix IV), a United States Senate subcommittee heard testimony concerning [7] "Soviet principle 10. It was a plan to break America's resistance without resorting to war."
4. Intercepted Soviet cables reveal that the highest levels of the American government were infested with Soviet spies.
5. By establishing the 10th Amendment, our found-

ing fathers created a government in which the power to govern the lives of the individual states was left in the hands of the American people. The socialist-controlled Supreme Court illegally and unconstitutionally used the 14th Amendment to destroy the provisions of the 10th Amendment, turning America into a socialist state controlled by the Supreme Court.
6. Madalyn O'Hair, one of the main litigants in the Supreme Court case that officially kicked God out of American society, was a communist.

In the now infamous court case *Abington School District. v. Schempp*, which took place in 1963, two cases were decided simultaneously: *Abington School District v. Schempp* and *Murray v Curlett*.

Famed atheist Madalyn Murray O'Hair felt so slighted that the now famous case became known as *Abington School District v. Schempp* and was not called *Murray v Curlett* that she felt the need to write *The Matter of Prayer*. I will allow her to speak for herself:

> [8] "It was thus that, as an Atheist, my unhappiness concerned with prayer culminated in a lawsuit. My complaint against those school prayers, begun in the fall of 1959, continued until the decision of *Murray v Curlett* was handed down— almost four years later—by the Supreme Court of the United States on June 17, 1963... There is no "Lord's Prayer" in the public schools of the United States because I, as an Atheist, challenged it specifically. I want that shown in the records of our culture as it is shown in the legal records of what went on 'back then' in the early 1960s."

Madalyn O'Hair was a communist and an atheist. Along with her communist allies on the Supreme Court, she robbed America of its very soul. William J. Murray, son of the famous atheist and author of the book *My Life Without God*, is now a Christian evangelist. He had this to say about his mother's lifestyle and affiliations:

> [9] "I was born into a home of near constant rage and violence. My mother never married my father or my brother's father. As a result of my mother's constant angry outbursts she could not hold down a job and she, my brother and I lived with her parents and my unmarried uncle in a small row house in Baltimore, Maryland. My grandfather had never filed an income tax return and most of what he did do during his life was illegal or ill advised... My uncle kept hoards of pornography in his room and my mother filled the house with statues of mating animals which she worshipped.
>
> "My mother accepted the communist doctrine when I was about ten years old and from that time on there were socialist and communist study group meetings in the basement of our Baltimore home . . ."

7. The ACLU is a socialist-communist front organization that for decades has been on a mission to have God completely removed from American society. Its founder, Roger Baldwin, stated:

> [10] "We are for *Socialism*, disarmament, and ultimately for abolishing the state itself... We seek the social ownership of property, the abolition of the propertied class, and the *sole control* of those who produce wealth. *Communism* is the goal... I don't re-

gret being part of the communist tactic. I knew what I was doing. *I was not an innocent liberal.* I wanted what the communists wanted and I traveled the United Front road to get it."

Newswatch magazine recently ran an article concerning the Ten Commandments story in Alabama, featuring an aspect of the story that other secular news agencies failed to cover. It exposes the plan of the ACLU from a man who was once a part of their organization:

> [11] "Herbert Titus, one of three attorneys defending Chief Justice Roy Moore of the Alabama Supreme Court, knows firsthand about the ACLU [American Civil Liberties Union] and its aims. A Harvard Law School graduate who served in the Justice Department under Robert Kennedy, Titus taught law at the University of Oregon Law School.
>
> "He pursued legal activism, signing on to serve as an ACLU attorney. He knows better than most what the ACLU's true objectives are and what is at stake in the lawsuit filed against Chief Justice Moore. Titus, who professed Christ in 1975, later taught law at the Oral Roberts University School of Law and served as the founding Dean of the College of Law and Government at Regent University.
>
> "A highly regarded constitutional scholar, Titus said... The ACLU, says Titus, wants nothing less than to scrub the American landscape clean of all 'vestiges of the religious foundation of law and liberty in America.' And it seeks vulnerable targets in its campaign to purge religion from public life. 'Chief Justice Moore,' he said, 'is a vulnerable target, just as cities and towns and states across the country have

been vulnerable targets to this assault on America's Christian tradition.'

"Small victories, he said, build precedents for larger cases. Given enough courtroom conquests, the ACLU will go on to challenge '*any* reference to God in any public place, in any public ceremony of any kind.' That includes, he said, '*In God We Trust* on our money, and *Under God* in the Pledge of Allegiance.'

"'I know,' he said. 'I used to be an ACLU co-operating attorney. In the 1960s there was a *definite plan* to rid this nation of all public displays of any religious symbol of this nation's founding.' The case against Moore, he said, is 'just part of that plan,' and the reason why the outcome is so critical.

"'What's at stake in the case involving Chief Justice Moore and the monument that contains the Ten Commandments is the very future of the nation,' said Titus.

"Are we going to be a nation under God with liberty and justice for all? Are we going to be a nation that *rejects* God and says that God belongs only behind the four walls of the church or the four walls of our home? That's the issue in this case."

Is it just a coincidence that the first time religious freedoms were overturned in America is right about the same time that these left-wing Communists and Socialists began infiltrating our country and our government? Many congressmen and even State Supreme Court Justices at the time of these rulings felt that America was being taken over by a handful of judges, and that the right of self-rule was being stripped from the states and from the American people.

The following men and woman came from every level of society, and they will tell you for themselves what they thought about the left-wing communist-supporting Supreme Court and its decisions of the time. These quotes are from the book *The Warren Court and its Critics:*

What They Had To Say:

> [12] "Though Roosevelt, Truman, and Eisenhower have led the country 'down the road to socialism,' the John Birch Society views the Chief Justice (Warren) as the power behind the 'whole socialist machines.' In January 1961, the Birch society instituted a campaign to 'impeach Earl Warren'."

After you see what most prominent Americans had to say about many of the "Warren Court" decisions, you will understand why they wanted him impeached. Please note that this criticism come from Republicans and Democrats, Catholics and Protestants alike.

- [13] "Claire Hoffman (R. Mich.) called for impeachment of the Justices *because their decisions were resulting in the virtual overthrow of the government* through fallacious reasoning, rendering decisions *which made constitutional provisions void."*

- [14] "In response to the school prayer decision, Roman Catholic clergy were adamant in their criticism of the Court's position. Cardinal Spellman stated that he was 'shocked.' Cardinal McIntyre viewed the holding as 'scandalizing' and one which 'puts shame on our faces *as we are forced to emulate (Soviet Premier) Mr. Khrushchev.'* Americans characterized the decision as a 'stupid... doctrinaire decision, an unrealistic decision, *a decision that spits in the face of our history, our tradition, and our heritage as a religious people'*."

- [15] "Representative Dale Alford (D. Ark.) rose in the House and delivered the following attack on the court: 'The greatest enemy that confronts our country today is not the Soviet or Red China or Berlin crisis or inflation; *it is the destruction of the Constitution of the United States of America by oath-breaking usurpers who are now members of the Supreme Court'*."
- [16] "In a similar vein, Rep. Mendel Rivers (D. S.C.) has characterized the Supreme Court as a 'greater threat to this Union than the entire confines of Soviet Russia'."
- [17] "Sen. Richard Russell (D. Ga.) noted that 'if the people really value their freedom, they will demand that the Congress curtail and limit the jurisdiction being exercised by this group (the Supreme Court) before it's too late.'"
- [18] "Radio announcer Dean Clarence Manion said that 'Nothing strikes more dangerously at our liberties *then tampering with the Constitution by a Communist brainwashed Supreme Court...* Only a strong self-conscious Congress and vigilant sacrificial self-reliance on the part of the states can now save the American Republic'."
- [19] "Sen. James Eastland (D. Miss.) said that Chief Justice Earl Warren *'sides for the Communists* whenever the issue is clearly between them and the security of the United States'."
- [20] "Attorney Andrew Wilson Green noted that 'There are those who suspect one member of the

Court as being under Communist discipline, another as being subject to Communist blackmail, another as knowingly following Communist desire out of political ambition, another as being sympathetic because so many of his friends are Communists, including members of his family, and a fifth as being motivated by resettlement of a religious nature'."

- [21] "Rep. Howard Smith (D. Va.), the powerful chairman of the House Rules Committee, stated that he could not recall a single case decided by the Warren court which the Communists had lost."
- [22] "George J. Thomas, representing the Congress of Freedom (comprised of the delegates of some 500 separate organizations), interpreted the recent Supreme Court decisions as 'National red lights of warning of the destruction of our government and our liberties.' In addition, Thomas went on to attack the law clerk system which 'has a leftist tendency' as well as Justice Frankfurter And the late Justice Holmes for 'utter contempt for God, and the ideal of God'."
- [23] "Former FBI agent Dan Smoot and writer of the weekly periodical the *Dan Smoot Report*... attacked Warren for not having a sufficient background to be a justice of the peace, let alone a Chief Justice of the Supreme Court. In addition, he claimed that Warren was *'abysmally ignorant' in the field of constitutional law, a socialist, and in favor of unlimited governmental expansion.*"
- [24] "Representative Coleman (D. Ala.) called attention *to articles in Communist newspapers*

praising certain Supreme Court decisions. A related item found a British Communist newspaper praised Justice Black for his decision in one of the more controversial cases. Coleman, having made the connection between communism and Black, then appealed to Congress to take action *'before the court destroys this nation'*."

- [25] "Robert Welch, of the John Birch Society, said *'Communism and socialism are almost one and the same, and that the whole Supreme Court is a nest of socialists* and even worse'."
- [26] "Equally bitter was an editorial in Columbia, South Carolina, which stated that 'In the exercise of dictatorial powers, *the difference between the Kremlin and the Supreme Court is that the Kremlin is composed of eleven men and the Supreme Court only nine'*."
- [27] "In the book *Nine Men Against America* by Rosalie Gordon the author traces the 'historical disintegration' of the Supreme Court from the time of President Franklin Roosevelt. With respect to the old guard—Justices Butler, Sutherland, McReynolds and Van Devanter—she felt that whatever their philosophy, it was 'basically American.' In examining the various justices, Black is condemned for being far more favorable to Communists than to American businessmen, Frankfurter as an 'opportunistic thinker,' and Douglas as no more than a publicity seeker and an 'out and out leftist.' These Justices, she argued, *'went about their demolition job on the Constitution* in the manner characteristic of our social revolutionaries for the past twenty

years'."
- [28] "Marlin T. Phelps, former Justice of the Supreme Court of Arizona, spoke similarly of the Court. In a broadcast... entitled *'Supreme Court—Communist's Most Precious Asset,'* Phelps attacked the court for not adhering to the rules of strict constitutional interpretation... *and chastises those persons who feel that the Constitution and the Bible are "outmoded and outworn."*
- [29] "Former Supreme Court Justice James Byrnes wrote a biting article for *U.S. News and World Report* entitled *'The Supreme Court Must Be Curbed'.'"*
- [30] James Davis (D. Ga.) noted *'The Court has dedicated itself to the complete destruction of the states'."*

All of these people believed that the Supreme Court led by Earl Warren was destroying the American Republic and its Constitution.

While I believe the proof is undeniable, we may never be able to conclusively prove whether or not there was (or is) an active conspiracy to destroy the Constitution. Were these individuals and organizations working in concert, or was it only similar ideology working independently to achieve the same objective?

While the answer to that question may go unanswered, the results are undeniable. The form of government that our founding fathers guaranteed to us in the Constitution has all but been destroyed and replaced with tyrannical government that has swallowed up the rights and freedoms of the people and the states. Almost everyone quoted above understood that a revolution was taking place. They saw this as a "bloodless coup d'état" in which America, its laws and its policies were taken over by those seeking to make America resemble a communist/socialist state rather than the Constitutional Republic our founding fathers created. And the war is not over.

If we as Americans want to save the American Republic and the blessings that flow from true freedom and liberty for our children and grandchildren, we are going to have to act quickly. We must fight *"The Next American Revolution."*

America's Future
Present - ?

[1] *"If we and our prosperity reject religious instruction and authority, violate the rules of eternal justice, trifle with the injunctions of morality, and recklessly destroy the political constitution which holds us together, no man can tell how sudden a catastrophe may overwhelm us that shall bury all our glory in profane obscurity."*

Daniel Webster

Chapter 13

The Next American Revolution

> *"The accumulation of all powers, legislative, executive, and judiciary, in the same hands, whether of one, a few, or many, and whether hereditary, self-appointed, or elective, may justly be pronounced the very definition of tyranny."*
>
> **James Madison, Federalist No. 48**

> *"Whenever any Form of Government becomes destructive of these ends, it is the Right of the People to alter or to abolish it, and to institute new Government."*
>
> **Declaration of Independence**

In order to return America to the moral, orderly society that it was before the 1940s—a society that possessed more freedom, peace, liberty and happiness than we presently enjoy—individual Americans all over this great nation must actively participate in The Next American Revolution. Again, the definition of the word "revolution" is:

> [1] "Overthrow of a government, form of government, or social system by those governed... with another government or system taking its place."

I do not refer to a military coup. Violence itself violates the tenets of Christianity and the teachings of Christ. Marin Luther King never resorted to violence to ensure the civil rights of the African-American community, and neither should we. Just as Dr. King peacefully fought for civil rights, we must also fight for the civil rights that both God and our founding fathers have granted us. The truths presented in this book will not be taught by any other segment of American society; therefore, those organizations who still believe in the Constitutional Republic of our founding fathers must shoulder the responsibility.

To understand what the Next American Revolution is to be, let us first briefly recap the first five "revolutions" that America has experienced.

The First American Revolution took place when the original 13 colonies felt that the British government was growing far too restrictive in its laws and refused to allow the colonies to govern themselves as they deemed best. Because of their firmly held beliefs, the colonists felt that their only recourse was to break from Great Britain. The colonies felt the need to secede from Britain's rule for four primary reasons:

1. Britain restricted the colonies' religious liberties

2. Britain imposed oppressive taxation
3. Britain rejected an appeal to allow the colonies the right of self-government
4. Britain had trampled upon the rights of the people to own property free from government seizure

The colonists wrote a document now known as the *Declaration of Independence* to inform Great Britain and its King of their intentions and reasons. In this document, the colonists expressed the belief that their rights had been given by the hand of God, and that government was to receive its power from the consent of the people. Since the will of the people was being ignored, they felt that "whenever any Form of Government becomes destructive of these ends, it is the Right of the People to alter or to abolish it, and to institute new Government." This is why the first American Revolution was fought.

The Second American Revolution took place as a result of the Supreme Court case *Marbury v. Madison*. This was a *revolutionary* departure from the system of government that the founding fathers created, in that it resulted in the Supreme Court giving itself the power of judicial review. For the first time in America's short history, the power to determine which laws were to be enacted had been taken from the hands of the American people and their representatives, and subjected to a majority on the Supreme Court. The Marshall-led court had now determined for itself that it would be the final arbitrating authority on what was constitutional and unconstitutional, legal and illegal, and eventually what is moral and immoral in American society

The Third American Revolution culminated with the ratification of the 14th Amendment to the Constitution. Written in 1868, this amendment provided citizenship for the slaves who had been freed by the 13th Amendment. For

60 years, every American court saw the 14th Amendment for what it was: a civil rights amendment that gave the federal government the power to dictate policy to the states only with regard to the citizenship rights of former slaves, and did not contemplate that the 14th Amendment was a shorthand incorporation of the first eight amendments, making them applicable as explicit restrictions upon the states.

However, ratification of this amendment allowed the federal government for the first time in American history to "get its foot in the door" with regard to states' rights. This *revolutionized* the American form of government in that it, for the first time, gave the federal government a small amount of power over what the founding fathers had created as sovereign states, free from federal rule or policy.

For many in the South, the issue was not slavery as much as it was about states' rights. Those in the South felt that once the federal government was allowed to dictate to the states what they could and could not do, it would never stop. In the minds of those in the South, the end result would be the same type of tyrannical government from which their fathers and grandfathers had fought so hard to break free.

The Civil War and the debate over slavery exposed the one major weakness in the U.S. Constitution: it was written for a people who would be responsible enough to govern themselves according to biblical principles. As John Adams, the Second President of the United States and delegate to the Constitutional Convention, said:

> [2] "Our Constitution was made only for a moral and religious people. *It is wholly inadequate to the government of any other.*"

Our Constitution was written to govern the lives of those committed to living according to Judeo-Christian principles. If a people desire to live without the government on their back, they must first be responsible enough to govern themselves. When those in charge of government in the South failed to rule themselves according to Christian principles, which clearly forbid slavery, the federal government felt a moral obligation to intercede.

While the actions of the North in seeking to abolish slavery were noble and just, their actions set a dangerous precedent that those later in American history would exploit to their advantage in their lust for power.

The Fourth American Revolution was a political revolution that took place when the Supreme Court, ignoring the original intent of the 14th Amendment and ignoring nearly 60 years of judicial precedent, ruled that it now had not only the power to declare federal laws unconstitutional, but the 14th Amendment had also given them the constitutional authority to declare state laws and state Constitutions void.

In a series of unprecedented rulings, the Supreme Court decided that the ratification of the 14th Amendment granted the federal government authority to rule on all provisions of the Bill of Rights. The Supreme Court decided it was now the final authority over every aspect of American life, and that the states and the people were no longer competent to govern themselves. As we saw earlier, Thomas Jefferson himself stated that the Constitution had "created no such tribunal."

These rulings resulted in a government that is no longer a nation "of the people" and "by the people," but rather "of the court" and "by the court." Since that time, the right of self-government for the states has been illegally and unconstitutionally taken away, in much the same way that the colonists were not allowed to govern themselves.

In the Supreme Court case of *Walz v. Tax Commission* in

1970, Supreme Court Justice William Douglas stated the Supreme Court had created *an American Revolution* that began to take away the articles of the Bill of Rights from the states, in direct opposition to the true intent of the Constitution's framers.

> [3] "In affirming this judgment the Court largely overlooks the *revolution* initiated by the adoption of the Fourteenth Amendment. That *revolution* involved the imposition of new and far-reaching constitutional restraints on the States. Nationalization of many civil liberties has been the consequence of the Fourteenth Amendment, reversing the historic position that the foundations of those liberties rested largely in state law."

After this *"revolution,"* which *"involved the imposition of new and far-reaching constitutional restraints on the States,"* what remained was a government with far more in common with the tyrannical government our founding fathers broke away from than the type of government that they had created to ensure "Life, Liberty and the pursuit of Happiness."

The Fifth American Revolution was a cultural revolution in that it resulted in the moral and social overthrow of America by those who wished to impose their debauchery on an otherwise Judeo-Christian nation. Thomas Jefferson warned that it would break up the foundations of the Union if the ability of the states to rule on the morality of their societies was taken away: "'Taking from the States the moral rule of their citizens, and subordinating it to the [federal government]... would... break up the foundations of the Union."

This revolution reached its fulfillment when the Supreme Court of the 1940s– 1960s altered the original intent of the Constitution to push its secular humanist agenda on an unsuspecting America. *Engel v. Vitale* 1962 and *Abington School District v. Schempp* 1963 kicked God out of America by erecting a "a wall of separation between Church and state," which had never before existed in America.

Therefore, the Next American Revolution must resemble the First American Revolution in its scope and purpose. We must cast off the tyrannical form of government that the United States federal government has become, led primarily by the Supreme Court.

The tyrants of today's government are guilty of committing the same abuses of power that the British committed against the people of the colonies:

1. They have restricted the states' religious liberties
2. They have imposed oppressive taxation
3. They have rejected an appeal to allow the states the right of self-government
4. They trampled upon the rights of the people to own property free from seizure by the government.

The American people, like our founding fathers, must remind the federal government that our founders believed a government receives its power from the consent of the people and that the states must be returned the power to rule their own lives and own societies as they see fit. The "Declaration of Independence II" found on my website **TheRiseofAmerica.com** could be incorporated as a means of informing the government of our intentions.

Declaration of Independence II

Recently, I again read the Declaration of Independence. It was almost eerie how much of what I have written here matches what our founding fathers wrote over two-and-a-quarter centuries ago in the Declaration of Independence. Americans must call for another American Revolution, just as our founding fathers so boldly did.

Many Americans are sick of a government that infringes on the rights of its citizens, especially those rights given by the hand of God. We must inform those who have hijacked our Constitution and those who rule according to the illegal Supreme Court decisions of a generation ago that we no longer recognize their authority, because they are acting outside the authority given to them by the founding fathers and the U.S. Constitution, which is the ultimate law of the land.

If you have never read the Declaration of Independence in its entirety, please do so. Upon reading this document, notice the uncanny similarity between the documents that our founders created and what we as Americans should be calling for today, if we want our government and our society back.

Our founding fathers held to the belief that all government was to be left in the hands of the people, and that when this power is taken from the people, those in government responsible for the usurpation of power should be removed. This is why the Declaration of Independence reads:

> "That whenever any Form of Government becomes destructive of these ends, *it is the Right of the People to alter or to abolish it, and to institute new Government,* laying its foundation on such principles and organizing its powers in such form, as to them shall seem most likely to effect their Safety and Happiness. Prudence, indeed, will dictate that Governments long established should not be changed for light and transient causes; and accordingly all experience hath shown that mankind are more disposed

to suffer, while evils are sufferable, than to right themselves by abolishing the forms to which they are accustomed. *But when a long train of abuses and usurpations, pursuing invariably the same Object evinces a design to reduce them under absolute Despotism, it is their right, it is their duty, to throw off such Government, and to provide new Guards for their future security."*

As Britain so dominated our founding fathers, America has become a government ruled by despotism. The word "despotism" means "[4] Absolute power; authority unlimited and uncontrolled by men, *Constitution* or laws."

On, December 14, 1787, Federalist Alexander Hamilton wrote the following in the Federalist papers No. 22 concerning where the power of American government should lie: "The fabric of American empire ought to rest on the solid basis of THE CONSENT OF THE PEOPLE. The streams of national power ought to flow from that pure, original fountain of all legitimate authority."

Our country is no longer controlled by a Constitution (at least not the one originally established over 200 years ago). We no longer have a government that receives its power from the consent of the people. We are no longer a country that operates by a separation of power. We are governed by an out-of-control federal court system that no longer feels it must answer to any other political body, nor to the American people. The Supreme Court has so twisted the Constitution that those civil liberties which our founding fathers fought so hard to protect are all but gone.

I am not calling for an overthrow of the American government and replacing it with another form of government, i.e. communism/socialism, etc.; as we have seen, we are well on our way toward that already. I simply demand that our government be returned to the people—that the government be *restored* to the type of government our founding fathers created, and that we are guaranteed in Article 4 Section 4 to the Constitution and by the 10th Amendment.

Even if I called for the abolishing of our system government, do I not have that right? How is this so different than what our founding fathers did when their God-given, unalienable civil rights and pleas for self-government were refused? Read again our founding fathers' response to the infringement upon their rights, and their pleas for self-government all but ignored:

> "That whenever any Form of Government becomes destructive of these ends, *it is the Right of the People to alter or to abolish it, and to institute new Government...* when a long train *of abuses and usurpations*, pursuing invariably the same Object evinces a design to reduce them under absolute Despotism, *it is their right, it is their duty, to throw off such Government."*

The Declaration of Independence not only gives the American people the right to change a government that treats its people as we are treated today, but our founders felt that we had "a duty" to throw out this type of repressive government.

The *World Book* encyclopedia says this about the principles laid out in the Declaration of Independence:

> [5] "People may alter their government *if it fails in its purpose.* Or they may set up a new government. People should not, however, make a revolutionary change in long-established governments for unimportant reasons. *But they have the right to overthrow a government that has committed many abuses and seeks complete control over the people."*

When writing the Federalist Papers, on January 3, 1788, Alexander Hamilton had the following to say in Federalist No. 33 with regard to tyranny and what the American people must do about it:

> "If the federal government should overpass the just bounds of its authority and make a tyrannical use of its powers, the people, whose creature it is, must appeal to the standard they have formed, and take such measures to redress the injury done to the Constitution as the exigency may suggest and prudence justify."

In his first inaugural address, Abraham Lincoln said, "This country, with its institutions, belongs to the people who inhabit it. Whenever they shall grow weary of the existing government, they can exercise their constitutional right of amending it, or exercise their revolutionary right to overthrow it."

When our tyrannical Supreme Court overstepped its Constitutional authority and sought complete control over its citizens to the point that our children cannot even pray, wear a cross and carry a Bible to school, I would say we have reached that point.

When convicted murderers who were found guilty of brutally beating a 71-year-old woman to death are released from prison by our federal court system because the prosecutor used seven words from the Bible in a courtroom, it is clear that our government is out of control and has lost touch with the American people.

When the Supreme Court gives large corporations and development firms the right to seize your land without your permission, do you think that the 5th Amendment is still intact?

When an entire state that had turned down a tax increase can have its collective will overturned by one federal judge, and when the socialists in the government feel they may help themselves to half of our income to further push their socialist agenda, American is closer to resembling Soviet Russia than the nation our founders established. Remember the phrase "taxation without representation"?

American has become a nation in which communities of people who primarily hold Judeo-Christian values are now told that they cannot place crosses in graveyards to remember their dead, nor do they have the right to place nativity scenes in city parks to celebrate Christmas. **This is so un-American it stinks.**

For years, organizations such as the America Center for Law and Justice (ACLJ) have appealed to the Supreme Court for many of these bogus rulings to be overturned. However, just as the appeals of our founding fathers to the tyrants who ruled over them fell on deaf ears, the many attempts to appeal to the Supreme Court's good sense and good judgment have done likewise.

Therefore, the American people have no other choice. We, like our founding fathers, can appeal to tyrants for only so long before we must realize that they will not surrender the power that they have usurped: *it must be taken from them.*

[6] "[Former] Supreme Court Justice James Byrnes wrote a biting article for *U.S. News and World Report* entitled 'The Supreme Court Must Be Curbed...' The former Justice concluded his article by reasoning that 'Power intoxicates men. It is never voluntarily surrendered. It must be taken from them. *The Supreme Court must be curbed'*."

Our founding fathers, following *years* of appeals to their tyrants, ultimately reached this same decision—that power intoxicates men and that it is never voluntarily surrendered; *it must be taken from them!*

Again, our founding fathers' greatest fear was that someday the federal government would grow so large and powerful that it would eventually control the everyday lives and freedoms of its citizens. Our founding fathers wrote the "Freedom of Speech" amendment into the Constitution to keep the government from suppressing the voices of the American public when the day came to speak out against the tyranny that they experienced and that we see today.

What many Americans do not understand is that the Declaration of Independence gives us the *"Unalienable right"* to change our government when it reaches the tyrannical state it is in today, and that the ratification of the Constitution has never done away with, superseded or otherwise replaced the Declaration of Independence as a binding and legal federal document. This is again made clear by our founding fathers.

The last state to ratify the Constitution was Rhode Island on May 29, 1790. Samuel Adams, signer of the Declaration of Independence, had this to say about the Declaration of Independence while speaking to the Massachusetts Legislature on Jan. 17, 1794. Remember, this was four years after the last state had ratified the Constitution:

> [7] "Before the formation of this Constitution... [The] Declaration of Independence was received and ratified by all the states in the union *and has never been disannulled."*

As the debate continues over states' rights and the separation of church and state, the supporters of our founders often point to the Declaration of Independence as proof of the founders' intentions. Opponents try to convince everyone that the ratification of the Constitution has done away with, superseded or otherwise replaced the Declaration of Independence as a binding and legal federal document.

By Samuel Adams' testimony over a decade after the Constitution was written and four years after the last state ratified it, this is simply not true. The Declaration of Independence is as much a binding federal document today as when written. The only group empowered to disannul the Declaration of Independence as a binding federal document would be our founding fathers or the American people. Therefore, no modern-day judge, court ruling or Congress has the power to change that.

What then can the people do when a ruling by the Supreme Court is unconstitutional, or when the Court makes rulings that go beyond simple "opinions" and begins to act as if it is the final and absolute lawmaking body? What then can the people do when the Supreme Court rules on a case that it had no right to rule on? What can be done when the Supreme Court makes a ruling that the American people know is illegitimate, illegal or unconstitutional? Or, as Judge Andrew P. Napolitano asks in the sub-title of his book *Constitutional Chaos*: What Happens When the Government Breaks Its Own Laws?

Since there is no higher judicial body in place to correct the abuses of constitutional power by the Supreme Court, it is then left to the people and their elected officials. Americans must educate themselves about their own Constitution and their civil rights. They must learn the actual role of government and how much power our founding fathers actually gave each branch of the federal government in the Constitution.

In a free society, it is the responsibility of the people to know and understand their Constitution so that they may recognize when their government is abusing its constitutional authority. Former President John Adams said:

> [8] "We electors have an important constitutional power placed in our hands... It becomes necessary to every [citizen], then, to be in some degree a statesman and to examine and judge for himself... the... political principles and measures."

John Jay, considered one of the three founders most responsible for the ratification of the Constitution, and the original Chief Justice of the Supreme Court, declared, "Every member of the State ought diligently to read and to study the Constitution of his country... By knowing their rights, they will sooner perceive when they are violated and be the better prepared to defend and assert them."

Who then will teach Americans that this was the opinion of our founding fathers? High schools and colleges are not allowed to, because of the fictitious theory of separation of church and state, and the secular media refuses to report on it because it conflicts with their anti-Christian worldview. One of the primary reasons that America has been allowed to slip down the road to socialism is because the previous generation of Americans failed to teach their children the political and spiritual truths that our founding fathers held dear.

In 1961, Herbert Aptheker was the editor of the communist monthly *Political Affairs*, which is a Marxist magazine that is still active today. During a speech given at Wayne University, he was quoted as saying that the

> [9] "Neglect of parents to teach our youth Christianity and Americanism has made the communist

talk of deceiving American youth much easier."

If the church in America does not assume responsibility for teaching these truths, then the ideals of our founding fathers may be lost and forgotten forever by the next generation.

The church takes books like *The Purpose-Driven Life* and we teach them in our small groups, Bible studies and our Sunday Schools, but if we do not teach these historical truths with just as much dedication and commitment, our society will collapse around the church. The church cannot fulfill Christ's mandate to be the salt and the light to a dying society if it only stays within the four walls of the building itself.

Lawyer-turned-evangelist Charles G. Finney, one of the key figures of the Second Great Awakening, clarifies for us what the role of those who believe in God should be with regard to our government:

> [10] "God cannot sustain this free and blessed country which we love and pray for unless the church will take right ground. *Politics are a part of a religion...* Christians must do their duty to the country as a part of their duty to God... *He will bless or curse this nation according to the course they take."*

To focus only upon the spiritual needs inside the church without confronting the government, culture and society in which we live is like sweeping the floor of a building that is falling apart around us. For this reason I have created a study guide on the web site **TheRiseofAmerica.com** for any organization that will teach these truths in any type of setting (conference, special event, Bible study, small group study, etc.).

The elitists in the media attempt to portray lawyers

and judges as the only people intelligent enough or qualified enough to know and understand the U.S. Constitution, and that if an ordinary American citizen questions whether the government has gone beyond its allotted authority, the media immediately attacks the individual's legal credentials in an attempt to bring doubt as to whether the individual has the "legal expertise" to even make such an assertion.

In an interview in 2003, Dr. James Dobson was talking to a popular news talk show host about the fact that our Constitution is being twisted and distorted from its original intent. When the interviewer began to lose the argument, his only recourse was to say, "Are you a lawyer?"

This type of elitism is common in the secular media. This man was implying that since Dr. Dobson was not a lawyer, he could not understand what the Constitution really meant and that we should only trust lawyers for that. This is like trusting the fox in the chicken coop.

America's original Chief Justice of the Supreme Court, John Jay—who was not an elitist—did not feel that only lawyers would be able to understand the Constitution. He felt that a careful study of this document by *common, everyday citizens* would make them better able to not only defend their civil rights, but also to assert them. The church and other patriotic organizations must assume this responsibility.

The time for inaction is over. We must adopt the attitude of William Jennings Bryan, who once said:

> [11] "We do not come as aggressors. Our war is not a war of conquest; we are fighting in the defense of our homes, our families, and posterity. We have petitioned, and our petitions have been scorned; we have entreated, and our entreaties have been disregarded; we have begged, and they have mocked...

We beg no longer; we entreat no more; we petition no more. We defy them!"

Chapter 14

Restoring our Constitution

> [1] *"They keep talking about drafting a Constitution for Iraq. Why don't we just give them ours? It was written by a lot of really smart guys, it's worked for over 200 years and we're not using it anymore."*
>
> **George Carlin**

The greatest and most pressing challenge that we as Americans are currently facing is to reverse the socialists' advances over the last 80 years and preserve the "Great American Experiment" by restoring our founding fathers' perspective on government.

While a significant grassroots effort from the American people is necessary to restore America to its former glory, we are not alone. More and more politicians and other government officials are beginning to understand that our federal government and the Supreme Court are out of control. Although the fight to restore America to its former glory is suppressed by the secular mainstream media, in the last decade more momentum has been generated toward returning America to the society that it once was by those in high places of government. Former Alabama Attorney General and now federal judge Bill Pryor had this to say in a commencement speech to the 1997 McGill-Toolen graduating class. His words offer hope that men in important government positions will be willing to defend the Constitution and stand against the injustices perpetrated upon us:

> [2] "The American experiment is not a theocracy and does not establish an official religion, but the Declaration of Independence and the Constitution of the United States are rooted in a Christian perspective of the nature of government and the nature of man. *The challenge of the next millennium will be to preserve the American experiment by restoring its Christian perspective.* Catholic writer George Weigel explains the nature of the crisis in this way:
>
> 'Two decades into the third century of that experiment, it is no longer clear that the tri-centennial anniversary of the Declaration of Independence will take place in a country living in continuity with its moral-cultural roots. Should the historic American attempt to achieve a vital democratic pluralism in which self-governance is possible (because the people have formed and sustained the moral habits—the virtues--necessary for self-governance) collapse; should the American experiment decay into a republic of established and governmentally enforced secularism; *then the American experiment as understood*

by George Washington, James Madison, Abraham Lincoln... will have failed.'

"The external forms of democracy—elections, legislatures, governors and presidents, courts—may remain, but they will be hollow. And their endurance over time will be dubious, at best. For the American people, required to divest themselves of their deepest convictions in order to enter public life, will no longer be able to give a persuasive public account of their commitment to democratic republicanism.

"This crisis has two faces. *First is the increasing secularization of our country, and second is the erosion of self-government. The primary catalyst for both trends is, in my judgment, the Supreme Court of the United States.* In 1962, with its decision prohibiting prayer in public schools, the Supreme Court *started building a wall* that has increasingly excluded God and religion from our public life. The Supreme Court has excluded Nativity scenes from public buildings during Advent and prohibited prayers at public school graduation ceremonies. *Our government, succumbing to the Court's unsound mandates, has become hostile to religion.*

"Today in this State we debate and litigate whether a display of the Ten Commandments, the cornerstone of law for Western Civilization, can be kept in a courtroom in Gadsden. The American Civil Liberties Union, which is often uncivil and tramples upon liberty, wants to remove that display and end the practice of beginning jury assembly sessions with a Christian prayer led by an unpaid volunteer local clergyman, sometimes Catholic and other times Protestant. No taxpayer funds are involved and no one is required to participate.

"If these acknowledgments of God must be excluded from our state courtrooms, will the Supreme Court of the United States then remove the multiple references to the

Ten Commandments in its courtroom? Will federal courts end their practice of beginning sessions with the prayer, God save the United States and this Honorable Court? Will our national motto *In God We Trust* be removed from our currency? How far will we allow the proponents of secularism to go in excluding religion from public life? Or, will these practices survive merely because the Supreme Court determines that the practices no longer mean anything?

"In the years following the school prayer decision, it seems our government has lost God. This reminds me of a story about two children, Caroline and Victoria. The parents of these rambunctious little girls were having difficulty imposing discipline, as were the teachers at their school. Exasperated, the parents sought the assistance of their parish priest, who offered to speak with each girl separately. When Victoria, the youngest, met with the priest, sitting in a large chair that swallowed her, the priest sat behind a large desk and stared down at the shaken child. In a firm voice the priest asked Victoria, 'Where is God?' Victoria sat in silence and did not move a muscle. Again, a little louder, the priest asked, 'Victoria, where is God?' Victoria's eyes grew larger, but she said nothing. Finally the priest leaned over the desk and thundered, 'WHERE IS GOD?' At that, Victoria darted from the room, dashed down the hall and burst into the room where Caroline waited. 'What's wrong, Victoria?' Caroline asked. Victoria looked her sister in the eye, shed a tear, and whispered, 'The adults have lost God, and they are trying to blame us.'

"While our government may have lost God, I assure you our people have not. The second and closely related crisis created by our Supreme Court involves the erosion of self-government. On January 22, 1973, seven members of that court swept aside the laws of the fifty states and created—out of thin air—a constitutional right to murder an unborn child. Last year, the Court swept aside the vote of a majority of the people of Colorado to end any preferences or special privileges for homosexuals in their state. Recently, lower federal courts struck down laws that prohibit assisted suicide.

"The most important decisions of our time and our country are not being made by the people or their elected representatives. The Supreme Court has restructured our political community without the consent of our people, in my judgment, and has violated the Christian understanding of *tranquillitas ordinis* (The tranquility of the Social Order)...

"Our challenge, and especially your challenge, in this next millennium will be to *end this trend and restore the American experiment.* To meet the challenge, we must have, among others, the leadership of the graduates of Catholic schools, who follow in the footsteps of Clarence Thomas, Antonin Scalia, Supreme Court Justices who do understand, and the great graduate of McGill Institute, Admiral Jeremiah Denton.

"*The two greatest moral problems in American history—slavery and segregation—were resolved when Christians demanded justice. You must enter the public square and share your Christian heritage with your community and your government.* You must live the Gospel and teach it to your children. But I urge you not to be deceived by the false promise of utopians that we can somehow create the peace of Heaven here on earth. Our challenge is to build better structures for securing justice, whether in our economy, our culture, or our government. Thank you and God bless you."

Judge Pryor reiterates everything I have written in this book. He agrees that the Supreme Court is responsible for the tyranny we are now experiencing. The American people no longer have any say in the moral direction of their nation.

The Supreme Court has, in fact, made itself the final determiners of what is moral and what is immoral and it is forcing the rest of the nation to comply with its unconstitutional mandates. The Supreme Court has so overstepped its bounds regarding issues of morality that in the case of *County of Allegheny v. ACLU Greater Pittsburgh Chapter* in 1989, Justice Kennedy said that the Supreme Court has become "a national theology board."

The Supreme Court was never granted the constitutional authority to overturn or override the will of the people. Our founding fathers created the Supreme Court to review laws made by the federal legislature. However, these rulings were intended to be only "an opinion" and not a legal mandate to be forced on the American people. Whenever the Supreme Court rendered its "decision," our elected representatives should consult that decision, but were never to be legally bound by it.

As we saw earlier in the 1857 law book, *The Historical and Legal Examination of That Part of the Decision of the Supreme Court of the United States in the Dred Scott Case*, it is permissible to disregard the "opinion" of the Supreme Court because it was not given the constitutional power to exert its will upon the American people.

> [3] The power of the [Supreme] Court is judicial—so declared in the Constitution; and so held in theory, if not in practice. [The Supreme Court] is limited to cases *"in law and equity,"* and though sometimes encroaching upon political subjects, it is without right, without authority, and without the means of enforcing its decisions. It can issue no mandamus to Congress, or the people, nor punish them for disregarding its decisions, or even attacking them.

Nowhere in the Constitution did the founding fathers give the Supreme Court the power to veto legislation enacted by the American people, especially at the state level. During the Constitutional Convention, the delegates debated whether or not the Supreme Court should be given the power to veto federal legislation, and the notion was rejected. Instead, veto power was given to the President, as clearly stated in Section 7-2 of the Constitution. Had the constitutional delegates wanted to give the Supreme Court this power, it had an opportunity to do so and decided against it.

James Madison, the chief architect of the U.S. Constitution, was also the chief architect of the Virginia Constitution of 1776. He makes clear the spirit and intent of the founding fathers with regard to whether or not the will of the people should ever be overruled: "All power to suspend laws, or the execution of laws, by any authority, without the consent of the representatives of the people, is injurious to their rights, and ought not to be exercised."

Thomas Jefferson had this to say about the power that the founding fathers gave to the Supreme Court when drafting the Constitution:

> [4] "The opinion which gives to the judges the right to decide what laws are constitutional and what are not... would make the judiciary a despotic branch. To consider the judges as the ultimate arbiters of all constitutional questions is a very dangerous doctrine indeed, and one which would place us under the despotism (absolute power) of an oligarchy (form of government in which the supreme power is placed in a few hands)... The Constitution has erected no such single tribunal."

The most substantial power grabs by the Supreme Court

in American history occurred in the 1940s–1960s. Many of our elected representatives of the time, both Republicans and Democrats, recognized that the Supreme Court was consistently acting outside of its constitutional jurisdiction and needed to be stopped.

Senator Sam J. Ervin Jr. (D., N.C.) said, [5] "We are ruled in large measure by judicial oligarchy (a government by the few)... The court is destroying the power of the States and is encroaching on Congress and the Executive."

Sen. Richard Russell (D., Ga.) noted, [6] "if the people really value their freedom, they will demand that the Congress curtail and limit the jurisdiction being exercised by [the Supreme Court] before it's too late."

Senator Strom Thurman (D & R., SC.) emphatically stated, [7] "The [Supreme] Court has consistently moved to expand its power, till it threatens to be the dominating power of the government. The time has come for action by the Congress to call halt to this unconstitutional seizure of power by the third branch of government."

The Strategy

Anyone who understands military warfare tactics knows that in order to win a war, forces must concentrate on one important objective. Most military historians agree that Adolph Hitler lost the Second World War because he tried to fight a war on two fronts.

While he was fighting a war with only Western Europe, he was fighting a war on one front. At this point he was practically unstoppable. When he decided to attack the Soviet Union at the same time, he opened up a war on two fronts, which effectively divided his military troops and resources. Then, instead of having one almost unstoppable force, he had two considerably weaker and divided forces, which were much easier to overcome.

Those of us who believe in the type of government that our founding fathers created have divided ourselves into separate armies, each fighting for our own cause. We have pro-2nd Amendment, anti-tax, pro-family, pro-private property, pro-life, and pro-traditional American groups, each trying to accomplish a given objective, whether it is to stop flag burning, secure gun rights, revise the tax code or end homosexual marriage, abortion or pornography. We are all fighting a war on many fronts, which has effectively divided our troops and resources. This is why we have been so easy to defeat. If we can pool our resources and agree to fight this cultural war on one front, and focus our energies and resources on one specific objective, we can be unstoppable.

However, consolidating our forces is only part of the solution. An army of troops cannot be released without a clear and concise objective. Military strategists understand that the most effective way to win a war is to decapitate the enemy leadership. This will effectively leave the rest of the opposing army in a leaderless state of confusion.

Those in America who believe in the traditional type of government that our founding fathers created far outnumber those who do not, yet we have been unsuccessful in winning any of the battles because we have allowed the enemy leadership to retain power. Unless the Constitution is restored to the original intent of the founding fathers and the right of self-rule is placed back into the hands of the American people, we will never win the culture war.

The American people have known for years that something is very wrong with the American government and American society. Now that we have identified the problem and understand who is responsible, the question becomes—how do we fix it?

What do we, as 21st century Americans, do when, like our founding fathers, we have experienced a "long train of abuses and usurpations of power by the federal government"? Unlike the conflict between America and Britain, we cannot declare independence from each other, or even split America into red states and blue states. Anyone who truly loves America would not consider these as options. We can, however, restore America to the type of government that our Founders created and simply let red states be red and blue states be blue. Almost seems too simple, doesn't it?

The founding fathers created the best political Constitution that was, as former Prime Minister of Great Britain W. E. Gladstone put it, "The most wonderful work ever struck off at a given time by the brain and purpose of man." The problem we presently have in America is that we have abandoned that Constitution in favor of a socialist Constitution and a government that, depending on who is controlling it, is either trying to force red states to be blue or trying to force blue states to be red. And as Abraham Lincoln said in June of 1858: "A house divided against itself cannot stand."

Federal Judge Bill Pryor identified that problem when he said, "This crisis has two faces. First is the increasing secularization of our country, and second is the erosion of self-government. The primary catalyst for both trends is, in my judgment, the *Supreme Court of the United States*... Our challenge... in this next millennium will be to... restore the American experiment as understood by George Washington, James Madison, and Abraham Lincoln."

There was nothing wrong with the Supreme Court or the federal government that our founders originally created. That government simply no longer exists. To restore the

American experiment as understood by George Washington, James Madison, Abraham Lincoln, we must bring America back to a Constitution Republic, in which each state has the sovereign right to determine how red or blue it wants to be.

State sovereignty is a truth that is expressed throughout the Constitutional Convention and the subsequent conventions at the state level. Alexander Hamilton, in a speech to the New York Ratifying Convention on June 17, 1788, stated that it would by politically repugnant to even consider that the federal government would ever encroach upon the sovereignty of the states:

"The State governments possess inherent advantages, which will ever give them an influence and ascendancy over the National Government, and will forever preclude the possibility of federal encroachments. That their liberties, indeed, can be subverted by the federal head, is repugnant to every rule of political calculation."

On November 22, 1994, thirty of our states Republican governors unanimously adopted the Williamsburg Resolve. In it, they said: "The challenges to the liberties of the people... comes from our own Federal government that has defied, and now ignores, virtually every constitutional limit fashioned by the framers to confine its reach and thus to guard the freedoms of the people" and that "Federal action has exceeded the clear bounds of... the Constitution, and thus violated the rights guaranteed to the people."

In recent years there has been much debate over what to do about the problem of judicial tyranny, and many solutions have been offered. Our founding fathers have given the American people six options for dealing with a federal government that has a history of a "long train of abuses and usurpations of power." Actually, they gave us seven options, but armed conflict with my fellow American is not an option that I wish to contemplate. Let us look at these six constitutional options and see if we can determine which is most feasible.

1. *Get Congress to do its job*—Congress has the Constitutional authority to limit the jurisdiction of the Supreme Court. Each Congressman has each taken a solemn oath to "Support and defend the Constitution of the United States of against all enemies, foreign and domestic." However, it is clear that Congress has failed miserably in defending the Constitution. The political atmosphere in Washington has become so venomous and bi-partisan that getting Republicans and Democrats to agree on anything is highly unlikely, even when one side presents a very good idea. As we have seen from the numerous quotes in Chapters 10–12, the criticism attacking the Supreme Court for turning America down the road to socialism came from Republicans and Democrats, Catholic and Protestant and orthodox Jews alike. This truly is a non-partisan issue, at least among the American people. This fight is between those in America who are "American," and those who are "Anti-American."

   It is clear that the members of Congress have known about this unconstitutional usurpation of power for over 60 years now, and what have they done about it? Nothing! One must begin to wonder if they really want to deal with the problem at all. But I guess they do have more important issues to deal with than the oaths they took before Almighty God to defend and protect the Constitution. After all, Major League Baseball does have that steroid problem to worry about.

2. *Impeach Judges*—The Constitution has given the American people the option to impeach judges for breaking the law. Willfully voiding the 1st and 10th Amendments of the Constitution without the consent of the American people to push their personal political agenda is violation of their oath of office and an impeachable offense.

It must be fully understood that the Supreme Court does not have the constitutional authority to alter amendments to the Constitution from which it alone derives its power. The only legal way to repeal a constitutional amendment is by the consent of the people. Let us look at the only way that this may be legally done, by examining the only constitutional amendment ever repealed—the 18th Amendment.

On Jan. 16, 1919, the United States ratified the 18th Amendment to the Constitution. This Amendment deemed the manufacture, sale, transport, import or export of intoxicating liquors to be illegal. Fourteen years later, when the people decided to repeal this amendment, they could not simply ignore or erase it. The only way to repeal a constitutional amendment is through another constitutional amendment. Therefore, the 21st Amendment was created and ratified on Dec. 5, 1933, and reads: "The eighteenth article of amendment to the Constitution of the United States is hereby repealed."

It is crucial to understand that the 18th Amendment was created by the people, and to be repealed, it must have the consent of the people. The Congress or the courts are powerless to do away with a constitutional amendment without the consent of the American people.

If the 10th Amendment, which grants states the sovereign right to govern their societies as they see fit, is to be repealed, it cannot be repealed by judicial decree or by an act of Congress. This amendment may only be repealed by the consent of the people. This can only be accomplished through another constitutional amendment, which must be ratified by the states. If the American people, when ratifying the 14th Amendment, intended it to repeal the 10th amendment, the 14th Amendment would have read: "The Tenth article of amendment to the Constitution of the United States is hereby repealed."

For more on the constitutionality of judicial impeachment, read *Restraining Judicial Activism* by David Barton. Unfortunately, the power to impeach a sitting federal or Supreme Court judge falls on the Congress and, as we have seen, the level of partisan politics in Washington makes the possibility of impeachment highly unlikely.

I am not personally in favor of this action because it seems pretty mean-spirited and vengeful, and would probably result in more deepening resentment and further divide the country instead of uniting it. Impeachment should be pursued only as a last resort.

3. *Appoint strict constructionist judges*—Ultimately, we should have Supreme Court judges who interpret the constitution as it was intended, following the rule of law and submitting to previous Supreme Court precedents without legislating from the

bench. A push has recently been underway to get more constructionist judges appointed to the federal benches and on the Supreme Court, to reverse some of the unconstitutional seizures of power. The problem is, once again, Congress. With the retirement of Supreme Court Justice Sandra Day O'Connor, we have seen the venomous, partisan politics that our two-party system never fails to provide for us. Politicians are great at two things: looking after their own best interests and compromising. And you know who always gets the short end of that stick—the American people.

Still, this leaves us with two problems. First, we never know what stand a judge will take *after* he is appointed to the Supreme Court, and is no longer elected and therefore, no longer accountable to the people. Take Earl Warren, for example. When he was appointed by Dwight D. Eisenhower, he was primarily considered a conservative governor from California. However, as we saw in Chapter 12, he presided over and supported most of the cases that have led us down the road to socialism.

Second, even if we could appoint honest, constructionist judges, this strategy still ignores the bigger problem of judicial tyranny. Even if more conservative, constructionist judges are appointed to the federal benches and on the Supreme Court, the problem will not be solved; America would still be ruled by a handful of federal judges who happen to agree with our political and social agenda.

People in blue states shouldn't have to live under the tyrannical rule of federal judges appointed by the people in red states, no more than red states like to live under the tyrannical rule of blue-state federal judges. The truth is, no state should be forced to live under the tyrannical rule of any federal judges.

No American should have to live in a state that does not match his or her social or moral ideology. Our founding fathers wanted to let every state determine for itself what type of state it would be.

Take religious freedom, for example. Virginia, from the beginning, pursued a policy of disestablishmentarianism; that is, it did not want to establish a state church. Massachusetts, on the other hand, had an established church until well into the 19th century. It is clear that our founding fathers intended to leave these issues in the hands of the states and not be imposed on the individual states by the federal courts. When the 10th Amendment is restored, this will no longer be an issue.

4. *Get the Supreme Court cases reversed*—Four major Supreme Court cases, *Gitlow vs. New York* 1925, *Cantwell vs. Connecticut* 1940, *Murdock vs. Pennsylvania* 1943 and *Everson vs. Board of Education* 1947, have, for all practical purposes, voided the 10th Amendment by judicial decree. Again, this is a blatant judicial rewriting of the Constitution. Reversing these cases would require years and years and cost millions and millions of dollars, and still the outcome would be uncertain. Our founding fathers realized that you can only appeal to tyrants for so long before you must take matters

in your own hands. Call me a pessimist, but due to the activist nature of some modern Supreme Court Justices, somehow I do not think that asking the Supreme Court to please give us our civil and states rights back is going to work. Remember, former Supreme Court Justice James Byrnes said, "Power intoxicates men. It is never voluntarily surrendered. It must be taken from them."

Fighting every court case in which our civil rights have been violated is like pulling dandelions. Allow me to explain. A dandelion is a weed, and once the flower has been pulled off it, it will not die; the flower will return in a couple of days. To effectively deal with dandelions, one must go directly to the root. Once the root is removed, the rest of the weed will die and no longer present a problem. The same may be said about the unconstitutional seizure of our civil rights. If we simply fight a court battle every time our constitutional and states rights are attacked and violated, we will be fighting forever. Considerable time, energy and money would be wasted without ever winning the war. We would simply go from one battle to the next. However, by going to the root of the problem—the illegal and unconstitutional Supreme Court rulings that have voided the 10th Amendment —much of the problem will resolve itself.

5. *Federal Constitutional Amendments for individual issues*—The Supreme and federal courts have forced many things on the American people that they have not voted for or consented to. Flag burning, taking "under God" out of the pledge, seizure of property rights, gun control, income taxes, banning

religious displays, etc. It is clear that the American people care about their Constitutional rights, but it seems that everyone has his or her own particular issue or cause that he or she cares about. Therefore, there is often times not enough popular support on any one single issue to pass a single constitutional amendment to protect these rights. The real problem with these issues is not that we need to change the Constitution; we simply need to change it back so that all these issues are in the hands of the people and the individual states, where our founding fathers placed that power initially—especially when it comes to moral issues. Thomas Jefferson, in correspondence with Supreme Court Justice William Johnson, reminded him of this fact:

[8] "Taking from the States the moral rule of their citizens, and subordinating it to the [federal government] ... would... break up the foundations of the Union... I believe the States can best govern our home concerns, and the [federal] government our foreign ones."

6. *Amending State Constitutions*--Why even attempt to amend state Constitutions anymore? Doesn't anyone else see that under the current state of affairs, this is simply delaying the inevitable? It does not matter what state Constitutional amendments we pass; if a federal judge or the Supreme Court does not agree with the people of that state, the federal bench pronounces their Constitutional amendment unconstitutional. I will cite two examples:

    For about 325 years, those who sought to serve in the public sector in the state of Maryland were *required by their state Constitution* to take an oath acknowledging their faith in God. This tradition continued until 1961, when the Supreme Court decided that this tradition, unchallenged for over 300 years, was in violation of the Constitution, even though the Maryland Constitution was in existence at the time the federal Constitution was proposed by our founding fathers and ratified by the state of Maryland. Apparently the founders and the Maryland delegates did not see a conflict between the federal Constitution and Maryland's state Constitution.

Voters in Nebraska in the year 2000 overwhelmingly passed a constitutional ban on same-sex marriage which defined marriage as a union between a man and a woman. Nebraska's Constitutional amendment was struck down by *a single federal judge.*

If the power of the federal courts is not restricted, you can be sure that these tyrannical rulings will continue. Until the American people come to the realization that they no longer have any say in the affairs of the government or their society, we will continue to have our civil rights taken from us.

You will often hear those opposed to the reigning-in of the federal courts scream that this would destroy the independence of the judiciary. In a letter to Thomas Ritchie on December 25, 1820, Thomas Jefferson makes it clear that an "independent" judiciary meant independence from the other branches of government, and not independence from the people: "A judiciary independent of a king or executive alone, is a good thing; but independence of the will of the nation is a [absurdity], at least in a republican government."

As I stated earlier, we can either go after the dandelion, or we can go after the root. When you kill the root, you kill the whole weed; therefore, if you want to go after these unconstitutional seizures of power, you also need to go for the root. The place from which all other usurpations of state power have originated is the distorted interpretation of the 14th Amendment, in which the Supreme Court *gave itself* the jurisdiction to rule on states' issues, laws and Constitutions.

Therefore, in order to restore states' rights, we must restore the original intent of the 10th Amendment, by deeming it unconstitutional for federal judges to nullify state laws, state constitutions or state sovereignty.

The founding fathers created a government of the people and by the people. Article 4, Section 4 of the Constitution reads, "The United States shall guarantee to every state in this Union a republican form of government."

Remember, a Republic is defined as a "state in which the exercise of the sovereign power is lodged in representatives elected by the people." It does not read "the exercise of the sovereign power is lodged in federal courts."

Yet, for over two hundred years, the Supreme Court has gradually, silently and systematically taken over the American government and appointed itself the supreme rulers of America, while delegating some power over the states to the federal Congress that was not granted them by Section 8 of the Constitution.

The Anti-Federalists warned about this gradual usurpation of power by the federal judiciary during the Constitutional convention—unfortunately, no one listened. By the year 1820, one of the leading Anti-Federalists, Thomas Jefferson, wrote a letter to Thomas Ritchie in which he expressed grave concern about the federal courts undermining the Constitution.

> "The judiciary of the United States is the subtle corps of sappers and miners constantly working underground to undermine the foundations of our confederated fabric. They are construing our constitution from a co-ordination of a general and special government to a general and supreme one alone."

Even as early as 1820, some of our founding fathers recognized that the Supreme Court was slowly transforming America from a federal into a national government. This has been accomplished so slowly and secretively that its usurpation of power has gone relatively unnoticed by most Americans.

James Madison warned the American people from the floor of the Constitutional Convention that this is usually the way in which individual freedoms are taken—gradually.

> [9] "Since the general civilization of mankind, I believe there are more instances of the abridgement of the freedom of the people by gradual and silent encroachments of those in power than by violent and sudden usurpations."

Thomas Jefferson actually went as far as telling us which branch of government he believed would ultimately be responsible for the destruction of our Constitutional Republic.

> [10] "It has long been my opinion... that the germ of dissolution of our federal government is... our *Federal Judiciary*; an irresponsible body... working like gravity by night and by day, gaining a little to-day and a little tomorrow, and advancing its

noiseless step like a thief, over the field of jurisdiction, until all shall be usurped from the States, and the government of all be consolidated into one."

The founding fathers did not set up the Supreme Court to reign over the other branches of government and, ultimately, over the people. The Supreme Court was created to be the weakest of the federal government branches, never to be granted power over the other two federal departments (i.e. the Congress and the President) or over the affairs of the individual sovereign states.

While writing the Federalist papers, which sought to alleviate the fears that many of the American people had about the power given to federal judges under the new Constitution, Federalist Alexander Hamilton, signatory of the Constitution, had this to say about the amount of power that the proposed Constitution was granting to the Supreme Court:

> [11] "The Judiciary is beyond comparison the weakest of the three departments of power... it can never attack, with success, either of the other two... The judiciary, from the nature of its functions, will always be the least dangerous to the political rights of the Constitution; because it will be least in a capacity to annoy or injure them."

This was the original intent of the founders of this nation. The doctrine of judicial review in which the Supreme Court decides the constitutionality of laws enacted by the American people and their respective states is a power never granted in the Constitution.

Former U.S. Attorney General Edwin Meese III is quoted in the book *Men in Black: How the Supreme Court is Destroying America*, about the founding fathers' intentions when founding the American form of government:

> [12] "Not a single participant at the Constitutional Convention, not a single legislator of the ratifying states, and not a single leading political theorist at the time argued that the judiciary should be the branch of government to hold sway over the others...[T]he framers had no intention of trading one form of tyranny for another. They had no intention of creating a government where a mere handful of unelected officials, appointed for life, would dictate policy to Congress, the states, and ultimately the people. The purpose of the judiciary was straightforward: to decide case and controversies and interpret—narrowly—the Constitution. It was not granted broad authority to sculpt a new Constitution, negate legislation at will, or advance political causes through judicial opinions."

If America is to be returned to its former glory, the power that the Supreme Court has seized from the American people over the last 80 years must be taken back. The Court must be demoted to the weakest of the three departments of power, without the ability to attack the will of the American people and their elected representatives.

Therefore, we need a constitutional amendment to restore the original intent of the founding fathers with regard to the role of the federal government, and especially the federal judiciary. The only solution is to put the power of their government back into the hands of the American people. Therefore, I propose the following amendment be added to both the U.S. Constitution and the Constitutions of each individual state.

Section 1 - That each State in the Union shall retain its

sovereignty, freedom and independence, and every power, jurisdiction and right which is not by this Constitution expressly delegated to the Congress of the United States.

Section 2 - All power to suspend the execution of state laws and state Constitutions by any member of the federal judiciary, without the consent of the representatives of the people, is injurious to their rights, and ought not to be exercised.

This amendment, proposed as the 28th Amendment, would accomplish two things. First, it would prohibit federal judges and federal courts from nullifying the execution of state laws and state Constitutions by judicial decree without the consent of the people of the individual states, thus doing what Congress have failed to do over the last 80 years— limiting the power of the federal judiciary and restoring their jurisdiction to its proper place: oversight over the other two branches of the federal government.

Second, it would restore state sovereignty, which the founding fathers originally intended to leave in the hands of the states and the American people. This would restore the original intent of the 10th Amendment of the Constitution and negate the usurpations of power that the Supreme Court has amassed in its distorted interpretations of the 14th Amendment.

This type of proposal for a constitutional amendment to end judicial tyranny is not however a new one. Robert Bork, the conservative American legal scholar who was nominated in 1987 to the Supreme Court by President Ronald Reagan, had the following to say in his 1996 book *Slouching Towards Gomorrah:*

> [13] "There appears to be only one means by which the federal courts, including the Supreme Court, can be brought back to constitutional legitimacy. That

would be a constitutional amendment making any federal or state court decision subject to being overruled by a majority vote of each house of Congress. The mere suggestion of such a remedy would bring down cries that this would endanger our freedoms. To the contrary, as already noted, it is the courts that are not merely endangering our freedom, but actually depriving us of them, particularly our most precious freedom, the freedom to govern ourselves democratically unless the constitution actually says otherwise. The United Kingdom has developed and retained freedom without judicial review."

This amendment is almost a word-for-word duplicate of George Mason's Master Draft of the Bill of Rights that was proposed to the Federal Constitutional Convention, on September 12, 1787, proving that this was the original intent of the founding fathers. Similar Amendments were proposed by the Constitutional Conventions of New York, Virginia, Maryland, North Carolina, and Vermont. All the proposals were nearly a verbatim copy of Mason's master draft.

Section 1 of this Amendment is simply a rewording and re-emphasis of the original intent of the 10th Amendment, which was written to limit the amount of power that the federal government would hold over the American people and the individual states. *World Book* encyclopedia explains the original intent of the Constitution's framers when adopting the 10th Amendment:

> [14] "This amendment was adopted to reassure people that the national government would not swallow up the states. It confirms that the states or the people retain all powers *not given to the national government.*"

This Constitutional amendment should be ratified by the American people, because many of our politicians, in their lust for power, have not had the political courage to stand up to the Federal and Supreme Courts' unconstitutional seizures of power.

This does absolutely nothing to upset the separation of power between the federal branches of government; it simply restores the original intent of the founding fathers when the American people ratified the 10th Amendment.

The Supreme Court and the federal courts could continue to oversee the two other federal branches of government (the President and Congress), and the state courts and the state Supreme Court would still have the power to rule on state laws and state Constitutions. This is how the founding fathers originally designed the government to operate before it was illegally changed by the Supreme Court. The Supreme Court should not be excluded from the process; it simply needs to be put back into its proper constitutional place. As Abraham Lincoln put it, "We the People are the rightful masters of both Congress and the Courts—not to overthrow the Constitution, but to overthrow the men who pervert the Constitution..."

This amendment would restore the power of American government back to the hands of the American people and return to the individual states the right of self-government guaranteed by Article 4, Section 4 and by the 10th Amendment, and would effectively reverse the usurpation of power that the Supreme Court bestowed upon itself.

The socialist and secularists who are opposed to this amendment will resort to all kinds of propaganda to defeat it. They will insist that we are trying to change the American system of government, when in reality we are simply attempting *to restore it*. Therefore, in order to fight this type of propaganda, education will be essential. We must teach the American people the truth surrounding the founding of this great nation and convince the American people that if America is to remain prosperous and blessed, we must restore our Constitutional Republic.

For this movement to be effective, we must make this a bi-partisan *"issue,"* because "issue proposals" are not nearly as political, nor are they as partisan as issues tied to a particular political party. Individual issues appeal to the convictions that many Americans already hold dear, regardless of their political affiliation.

Certain Americans are so partisan and politically divisive in their ideology that they would never vote for a person or an issue initiated by the opposing party. We must tell our elected officials to stop the political in-fighting and return our government to the American people.

Issue-based movements are easier to pass because addressing an individual issue, like the right to self-government, on its merits alone eliminates much of the political partisan politics as it does not attach a (D) or an (R) next to it. This allows the American people to decide on the issue without the trappings that accompany political bias.

Take the issue of same-sex marriage, for example. During the 2004 elections, 11 states had Constitutional amendments on their ballots banning same sex marriage. All 11 states passed their Constitutional amendments regardless of whether the state was Republican- or Democratic-controlled. This issue had broad bi-partisan support because it was not tied to a particular political party—it was based upon sound principle.

I also believe that this amendment to the Constitution will have broad bi-partisan support because the American people do not want to believe that they have absolutely no say-so in the affairs of their government and their societies.

From the founding of this nation, the American people have wanted to be in control of their government and do not wish to be ruled by tyrants, whether it be a king or a court.

I am a member of a labor union. Historically, union members have been known to vote Democratic. When I approached my union brothers and sisters, every one of them overwhelmingly and unanimously supported a Constitutional amendment that would return the power of American government to the people. I then approached those whom I knew voted predominantly Republican, and also received overwhelming support for taking absolute and total control from the hand of federal judges and placing power back into the hands of the states and of the American people.

Most of what is destroying our American culture can be traced either directly or indirectly to these and many other Supreme Court rulings over the last 50 years. Unless the American people take back their Constitutional right to rule their own state governments and societies as they see fit, I fear America, like all the great nations that have gone before us, may soon end up on the ash heap of history.

Most Americans believe in a nation that is governed by the people and not by a handful of tyrannical judges. The majority of Americans want the right of self-rule returned to them and to their states, whether they are Republicans, Democrats or Independents; liberals, conservatives or moderates; or whether they support the Constitution Party, the Libertarian Party or the Green Party.

When this amendment is pushed to the political forefront, it should be easy to see which politicians, lobbying groups and political parties support socialism and secularism and are opposed to the type of government that our founding fathers created. They will then need to be removed from office.

I believe that it would be politically suicidal for any candidate to appear to support socialism. When this amendment is pushed to the political forefront, those "closet socialists and secularists," whether Republican or Democrat, who feel that the American people are not competent enough to govern the affairs of their own states and their own government will be exposed for who they really are, and removed.

Those who are opposed to this amendment will attempt to use issues such as slavery and segregation to prove that it is dangerous to leave power in the hands of the people and in the hands of the states. In a letter to William Charles Jarvis, on September 28, 1820, Thomas Jefferson said the following concerning the taking of constitutional power out of the hands of the American people because they have abused their constitutional power:

> "I know no safer depository of the ultimate powers of the society but the people themselves; and if we think them not enlightened enough to exercise their control with a wholesome discretion, *the remedy is not to take it from them*, but to inform their discretion by education. This is the true corrective of abuses of constitutional power."

Issues such as slavery and segregation were not ended when atheists protested against its immorality, but when Christians such as Abraham Lincoln and Martin Luther King courageously took a stand for what was right. This stand cost both men their lives.

One of my favorite Americans, Democratic President John F. Kennedy, was vehemently opposed to communism. In his inaugural address given on Friday, January 20, 1961, he made it quite clear that his administration would oppose both the socialization and secularization of America:

"For I have sworn before you and Almighty God the same solemn oath our forebears prescribed nearly a century and three quarters ago. The world is very different now... And yet the same revolutionary beliefs for which our forebears fought are still at issue around the globe—the belief that the rights of man come not from the generosity of the state, but from the hand of God...

"And so, my fellow Americans: ask not what your country can do for you—ask what you can do for your country.

Finally, whether you are citizens of America or citizens of the world, ask of us the same high standards of strength and sacrifice which we ask of you. With a good conscience our only sure reward, with history the final judge of our deeds, let us go forth to lead the land we love, asking His blessing and His help, but knowing that here on earth God's work must truly be our own."

In his inaugural address, John F. Kennedy recognized the threat that socialism and secularism posed to the future of the American Republic and publicly committed to the American people and before Almighty God that he would resist the forces that were gaining political influence in America. It appears that this stand also cost him his life.

The federal government and Supreme Court are not the answer to society's problems; they are the problem. However, we must understand that the secular media in this country will not be sympathetic to our cause. Quite the contrary, as it was with the book *Bias* by Bernard Goldberg, the media will ignore the subject until it cannot be ignored any longer, and will then do whatever it can to discredit not only the cause but those who advocate it.

While many in the media may not personally attack the character of those who wish to take up this fight, they will have no objection to parading those with disparaging and slanderous comments across television screens and across their publications to discredit them, regardless of whether or not there is any proof to their allegations. Smear campaigns been one of their favorite tactics for over the last 60 years. In his book *The Far Left*, written in 1964, Billy J. Hargis shows us that this has always been how they operate:

> [15] "You would have to lead an Anti-communist movement to know what the liberals are capable of—the hatred, incriminations, intimidations and coercion they constantly throw at the leaders of the anti-communist cause.
>
> I cannot describe adequately the heartache and persecution heaped upon any leader of an anti-communist movement by the liberal left-wing. With unlimited finances and being in control of the national media—television, radio and publications—they can destroy a man without any shrug of conscience or regard for 'due process of law.' It is a lawless spirit that is preached by the communists, and practiced by far too many liberals that we oppose."

I do not mention this to keep the media from slandering those who wish to take up the cause; rather, I fully expect it. Jesus warned us that there would be those who would say evil things about us falsely for Christ's sake: [15] "Blessed are you when they revile and persecute you, and say all kinds of evil against you falsely for My sake."

I say this only to prepare those who take up the cause to be ready for slanderous attacks. Remember, Jesus said we would be blessed for it. The secular media in this country has an agenda and will gladly provide media exposure to anyone who opposes our agenda, regardless of the existence of proof.

When our civil rights have been so violated that our children cannot pray over their school lunches, yet Congress can open a session in prayer and the Supreme Court begins each sessions with the prayer, "God save the United States and this Honorable Court"; when schools, public courthouses and other state and federal government property are commanded to remove items of a religious nature, yet the Supreme Court displays Moses and the Ten Commandments carved into the façade and hanging in its chamber; when a student is denied the right to open and read his Bible at school, yet one of the first acts of the Continental Congress was to purchase 20,000 Bibles because the Revolutionary War had created a shortage, I would say that our constitutional, civil and inalienable rights given to us by God Himself and by our founding fathers have been and are continuing to be violated by a tyrannical, out-of-control court system that has usurped power until it has become the dominant branch of government.

If you let people push you around long enough, they will continue to do so until you say, *"Enough!"* Those of us who are sick and tired of the secular establishment dictating what we can and cannot do need to stand up for what our founding fathers wanted and not compromise nor settle for anything less than a *total and complete restoration of our American Republic and the Constitution, as it was intended.*

Those in government who cannot find the courage, moral strength and personal integrity to support and defend the Constitution as they swore before Almighty God Himself in their oath of office, or cannot find the moral and personal fortitude to stand against the barrage that will come from socialists and secularist in the media, we will replace them with officials who will.

Many politicians who are personally and secretly opposed to restoring America's liberties and the right of self-rule are content to allow the unelected courts do their dirty work for them. Once this issue is pushed to the political forefront and these politicians are forced to take a side, you will see these individuals' true colors.

Religious liberty, state sovereignty and judicial tyranny should be the primary focus of all political debate in the coming elections. This is akin to a national emergency. When these issues are restored to their rightful and Constitutional place, the American people will then have the right to decide on the issues for themselves. The truth will only be heard when millions of Americans who know and understand what is truly wrong with America stand up to be heard. When we are told to sit down and shut up, we will cry out even louder. We will not stop until our hijacked American Constitution and society is returned to us. This is essential if we as American's desire for God to "bless America."

Abraham Lincoln, another of America's "right-wing extremists" and one of America's most beloved Presidents, also knew what it would take for a nation to be "blessed":

> "It is the duty of nations, as well as of men, to owe their dependence upon the overruling power of God and to recognize the sublime truth announced in the Holy Scriptures and proven by all history, *that those nations only are blessed whose God is the Lord.*"

Abraham Lincoln knew that not only men, but nations as well, would be blessed by God only if they remained obedient to Him and dependent upon Him.

Chapter 15

Conclusion

> [1] *"History shows that great nations rise and great nations fall, but the autopsy of history is that all great nations commit suicide." I believe that America is headed in that direction."*
>
> **British Historian Arnold Toynbee**

Today's critics say, "We don't want God to have anything to do with today's morality. We want to determine what is right and wrong without God." They often offer the argument "you cannot legislate morality." As we will see, this is not a new argument.

Since the beginning of time itself, man has struggled over "Who is God?" Not so much "Who is the person of God" as much as "Is God the final authority over every standard of morality, or am I?" Will Man assume the rule of deity, determining for himself what is right and wrong, or will he allow God to be God and submit to His authority and what He has already determined to be right and wrong; moral and immoral? This struggle is older than mankind itself.

Beneath the surface of the political war there rages a spiritual war, the same war that began in the Garden of Eden and has been raging for countless centuries since, and America is its present-day battleground

In the year 1815, in the case of the *Commonwealth v. Sharpless*, the Supreme Court of Pennsylvania said the following about legislating morality and the struggle that this country has always faced—and is facing today:

> [2] "Morality is defined as the condition of conforming to the right principles. It pits right against wrong. To 'legislate' means to make law. Law imposes rules on conduct and enforces them with authority. What law has ever been enacted by any government in the history of man that has not named something wrong and its opposite right? *Every law establishes and legislates morality*. What today's critics are saying is—"We don't want God to have anything to do with today's morality. We want to determine what is right and wrong without God. *America has become the battleground between the world's two oldest religions*. The first religion to appear in the history of mankind worships God. The second worships man. In America, the first is expressed primarily by Christianity. The second is Humanism. It is not a question of whether morality can or should be legislated. It is a question of which religion's guidelines will under gird the legislation; religious guidelines that deify God, or religious guidelines that deify man."

In the year 1815, before our court system and legislatures were overrun by socialists and secular humanists, our courts and legislatures understood the monumental struggle that has always been, and is presently, taking place in American society. The Supreme Court of Pennsylvania understood and stated in its ruling that all morality comes from religion. One religion deifies God while the other deifies man. The question then becomes: who are we worshiping?

Our country is presently faced with, and will always face, this same decision. As we see, history repeats itself. As it was in 1815, *"America has again become the battleground between the world's two oldest religions."* Yes, you and I ultimately have the freedom to choose for ourselves whose morality we will legislate; God's or man's. That is what freedom and freewill are all about. But do not think for a minute that by choosing the latter God will ever "bless America"!

During the Civil War, Abraham Lincoln had this to say about the spiritual condition of America during his 1863 Thanksgiving Proclamation. This statement is as relevant today as it was in 1863.

> "We have forgotten God. We have forgotten the gracious hand which preserved us in peace and multiplied and enriched and strengthened us, and we have vainly imagined, in the deceitfulness of our hearts, that all these blessings were produced by some superior wisdom and virtue of our own. Intoxicated with unbroken success, we have become too self-sufficient to feel the necessity of redeeming and preserving grace, too proud to pray to the God that made us."

Abraham Lincoln recognized that America at the time of the Civil War was going through the same historical cycle that all great nations and civilizations go through. America today finds itself in exactly the same position. Since after World War II, American has become intoxicated with unbroken success and many have vainly imagined, in the deceitfulness of our hearts, that all these blessings were produced by some superior wisdom and virtue of our own. We have become too self-sufficient to feel the necessity of redeeming and preserving grace, too proud to pray to the God that made us.

We need to ask ourselves individually and as a nation the same question that Benjamin Franklin asked the constitutional delegates about America's dependence upon God when the Constitutional Convention was about to fall apart:

> [3] "Have we now forgotten this powerful friend? Or do we imagine we no longer need His assistance? I have lived, Sir, a long time, and the longer I live, the more convincing proofs I see of this truth—that God governs in the affairs of men. And if a sparrow cannot fall to the ground without His notice, is it probable that an empire cannot rise without His aid? We have been assured, Sir, in the sacred writings, that "except the Lord build the house, they labor in vain that build it." I firmly believe this; and I also believe that without His concurring aid, we shall succeed in this political building no better, then the builders of Babel... I therefore beg leave to move—that henceforth prayers imploring the assistance of heaven, and its blessing..."

America as a nation cannot fall much further from God than it is presently. Unless we reverse the course of this nation, I fear that like many nations before us, America will commit suicide and end up on the ash heap of history. Many prominent and intelligent men across America, both past and present, share this belief. However, since the media in this country is largely controlled by the opposition, these warnings and admonitions continue to go unheard by the American public.

U.S. Senator Zell Miller (Democrat—Georgia) stood on the Senate floor on Feb 12, 2004, and said the following:

[4] "Arnold Toynbee, who wrote the acclaimed 12-volume *A Study of History*, once declared, 'Of the 22 civilizations that have appeared in history, 19 of them collapsed when they reached the moral state America is in today.'

"Toynbee died in 1975, before seeing the worst that was yet to come. Yes, Arnold Toynbee saw the famine. The 'famine of hearing the words of the Lord.' Whether it is removing a display of the Ten Commandments from a courthouse or the Nativity scene from a city square. Whether it is eliminating prayer in schools or eliminating 'under God' in the Pledge of Allegiance. Whether it is making a mockery of the sacred institution of marriage between a man and woman or, yes, telecasting around the world made-in-the-USA filth masquerading as entertainment...

"Everyone today seems to think that the U.S. Constitution expressly provides for separation of church and state. Ask any ten people if that's not so. And I'll bet you most of them will say 'Well, sure.' And some will point out, 'It's in the First Amendment.'

"*Wrong*! Read it! It says, 'Congress shall make no law respecting an establishment of religion or prohibiting the free exercise thereof.' Where is the word 'separate'? Where are the words 'church' or 'state?'

"They are not there. Never have been. Never intended to be. Read the Congressional Records during that four-month period in 1789 when the amendment was being framed in Congress. Clearly their intent was to prohibit a single denomination in exclusion of all others, whether it was Anglican or Catholic or some other.

"I highly recommend a great book entitled *Original Intent* by David Barton. It really gets into how the actual members of Congress, who drafted the First Amendment, expected basic biblical principles and values to be present throughout public life and society, not separate from it.

"It was Alexander Hamilton who pointed out that 'judges should be bound down by strict rules and precedents, which serve to define and point out their duty.' Bound down! That is exactly what is needed to be done. There was not a single precedent cited when school prayer was struck down in 1962.

"These judges who legislate instead of adjudicate, do it without being responsible to one single solitary voter for their actions. Among the signers of the Declaration of Independence was a brilliant young physician from Pennsylvania named Benjamin Rush. When Rush was elected to that First Continental Congress, his close friend Benjamin Franklin told him, 'We need you.... we have a great task before us, assigned to us by Providence.'

"Today, 228 years later, there is still a great task before us assigned to us by Providence. Our founding fathers did not shirk their duty and we can do no less.

"By the way, Benjamin Rush was once asked a question that has long interested this senator from Georgia in particular. Dr. Rush was asked, are you a democrat or an aristocrat? And the good doctor answered, 'I am neither. I am a Christocrat. I believe He, alone, who created and redeemed man is qualified to govern him.' That reply of Benjamin Rush is just as true today in the year of our Lord 2004 as it was in the year of our Lord 1776.

"So, if I am asked why, with all the pressing problems this nation faces today, why am I pushing these social issues and taking the Senate's valuable time? I will answer: *Because, it is of the highest importance*. Yes, there's a deficit to be concerned about in this country, a deficit of decency.

"So, as the sand empties through my hourglass at warp speed, and with my time running out in this Senate and on this earth, I feel compelled to speak out. For I truly believe that at times like this, silence is not golden. It is yellow."

Everyone in America who is echoing these same thoughts is being ignored or vilified by the secular press because the press does not want America to go in the direction that is favored by most Americans or our founding fathers.

Another man trying to get Americans to see the reality of our nation is Gary Palmer, President of the Alabama Policy Institute. In an article written on November 20, 2003, he echoes these thoughts:

[5] "According to the British historian Arnold Toynbee, history shows that great nations rise and great nations fall, but '...the autopsy of history is that all great nations commit suicide.' *I believe that America is headed in that direction.*

"Many people believe that the string of recent court decisions to overturn state anti-sodomy laws, to ban the public display of the Ten Commandments, and to remove the words 'under God' from the Pledge of Allegiance indicate that the moral and spiritual foundations of the country have been destroyed. For many, this belief was reinforced by the decision of the Massachusetts Supreme Court to legalize marriage between people of the same sex. I am of a different opinion.

"Our nation was built on a foundation that cannot be moved or destroyed. It was founded on Biblical principles that will endure whether people respect them or reject them because they are immutable... they are permanent. Our founding documents are embedded with these principles. And even though our people are largely ignorant of the Declaration of Independence, the truths in it remain unchanged. Even though the courts, the liberal politicians and their leftist allies routinely violate the U.S. Constitution, its brilliance is not diminished. Combined, they form a solid rock that will endure no matter what the secular humanists, the atheists or the socialists bring to bear against it.

"Consequently, if America falls into the ash heap of history, as so many other nations before us have done, it will not be because the foundation crumbled under us. It will be because as a nation and as a people we allowed ourselves to creep to the very edge, dangle our feet dangerously and ultimately jumped off.

"Why should we care if that happens, if we abandon our strong moral and spiritual foundation? Because everything that makes America unique—the basis for our freedom and our rights as individuals—depends on our founding principles and the moral and Biblical truths on which they are based.

"As one writer stated, 'It has been the consistent practice of the totalitarians, the atheists, and the materialists to concentrate on undermining, ridiculing, or eliminating the basic truths of religion. They know that once these go, all the derivative truths and practices that depend on these primary principles become virtually meaningless. So first, last, and always they center their attack on Number One Truths. What are the *Number One Truths*? According to the writer they are a belief in:

1. The fact of a personal God, Who has created and spoken to the world
2. Jesus Christ, true God and true man
3. The Ten Commandments
4. The sacred character of the individual (i.e. the sacredness of human life)
5. The sanctity of the lifelong marriage bond
6. The sanctity of the home as the basic unit of the whole human family
7. The human rights of every person as coming from God, not the State
8. The right, based on human nature, to possess private property, with its consequent obligation to society
9. Due respect for domestic, civil, and religious authority; and
10. Judgment after death.

"While the writer could very easily have re-emphasized these truths in response to current events, these tenets were actually published in 1949 in a book of daily devotions as a warning to Christians to take action against the secular forces that were steadily gaining influence in America.

"Unfortunately, it appears that they were successful because the institutions that should protect the truths on which America was founded—our colleges, the free press, our legislative bodies and our courts—have largely been turned against us. And in the case of the courts, the very body which was to protect the Constitution has turned the Constitution against us. The courts are denying us the fundamental freedom of self-government and replacing it with government by the judiciary under the control of secularists.

"The courts have become the new clergy in America, imposing a secular religion that will force its subjects to accept a new standard that demands tolerance of obscenity or the killing of unborn children or sexual deviance or anything else—except religious faith. As Toynbee pointed out, great nations do not fall to outside forces; they fall from within.

"The nations that rise in power and strength do so around a strong belief in something that is larger than themselves. The truly great nations have a belief in a higher purpose and a Higher Being that gives them the sense of destiny that propels them to greatness.

"America had that once. As a nation we once stood on the Solid Rock... and now? It looks like we are about to jump off."

There is a saying that "those who fail to learn from the past are doomed to repeat it." Many in this country believe that America is dangerously close to that point. The Bible is full of accounts of nations that turned from God and were destroyed. If America thinks that it is somehow exempt from this type of future, it is sadly mistaken.

None of the men who founded this nation thought that America could turn its back on God and still remain blessed. George Washington said the following in his First State of the Union Address:

> [6] "We ought to be no less persuaded that the [favorable] smiles of Heaven, can never be expected on a nation that disregards the eternal rules of order and right, which Heaven itself has ordained."

Can we say that the same type of future awaits America if we continue to reject God's rule and authority over our lives? Our founding fathers seemed to think so. Here is what Daniel Webster had to say about it:

> [7] "If we and our prosperity reject religious instruction and authority, violate the rules of eternal justice, trifle with the injunctions of morality, and recklessly destroy the political constitution which holds us together, *no man can tell how sudden a catastrophe may overwhelm us that shall bury all our glory in profane obscurity.*"

Daniel Webster warned us by listing five things that Americans could do that would bring "a catastrophe" that will "overwhelm us" and "shall bury all our glory in profane obscurity." They are:

1. Reject religious instruction
2. Reject religious authority
3. Violate the rules of eternal justice
4. Trifle with the injunctions of morality
5. Recklessly destroy the political Constitution

I pray that by now you see that America as a nation has in fact fulfilled all five of these conditions. The majority of Americans have not chosen this path for their nation; it has been forced upon them by a few socialists and secular humanists who have infiltrated every area of society from the press, government, courts, media, church and the educational system.

I personally know many good, righteous people in the country who are doing nothing to contribute to America's moral or political downfall and do not agree with the direction in which the nation is heading, but these same people are not actively doing anything to prevent it.

British statesman Edmund Burke once said, "Nobody made a greater mistake than he who did nothing because he could do only a little." Therefore, we must keep this motto in mind: **"Do a little or do a lot—but do something!"** Do not let this opportunity pass without doing something, either small or great, to help return America to a nation "of the people and by the people."

If we as Americans wish to pass on to our children a nation blessed by God, we must do far more. We must heed the words of President Dwight D. Eisenhower and Charles G. Finney who said, "Politics ought to be the part-time profession of every citizen who would protect the rights and privileges of free people and who would preserve what is good and fruitful in our national heritage."

> [8] "Christians must do their duty to the country as a part of their duty to God... *He will bless or curse this nation according to the course they take.*"

If we feel that the cares of this world, the deceitfulness of riches and the desire for material things are more worthy of our time than defending traditional American society, then we as Christians must spend more time in our churches teaching our children how to die as saints and martyrs. If you feel that this statement is a bit strong, I recommend reading *Persecution: How Liberals Are Waging War Against Christianity* by David Limbaugh.

Traditionalists in America must realize that for the last 40 years, we have already lost practically every battle and are on the verge of losing the war. If we desire to return America to its former glory, we must insist that our state and federal representatives return the power and right of self-rule in this nation to the hands of the people so that, as Abraham Lincoln said in his Gettysburg address, "This nation shall have a new birth of freedom, and that government of the people, by the people, for the people shall not perish from the earth."

Therefore I make the same appeal to you that Benjamin Rush made to Benjamin Franklin when he told him, 'We need you... we have a great task before us, assigned to us by Providence.'

Therefore, coupled with our prayers to Almighty God to preserve our nation, we must begin to fight **The Next American Revolution**. I leave you with four quotes that need to express our attitude and commitment during this time:

The time is now near at hand which must probably determine whether Americans are to be freemen or slaves; whether they are to have any property they can call their own; whether their houses and farms are to be pillaged and destroyed... The fate of unborn millions will now depend, under God, on the courage and conduct of this army. Our cruel and unrelenting enemy leaves us only the choice of brave resistance, or the most abject submission. We have, therefore, to resolve to conquer or die.

George Washington (1776)

"We do not come as aggressors. Our war is not a war of conquest; we are fighting in the defense of our homes, our families, and posterity. We have petitioned, and our petitions have been scorned; we have entreated, and our entreaties have been disregarded; we have begged, and they have mocked... We beg no longer; we entreat no more; we petition no more. We defy them!"

William Jennings Bryan

> *"In the beginning of a change, the patriot is a scarce and brave man, hated and scorned. When his cause succeeds however, the timid join him, for then it costs nothing to be a patriot."*
>
> **Mark Twain**

> *"These are the times that try men's souls. The summer soldier and the sunshine patriot will, in this crisis, shrink from the service of their country... Tyranny, like hell, is not easily conquered... If there must be trouble, let it be in my day, that my child may have peace."*
>
> **Thomas Paine 1776**

References

Foreword

1. *The Shawshank Redemption* © 1994, Castle Rock
2. Rom 8:24-25, 2 Cor 3:12, Heb 6:11-12 NKJV

Introduction

1. *Webster's New World Dictionary and Thesaurus.* Accent Software International, ©1998, Macmillan Publishers
2. *The Sovereign States.* James Kilpatrick, © 1957, Henry Regnery Co., Chicago, p. 37
3. Commencement Speech by Attorney General Bill Pryor to the 1997 McGill-Toolen Graduating Class. http://www.ago.state.al.us/issue/mcgill_grad.htm. Last accessed 18 Dec 2005
4. Abraham Lincoln: The Perpetuation of Our Political Institutions. Address to the Young Men's Lyceum of Springfield, Illinois January 27, 1838.
5. World Book online. © 2005. http://www.worldbookonline.com. Last accessed 18 Dec 2005
6. Bartleby.com. © 2004 Bartleby.com - http://www.bartleby.com/73/1749.html. Last accessed 18 Dec 2005
7. Musings on Winston Churchill. © 2002, 2003, 2004, 2005. http://www.alsindependence.com/Musings_On_Winston_Churchhill.htm. Last accessed 18 Dec 2005

Stolen History

1. President Woodrow Wilson. *Duty is Ours, Results Are God's.* http://dutyisours.com/duty.htm © 1999, 2000, 2003, 2004 Dio, Inc. Last accessed 18 Dec 2005
2. President Woodrow Wilson. *Duty is Ours, Results Are God's.* http://dutyisours.com/duty.htm © 1999, 2000, 2003, 2004 Dio, Inc. Last accessed 18 Dec 2005
3. *Faith of our Founding Fathers.* Tim Lahaye, ©1990, Masterbook Inc, Green Forest, AR, p. 1

4. *Censorship: Evidence of Bias in Our Children's Textbooks.* Paul C. Vitz, © 1986, Ann Arbor, Mich, Servant Books, p. 77.
5. http://www.pastornet.net.au/fwn/1999/oct/art09.html Last accessed 18 Dec 2005
6. *The Nation's History.* Arthur Leonard & Bertha Jacobs, ©1924, Henry Holt and company, New York, p. iii
7. "Jumping off the Solid Rock." Gary Palmer, November 20, 2003. http://www.alabamapolicyinstitute.org/gary-2003-11-20.html, Last accessed 18 Dec 2005
8. *God in the White House.* Richard G. Hutcheson, © 1988, Macmillan Publishing Company, New York, p. 27

What Do Americans Believe?

1. *Lectures on Revivals of Religion.* Charles G Finney, ©1868, Fleming H Revell Co., New York (first published in 1835, Lecture XV, pp. 281–282.
2. *The Empty Church: The Suicide of Liberal Christianity.* Thomas C. Reeves published by Free Press, a division of Simon & Schuster, Inc. © 1996. pp. 16-21.
3. James 3:3-4 NKJV
4. *Webster's New World Dictionary and Thesaurus.* Accent Software International, ©1998, Macmillan Publishers.
5. Revealing FACTS on the ACLU from its own writings. Diane Dew http://dianedew.com/aclu.htm. Last accessed 18 Dec 2005
6. State v. John Scopes ("The Monkey Trial") University of Missouri-Kansas City School of Law. © 2001 UMKC Law School DMCA. http://www.law.umkc.edu/faculty/projects/ftrials/scopes/evolut.htm. Last accessed 18 Dec 2005
7., *Lectures on Revivals of Religion.* Charles G Finney, © 1868, Fleming H Revell Co., New York (first published in 1835), Lecture XV, pp. 281–282.
8. The U.S. National Archives and Records Administration http://www.archives.gov/national-archives experience/charters/constitution_q_and_a.html. Last accessed 18 Dec 2005
9. Merriam-Webster online dictionary © 2005 Merriam-Webster, Incorporated. Last accessed 18 Dec 2005
10. *The Far Left.* Billy James Hargis. ©1964 Christian Crusade, Tulsa pp. 107–108, 105.

11. The Warren Court and its Critics, by: Clifford M. Lytle.
© 1968 University of Arizona press. Tucson. p. 23
12. 1936 CONSTITUTION OF THE USSR Bucknell University
© 1996 Robert Beard
http://www.departments.bucknell.edu/russian/const/
36cons04.html. Last accessed 18 Dec 2005
13. *The Far Left.* Billy James Hargis ©1964. Christian Crusade, Tulsa, p. 18

America's Rise

The First American Revolution

1. The Declaration of Independence, 1776
2. *Five Lies of the Century*. Davis T. Moore. © 1995 Tyndale House Publishers, Wheaton, Illinois. pp 9–10.
3. *Faith of our Founding Fathers*. Tim Lahaye, ©1990, Masterbook Inc, Green Forest, AR, p. 102
4. World Book online. http://www.worldbookonline.com Last accessed 18 Dec 2005
5. "George Washington's Speech to Delaware Indian Chiefs on May 12, 1779," in John C. Fitzpatrick, editor, *The Writings of George Washington*, Vol. XV,1932, Washington: U.S. Government Printing Office,, p. 55.
6. *Liberty! Cry Liberty!* Harold K. Lane, © 1939, Boston: Lamb and Lamb Tractarian Society), pp. 32–33. See also Fedrick Nyneyer, *First Principles in Morality and Economics: Neighborly Love and Ricardo's Law of Association*, © 1958, South Holland Libertarian Press, p. 31.
7. John Adams Inaugural Address in the City of Philadelphia, Saturday, March 4, 1797.
8. *Original Intent*. David Barton. ©1996, Wallbuilder Press, Aledo, Tx, p. 162.
9. *Faith of our Founding Fathers*. Tim Lahaye, ©1990, Masterbook Inc, Green Forest, AR, p. 116
10. *James Madison: The Papers of James Madison*, June 28, 1787. Henry D. Gilpin, editor, © 1840, Washington: Langtree and Sullivan. Vol. II, pp. 984-986,.
11. World Book online. http://www.worldbookonline.com Last accessed 18 Dec 2005
12. *James Madison and Religious Liberty*. Gaillard Hunt,

© 1902, Washington: American Historical Association, Government Printing Office,, p. 166
13. Everson v. Board of Education, 330 U.S. 1 (1947)
14. World Book online. http://www.worldbookonline.com Last accessed 18 Dec 2005
15 Library of Congress: Time Line, America During the Age of Revolution, 1776–1789: http://memory.loc.gov/ammem/bdsds/timeline.html Last accessed 18 Dec 2005
16. *Original Intent.* David Barton. ©1996, Wallbuilder Press, Aledo, Tx, pp. 203–204
17. Reynolds v. United States, 98 U.S. 145, 164 (1878).
18. *The Causes of the American Revolution.* John C. Wahlke, ©1973, D.C. Heath and Co., London, p. 68
19. *The Causes of the American Revolution.* John C. Wahlke, ©1973, D.C. Heath and Co., London, p. 69
20. *The Causes of the American Revolution.* John C. Wahlke, ©1973, D.C. Heath and Co., London, p. 70
21. Individual Freedom and the Bill of Rights. Chapter 9 Property Rights
U.S. Department of State's Bureau of International Information Programs.
http://usinfo.state.gov/products/pubs/rightsof/property.htm Last accessed 18 Dec 2005
22. World Book online. http://www.worldbookonline.com Last accessed 18 Dec 2005
23. *The Jubilee of the Constitution. A Discourse delivered at the request of the New York Historical Society, in the city of New York, on Tuesday, Apr 30 1839, Being the Fifteenth Anniversary of the Inauguration of George Washington as President of the United States, on Thurs Apr 30, 1789* John Quincy Adams, © 1839, New York: Samuel Colman, pp. 13–14
24. "The U.S. House Judiciary Committee Report." New York Christian Coalition. http://www.nychristiancoalition.org/SEPARATION.HTM Last accessed 18 Dec 2005

The U.S. Constitution

1. The U.S. National Archives and Records Administration http://www.archives.gov/national-archives experience/charters/constitution_q_and_a.html. Last accessed 18 Dec 2005

2. *The Life and Public Services of Samuel Adams.* William V. Wells, © 1865, Boston: Little, Brown, and Co, Vol /iii, p.273, to Richard Henry Lee on Aug 24, 1789. See also *Samuel Adams: The Writings of Samuel Adams*, Henry Alonzo Cushing, editor, © 1904, New York: G.P. Putnam's Sons, Vol IV, p. 334

3. "Thomas Jefferson, Memoir, Correspondence, and Miscellanies," from *The Papers of Thomas Jefferson*, Thomas Jefferson Randolph, editor, © 1830, Boston: Gray and Brown, Vol. IV, p. 373, to Judge William Johnson on June 12, 1823.

4. Bill of Rights Quiz by Tina Terry © 2004 http://www.jpfo.org/paysonquiz.pdf. Last accessed 1-24-2006

5. *The Life and Public Services of Samuel Adams*, William V. Wells, © 1865, Boston: Little, Brown, and Co, Vol /iii, p.273, to Richard Henry Lee on Aug 24, 1789; See also *Samuel Adams, The Writings of Samuel Adams*, Henry Alonzo Cushing, editor, © 1904, New York: G.P. Putnam's Sons, Vol IV, p. 334

6. "Thomas Jefferson, Memoir, Correspondence, and Miscellanies," from *The Papers of Thomas Jefferson*, Thomas Jefferson Randolph, editor, © 1830, Boston: Gray and Brown Vol IV, Pg. 374, to Judge William Johnson on June 12, 1823

7. World Book online. © 2005. http://www.worldbookonline.com. Last accessed 18 Dec 2005

8. Abuses and Usurpations. The Constitution Society. http://www.constitution.org/cs_abuse.htm Last accessed 18 Dec 2005

9. *The Journal of the Constitutional Convention.* James Madison. Edited by E.H. Scott. ©1893, Scott Foresman and Co., New York, p. 29

10. *The Sovereign States.* James Kilpatrick. ©1957, Henry Regnery Co., Chicago, p. 32

11. *The Sovereign States.* James Kilpatrick. ©1957, Henry Regnery Co., Chicago, p.. 38

12. *The Sovereign States.* James Kilpatrick. ©1957, Henry Regnery Co., Chicago, p. 37

13. *The Sovereign States.* James Kilpatrick. ©1957, Henry Regnery Co., Chicago, p. 36

14. *The Sovereign States.* James Kilpatrick. ©1957, Henry

Regnery Co., Chicago, p. 36
15. *Noah Webster's 1828 Dictionary.* Christian Technologies. © 2000, Independence, Missouri.
16. *The Sovereign States.* James Kilpatrick. ©1957, Henry Regnery Co., Chicago, p. 36
17. *The Sovereign States.* James Kilpatrick. ©1957, Henry Regnery Co., Chicago, p.138
18. *The Sovereign States.* James Kilpatrick. ©1957, Henry Regnery Co., Chicago, p. 138
19. *Noah Webster's 1828 Dictionary.* Christian Technologies. © 2000, Independence, Missouri.
20., *History of the United States from the Discovery of the American Continent.* Noah Webster © 1859, Boston: Little, Brown and Co., Vol. V, p. 24
21 John Adams, The Works of John Adams, Second President of the United States, Charles Frances Adams, editor (Boston: Little, Brown and Co., 1854), Vol. VI, p. 484, to John Taylor on Apr 15, 1814.
22. *The Letters of Benjamin Rush.* L.H. Butterfield, editor, © 1951, Princeton: Princeton University Press for the American Philosophical Society, Vol. I, p. 523, to John Adams on July 21, 1789.
23., *The American Spelling Book: Containing an easy Standard of Pronunciation: being the First Part of a Grammatical Institute of the English Language, To Which is Added, an Appendix, Containing a Moral Catechism and a Federal Catechism.* Noah Webster, © 1801, Boston: Isaiah Thomas and Ebenezer T. Andrews, pp. 103–104.
24., *The Jubilee of the Constitution. A Discourse delivered at the request of the New York Historical Society, in the city of New York, on Tuesday, Apr 30 1839, Being the Fifteenth Anniversary of the Inauguration of George Washington as President of the United States, on Thurs Apr 30, 1789.* John Quincy Adams, ©1839, New York: Samuel Colman, p. 53.
25. America and its people, James Martin, Randy Roberts, Steven Mintz, Linda O. McMurry, James Jones. ©1993, HarperCollins Publishing. New York p. 52
26., *The Pulpit of the American Revolution.* John Wingate Thornton, ©1860, reprinted 1970, NY, Burt Franklin, p. XXIX.
27. *Webster's New World Dictionary and Thesaurus.* Accent

Software International, ©1998, Macmillan Publishers.
28. *Noah Webster's 1828 Dictionary*, Christian Technologies. © 2000, Independence, Missouri.
29. *History of the United States from the Discovery of the American Continent.* Noah Webster © 1859, Boston: Little, Brown and Co., Vol. V, p. 6
30. One Nation Under God: America's Christian Heritage. James Madison. Published by the Christian Defense Fund. © Copyright 1997 Last accessed 18 Dec 2005 http://www.leaderu.com/orgs/cdf/onug/madison.html
31. *The Patriot* © 2000, Sony Pictures

The Second American Revolution

1. *Impeachment: Restraining an Overactive Judiciary.* David Barton, © 1996, Wallbuilders, Aledo, TX., pp. 19–21
2. *The Sovereign States.* James Kilpatrick. © 1957, Henry Regnery Co., Chicago, p. 38
3. *The United States Supreme Court—Lawmaking in the Third Branch of Government.* William C. Louthan, ©1991, New Jersey, Prentice-Hall, Inc., p. 49.
4. *The United States Supreme Court—Lawmaking in the Third Branch of Government.* William C. Louthan, ©1991, New Jersey, Prentice-Hall, Inc., p. 49.
5. *The United States Supreme Court—Lawmaking in the Third Branch of Government.* William C. Louthan, ©1991, New Jersey, Prentice-Hall, Inc., p. 50
6. *Men In Black—How the Supreme Court is Destroying America.* Mark Levin, © 2005, Regnery Publishing. Washington, DC., p. 24
7. *Impeachment: Restraining an Overactive Judiciary.* David Barton, © 1996, Wall builders, Aledo, TX., pp. 19–21
8. George Mason's Master Draft of the Bill of Rights. The Constitution Society. http://www.constitution.org/gmason/amd_gmas.htm Last accessed 18 Dec 2005
9. *The Federalist Papers #78.* Alexander Hamilton, © 1788, The Judiciary Department..
10. *The Historical and Legal Examination of that Part of the Decision of the Supreme Court of the United States in the Dared Scott case.* Thomas H. Benton, © 1857, New York: D. Appleton and Co., p. 4

11. *Impeachment: Restraining an Overactive Judiciary.* David Barton, © 1996, Wall builders, Aledo, TX., pp. 19-21
12. *Original Intent.* David Barton. ©1996, Wallbuilder Press, Aledo, Tx, pp. 270-271
13. *The Sovereign States.* James Kilpatrick. ©1957, Henry Regnery Co., Chicago, p. 41

The American Civil War

1. Abraham Lincoln Saved the Union, But Did He Really Free the Slaves?
Editorial by: Mackubin T. Owens. March 2004. http://www.ashbrook.org/publicat/oped/owens/04/guelzo.html Last accessed 18 Dec 2005
2. *April 1865.* Jay Winik, © 2001, NY, HarperCollins Publishers, p. 315
3. *The Civil War and Reconstruction.* William L. Barney, © 2001, Oxford Press, NY, p. 122
4. *Final Freedom.* Michael Vorenberg, © 2001, Cambridge University Press, UK, p. 228
5. *Final Freedom.* Michael Vorenberg, © 2001, Cambridge University Press, UK, p. Pg. 230
6. Mysteries of Canada. The Provinces Must Go Last accessed 16 Mar 2005
http://www.mysteriesofcanada.com/The_Provinces_Must_Go/provinces_chapter_1.htm
7. *American Constitutional Law.* Alpheus Mason, William Beaney, Donald Stephenson Jr. Englewood Cliffs, N.J. Prentice-Hall Publishers © 1983, p. 54
8. *American Constitutional Law.* Alpheus Mason, William Beaney, Donald Stephenson Jr. Englewood Cliffs, N.J. Prentice-Hall Publishers © 1983, p. 55
9. Roger B. Taney Wikipedia – The Free Encyclopedia http://en.wikipedia.org/wiki/Roger_Brooke_Taney Last accessed 18 Dec 2005
10. *John Adams: The Works of John Adams, Second President of the United States.* Charles Frances Adams, editor, © 1854, Boston: Little, Brown and Co., Vol. IX, p.229. To the officers of the first brigade of the third division of the militia of Massachusetts on Oct 11, 1798.
11. *Religion in American Politics.* Mark A. Noll, © 1990,

Oxford University Press, New York, p. 71
12. *Noah Webster's 1828 Dictionary*, Christian Technologies, © 2000, Independence, Missouri.
13. *Address of George Washington, President of the United States...Preparatory to his Declination.* George Washington, © 1796, Baltimore, George and Henry S. Keatinge, pp. 22–23.

The Third American Revolution

1. Walz v. Tax Commission, 397 U.S. 664, 672 (1970).
2. *Webster's New World Dictionary and Thesaurus.* Accent Software International, © 1998, Macmillan Publishers.
3. *The Sovereign States.* James Kilpatrick. ©1957, Henry Regnery Co., Chicago, p. 37
4. George Washington, Addresses of George Washington, President of the United States (Baltimore: George and Henry S. Keatinge, 1796
5. *Final Freedom.* Michael Vorenberg, © 2001, Cambridge University Press, UK, p. 236
6. *Final Freedom.* Michael Vorenberg, © 2001, Cambridge University Press, UK, p.109
7. Walz v. Tax Commission, 397 U.S. 664, 672 (1970).
8. *Final Freedom.* Michael Vorenberg, © 2001, Cambridge University Press, UK, p.134
9. *Final Freedom.* Michael Vorenberg, © 2001, Cambridge University Press, UK, p. 134
10. *Final Freedom.* Michael Vorenberg, © 2001, Cambridge University Press, UK, p. 238
11. *God in the White House.* Richard G. Hutcheson, © 1988, Macmillan Publishing Company, New York, p 40
12. *God in the White House.* Richard G. Hutcheson, © 1988, Macmillan Publishing Company, New York, p 45
13. *The American Nation: A History.* Albert Hart, ©1907, Harper and Brothers Publishers, New York, Vol. 26, P. 214

America's Fall
The Fourth American Revolution

1. *The 14th Amendment and the Bill of Rights*. Raoul Berger, ©1989, University of Oklahoma Press, Norman and London, pp. 13-14
2. *Webster's New World Dictionary and Thesaurus*. Accent Software International, © 1998, Macmillan Publishers.
3. . The Warren Court and its Critics, by: Clifford M. Lytle. © 1968 University of Arizona press. Tucson. p. 26
4. . The Warren Court and its Critics, by: Clifford M. Lytle. © 1968 University of Arizona press. Tucson p. 9
5. *The Supreme Court Reborn: The Constitutional Revolution in the Age of Roosevelt*. William E. Leuchtenburg, ©1995, Oxford University Press, New York, pp. 133, 132
6. *The Supreme Court Reborn: The Constitutional Revolution in the Age of Roosevelt*. William E. Leuchtenburg, ©1995, Oxford University Press, New York, p. 139
7. *The Supreme Court Reborn: The Constitutional Revolution in the Age of Roosevelt*. William E. Leuchtenburg, ©1995, Oxford University Press, New York, p. 139
8. *The Supreme Court Reborn: The Constitutional Revolution in the Age of Roosevelt*. William E. Leuchtenburg, ©1995, Oxford University Press, New York, pp. 218-219, 215
9. *The Supreme Court Reborn: The Constitutional Revolution in the Age of Roosevelt*. William E. Leuchtenburg, ©1995, Oxford University Press, New York, pp. 216, 142, 218
10. Barron v. Baltimore, 32 U.S. 243, (1833)
11. *The Supreme Court Reborn: The Constitutional Revolution in the Age of Roosevelt*. William E. Leuchtenburg, ©1995, Oxford University Press, New York, pp. 241-242
12. *The Supreme Court Reborn: The Constitutional Revolution in the Age of Roosevelt*. William E. Leuchtenburg, ©1995, Oxford University Press, New York, p. 242
13. *American Constitutional Law*. Alpheus Mason, William Beaney, Donald Stephenson Jr. Englewood Cliffs, N.J. Prentice-Hall Publishers © 1983, p. 472
14. *The Supreme Court Reborn: The Constitutional Revolution in the Age of Roosevelt*. William E. Leuchtenburg, ©1995,

Oxford University Press, New York, p. 243
15 *American Constitutional Law*. Alpheus Mason, William Beaney, Donald Stephenson Jr. Englewood Cliffs, N.J. Prentice-Hall Publishers © 1983, p. 473
16. "Thomas Jefferson, Memoir, Correspondence, and Miscellanies," from *The Papers of Thomas Jefferson*. Thomas Jefferson Randolph, editor, © 1830, Boston, Gray and Brown, Vol. IV, p. 373. To Judge William Johnson on June 12, 1823.
17. *The Sovereign States*. James Kilpatrick. ©1957, Henry Regnery Co., Chicago, p. 40
18. *The Sovereign States*. James Kilpatrick. ©1957, Henry Regnery Co., Chicago, p. 41
19. *The Sovereign States*. James Kilpatrick. ©1957, Henry Regnery Co., Chicago, p. 41
20. *The 14th Amendment and the Bill of Rights*. Raoul Berger, © 1989, University of Oklahoma Press, Norman and London, pp. 13–14
21. *The Sovereign States*. James Kilpatrick. ©1957, Henry Regnery Co., Chicago, p. 38

The Fifth American Revolution

1. *Webster's New World Dictionary and Thesaurus*. Accent Software International, © 1998, Macmillan Publishers.
2. *God in the White House*. Richard G. Hutcheson, © 1988, Macmillan Publishing Company, New York, p. 45
3. *Noah Webster's 1828 Dictionary*. Christian Technologies, © 2000, Independence, Missouri.
4. James Madison Rights, Powers and Duties The Constitution Society. http://www.constitution.org/cs_power.htm
Last accessed 18 Dec 2005
5., *America's Dates with Destiny*. Pat Robertson, © 1986, Nashville, Thomas Nelson Publishers, p. 95
6. Bartkus v. Illinois, 359 US 121
7. Walz v. Tax Commission, 397 U.S. 664, 672 (1970).
8. Abington v. Schempp, 374 U.S. 203, (1963)
9. *The Writings of Thomas Jefferson*. Albert Bergh, editor, © 1904, (Washington, D.C., Thomas Jefferson Memorial Assoc. Vol XVI, pp. 281-282, to the Danbury Baptist

Association on January 1, 1802

The Battle Behind the Battle

1., *The Works of Daniel Webster.* Daniel Webster, © 1853, Boston, Little, Brown and Co, Vol. I, p. 403
2. *The Far Left.* Billy James Hargis, © 1964, Tulsa, Christian Crusade, p. 18
3. 1936 CONSTITUTION OF THE USSR Bucknell University © 1996 Robert Beard http://www.departments.bucknell.edu/russian/const/36cons04.html. Last accessed 18 Dec 2005
4. The Warren Court and its Critics, by: Clifford M. Lytle. © 1968 University of Arizona press. Tucson. p. 55
5. *The Works of Daniel Webster.* Daniel Webster, © 1853, Boston, Little, Brown and Co, Vol. I, p. 403
6. Shadow Government of The United States and the Decline of America Published: November 12, 1998 Author: Unknown. FreeRepublic.com Copyright © 1999 Free Republic, LLC http://www.freerepublic.com/forum/a37f592f42625.htmLast accessed 18 Dec 2005
7. City Council of Charleston v. S.A. Benjamin, 2 Strob. 508, 518-520 (Sup. Ct. S.C. 1846)

America's Enemies

1. *Religion in American Politics.* Mark A. Noll, © 1990, Oxford University Press, New York, p. 71
2. Scarborough Country transcripts for Oct. 21. © 2004 MSNBC.com http://www.msnbc.msn.com/id/6306955/ Last accessed 18 Dec 2005
3. Poor oppressed Christians Warliberal.com. Posted by: Michael at October 7, 2003 08:30 Last accessed 20 Mar 2005 http://warliberal.com/mt/blog/archives/2003/10/07/poor_oppressed_christians.html
4. Religion baiting — The elite media declared open season on the President and his supporters. Joe Scarborough Archives © 2004, MSNBC http://www.papillonsartpalace.com/relibaitgion.htm Last accessed 18 Dec 2005

5. Call Me An Atheist The War on Faith. http://thewaronfaith.com/callmeanatheist.htm Last accessed 18 Dec 2005

6. Benjamin Rush, *Essays, Literary, Mora and Philosophical* (Philadelphia: Thomas and Samuel Bradford, 1798),pg. 94, 100,

7. *Religion in American Politics.* Mark A. Noll, © 1990, Oxford University Press, New York, p. 71

8. *Address of George Washington, President of the United States... Preparatory to his Declination.* George Washington, © 1796, Baltimore, George and Henry S. Keatinge, pp. 22–23.

9. *A Selection of Orations and Eulogies...In the Commemoration of the Life...of Gen George Washington.* Charles Humphrey Atherton, editor, © 1800, Amherst, Samuel Preston, p. 81. From an oration by Jeremiah Smith, February 22, 1800.

10. Revealing FACTS on the ACLU from its own writings. http://dianedew.com/aclu.htm Last accessed 18 Dec 2005

11. Revealing FACTS on the ACLU from its own writings. http://dianedew.com/aclu.htm Last accessed 18 Dec 2005

12. *Not So Christian America.* Thomas C. Reeves, (c) 1996, First Things 66, October 1996: 16–21.

13. My Favorite Quotes - Founding Fathers and Presidents. http://www.cancertutor.com/Quotes/Quotes_Presidents.html Last accessed 18 Dec 2005

14. Excerpted From: Crime and Punishment in America The National Center for Policy Analysis June 1995© 2001 NCPA
http://www.ncpa.org/w/w80.html Last accessed 18 Dec 2005

15. DARRELL SCOTT. Before the House Judiciary Subcommittee
Thursday, May 27, 1999 Howard County Republican Club Newsletter. Vol 2 Issue 4, July 2004 http://hocogop.com/nl/July04.pdf. Last accessed 18 Dec 2005

16. *John Adams: The Works of John Adams, Second President of the United States,* Charles Frances Adams, editor, © 1854, Boston, Little, Brown and Co., Vol. IX, p.229. To the officers of the first brigade of the third division of the

militia of Massachusetts, on Oct 11, 1798.
17. *The Papers of James Madison*. Henry D. Gilpin, editor, © 1840, Washington, Langtree and Sullivan, Vol. II, pp. 984–986. June 28, 1787.
18. *John Adams: The Works of John Adams, Second President of the United States*, Charles Frances Adams, editor, © 1854, Boston, Little, Brown and Co., Vol. IX, p.229. To the officers of the first brigade of the third division of the militia of Massachusetts on Oct 11, 1798.

The Warren Court

1. The Warren Court and its Critics, by: Clifford M. Lytle. © 1968 University of Arizona press. Tucson Pg. 51
2. The Warren Court and its Critics, by: Clifford M. Lytle. © 1968 University of Arizona press. Tucson Pg 17
3. *God in the White House*. Richard G. Hutcheson, © 1988, Macmillan Publishing Company, New York, p. 27
4. *The Far Left*. Billy James Hargis, © 1964, Tulsa, Christian Crusade, pp. 39–40, 42–43, 45, 54.
5. *Treason*. Ann Coulter, © 2003, New York, Crown Publishing Group, pp. 36–37.
6. *Webster's New World Dictionary and Thesaurus*. Accent Software International, ©1998, Macmillan Publishers.
7. *The Warren Court and its Critics*. p. 55
8., The American Atheist. Madalyn Murray O'Hair, Volume 36, No. 3 http://www.americanatheist.org/smr98/T3/tmop.html Last accessed 18 Dec 2005
9 World Christian Resource Directory. Testimony of William Murray. http://www.missionresources.com/atheist.html Last accessed 18 Dec 2005
10. Revealing FACTS on the ACLU from its own writings. Diane Dew
http://dianedew.com/aclu.htm. Last accessed 18 Dec 2005
11. The Center for Reclaiming America. Titus Explains ACLU Plan to Sue Judge Moore Wednesday, January 02, 2002 Last accessed 18 Dec 2005
http://www.reclaimamerica.org/PAGES/NEWS/newspage.asp?story=185
12. The Warren Court and its Critics, by: Clifford M. Lytle. © 1968 University of Arizona press. Tucson p.. 52

13. The Warren Court and its Critics, by: Clifford M. Lytle. © 1968 University of Arizona press. Tucson p.. 23
14. The Warren Court and its Critics, by: Clifford M. Lytle. © 1968 University of Arizona press. Tucson p.. 64
15. The Warren Court and its Critics, by: Clifford M. Lytle. © 1968 University of Arizona press. Tucson. p.. 16
16. The Warren Court and its Critics, by: Clifford M. Lytle. © 1968 University of Arizona press. Tucson. p.. 16
17. The Warren Court and its Critics, by: Clifford M. Lytle. © 1968 University of Arizona press. Tucson p.. 9
18. The Warren Court and its Critics, by: Clifford M. Lytle. © 1968 University of Arizona press. Tucson p.. 54
19. The Warren Court and its Critics, by: Clifford M. Lytle. © 1968 University of Arizona press. Tucson p.. 9
20. The Warren Court and its Critics, by: Clifford M. Lytle. © 1968 University of Arizona press. Tucson p.. 57
21. The Warren Court and its Critics, by: Clifford M. Lytle. © 1968 University of Arizona press. Tucson p.. 15
22. The Warren Court and its Critics, by: Clifford M. Lytle. © 1968 University of Arizona press. Tucson p.. 57
23. The Warren Court and its Critics, by: Clifford M. Lytle. © 1968 University of Arizona press. Tucson. p.. 58
24. The Warren Court and its Critics, by: Clifford M. Lytle. © 1968 University of Arizona press. Tucson. p. 23
25. The Warren Court and its Critics, by: Clifford M. Lytle. © 1968 University of Arizona press. Tucson p.. 51
26. The Warren Court and its Critics, by: Clifford M. Lytle. © 1968 University of Arizona press. Tucson. p.. 52
27. The Warren Court and its Critics, by: Clifford M. Lytle. © 1968 University of Arizona press. Tucson. p. 59
28. The Warren Court and its Critics, by: Clifford M. Lytle. © 1968 University of Arizona press. Tucson. pp.. 96, 53
29. The Warren Court and its Critics, by: Clifford M. Lytle. © 1968 University of Arizona press. Tucson. p. 94
30. The Warren Court and its Critics, by: Clifford M. Lytle. © 1968 University of Arizona press. Tucson. p. 39

America's Future

The Next American Revolution

1. *Noah Webster's 1828 Dictionary*. Christian Technologies, © 2000, Independence, Missouri
2. *John Adams: The Works of John Adams, Second President of the United States*, Charles Frances Adams, editor, © 1854, Boston, Little, Brown and Co., Vol. IX, p.229. To the officers of the first brigade of the third division of the militia of Massachusetts, on Oct 11, 1798.
3. Walz v. Tax Commission
4. *Noah Webster's 1828 Dictionary*. Christian Technologies, © 2000, Independence, Missouri
5. World Book online. © 2005. http://www.worldbookonline.com. Last accessed 18 Dec 2005
6. The Warren Court and its Critics, by: Clifford M. Lytle. © 1968 University of Arizona press. Tucson pp. 94–95
7. *The Writings of Samuel Adams*. Harry Alonzo Cushing, editor, © 1908, New York, G.P. Putnam's Sons, Vol. IV, p. 357. To the Legislature of Massachusetts on Jan. 17, 1794
8. *Impeachment: Restraining an Overactive Judiciary*. David Barton, © 1996, Wallbuilders, Aledo, TX., p. 51
9. *The Far Left*. Billy James Hargis, © 1964, Tulsa, Christian Crusade, p. 255
10. *Lectures on Revivals of Religion*. Charles G Finney, © 1868, New York, Fleming H Revell Co. (first published in 1835), Lecture XV, pp. 281–282.
11. William Jennings Bryan, "Cross of Gold" speech given during the 1896 Democratic National Convention on 9 July 1896.

A Restored Constitution

1. World Internet News. © Copyright 2003-2004 by worldinternetnews.net http://www.winc.tv/artman/publish/article_116.shtml Last accessed 18 Dec 2005
2. Commencement Speech by Attorney General Bill Pryor to the 1997 McGill-Toolen Graduating Class. http://www.ago.state.al.us/issue/mcgill_grad.htm Last accessed 18 Dec 2005

3. *The Historical and Legal Examination of that Part of the Decision of the Supreme Court of the United States in the Dared Scott Case.* Thomas H. Benton, © 1857, New York, D. Appleton and Co., p. 4
4. *Impeachment: Restraining an Overactive Judiciary.* David Barton, © 1996, Wallbuilders, Aledo, TX., pp. 19-21
5. The Warren Court and its Critics, by: Clifford M. Lytle. © 1968 University of Arizona press. Tucson p. 26
6. The Warren Court and its Critics, by: Clifford M. Lytle. © 1968 University of Arizona press. Tucson p. 9
7. The Warren Court and its Critics, by: Clifford M. Lytle. © 1968 University of Arizona press. Tucson p. 26
8. "Thomas Jefferson, Memoir, Correspondence, and Miscellanies," from *The Papers of Thomas Jefferson.* Thomas Jefferson Randolph, editor, © 1830, Boston, Gray and Brown, Vol. IV, p. 374.
9. *The Sovereign States.* James Kilpatrick. ©1957, Henry Regnery Co., Chicago, p. 37
10. *Master Thoughts of Thomas Jefferson.* Benjamin S. Catchings, © 1907, The Bar of New York City, p. 139.
11. *The Federalist Papers #78.* Alexander Hamilton, © 1788. The Judiciary Department.
12. *Men In Black—How the Supreme Court is Destroying America.* Mark Levin, © 2005, Regnery Publishing, Washington, DC., p. 210
13. *Slouching Towards Gomorrah: Modern Liberalism and American Decline.* Robert H. Bork, 1996, New York, Harper Collins Publishers. Pg 117.
14. World Book online. http://www.worldbookonline.com Last accessed 18 Dec 2005
15. *The Far Left.* Billy James Hargis, © 1964, Tulsa, Christian Crusade, p.. 148
16. Matt 5:11 NKJV

Conclusion

1. "Jumping off the Solid Rock." Gary Palmer, November 20, 2003. http://www.alabamapolicyinstitute.org/gary-2003-11-20.html Last accessed 18 Dec 2005
2. Commonwealth v. Sharpless 2 Serg. & R.91 (Sup. Ct. Penn. 1817)

3. *The Papers of James Madison.* Henry D. Gilpin, editor, © 1840, Washington, Langtree and Sullivan, Vol. II, pp. 984–986. June 28, 1787.
4. Senator Zell Miller (D- Georgia), Feb 12 2004 on the floor of the United States Senate in support of the Constitution Restoration Act of 2004 (HR 3799 IH). http://www.americanfarm.com/Viewpoint4-27-04a.html Last accessed 18 Dec 2005
5. "Jumping off the Solid Rock." Gary Palmer, November 20, 2003. http://www.alabamapolicyinstitute.org/gary-2003-11-20.html Last accessed 18 Dec 2005
6. Washington's Inaugural Address. Given April 30, 1789. National Archives and Records Administration. Last accessed 18 Dec 2005
http://www.archives.gov/exhibits/american_originals/inaugtxt.html
7., *The Writings and Speeches of Daniel Webster.* Daniel Webster, © 1903, Boston, Little, Brown, & Company, Vol XIII, pp.492–493. From a speech on February 23, 1852.
8., *Lectures on Revivals of Religion,* Charles G Finney, © 1868, New York, Fleming H Revell Co. (first published in 1835), Lecture XV, pp. 281–282.

About the Author

John D. Diamond serves as the Director of Discipleship at Bible Community Church in Columbus, Ohio and holds a B.S. in Theology from Vision Bible College and is presently working towards his Master in Education through Zion University. He is a veteran of the United States Air Force. He is presently working as an electrical Lineman for American Electric Power (AEP) and is a member of the International Brotherhood of Electrical Works (IBEW) Local 1466.